Counterfeit Amateurs

ALLEN L. SACK

Foreword by Ara Parseghian

COUNTERFEIT AMATEURS

An Athlete's Journey Through the Sixties
to the Age of Academic Capitalism

The Pennsylvania State University Press
University Park, Pennsylvania

LIBRARY OF CONGRESS CATALOGING-IN-PUBLICATION DATA

Sack, Allen L.
  Counterfeit amateurs : an athlete's journey through the
  sixties to the age of academic capitalism / Allen L. Sack ;
  foreword by Ara Parseghian
    p.   cm.
Includes bibliographical references and index.
ISBN 978-0-271-03368-6 (cloth : alk. paper)
1. College sports—Economic aspects—United States.
2. College athletes—United States—Economic conditions.
3. National Collegiate Athletic Association.
I. Title.

GV350.S23 2008
796.04'30973—dc22
2007036480

The Pennsylvania State University Press is a member of the
Association of American University Presses.

It is the policy of The Pennsylvania State University Press to
use acid-free paper. This book is printed on Natures Natural,
containing 50% post-consumer waste, and meets the minimum
requirements of American National Standard for Information
Sciences—Permanence of Paper for Printed Library Material,
ANSI Z39.48–1992.

Book design/typesetting by Garet Markvoort/zijn digital

To Kent Waldrep

For his positive outlook and persistence against the odds

Contents

Foreword

Of all of the teams that have won national championships at Notre Dame, the 1966 team provokes the most debate, in large part because of the national controversy that exploded over my play calling in the closing minutes of that season's Michigan State game, which ended in a 10–10 tie. Instead of immediately putting the ball in the air, I decided— for reasons I have discussed exhaustively over the years—to stay with our ground game until we could get better field position.

The downside of that decision has been that I have been criticized over the years for allegedly settling for a tie. The upside, as I have told players from that team at various class reunions, is that after all these years, people still remember the 1966 team and its classic face-off against Michigan State. The game appears quite often on ESPN Classic, and a surprising number of people still remember the names of key players on both squads. This classic matchup and the controversy it inspired have given the 1966 team a special place in collegiate sports history.

Allen Sack, the author of this book, was a member of that 1966 team. One of the things I remember about Allen is that he came to Notre Dame as a much-sought-after high school quarterback and ended up playing defensive end. It is not unusual for players to switch positions, but a move like this one required a whole new mindset. By the start of his senior year, Allen was a serious contender for a starting position on the defensive line. He ended up starting a couple of games and saw quite a bit of action as our "go-to guy" behind Alan Page and Tom Rhoads. He was one of eight players from his class to be drafted by the NFL.

Allen also stands out as one of the few players from that team to pursue a career as a college professor. This may help to explain why he is very sensitive to the changes that have taken place in sports and higher education since the sixties. Many of these changes, in his opinion, have erased the distinction between amateur college athletics and the pros. Twenty years ago, Allen's views seemed radical. Today, even the prestigious Knight Foundation Commission, co-chaired by Notre Dame's former president, Father Theodore Hesburgh, warns that college athletics has become a big business in which "the historic link between playing field and classroom is all but severed in many institutions."

Reasonable people will disagree about what Allen has written in this book, and Allen and I certainly have some substantial differences of opinion, especially over the issue of paying college athletes openly. It seems beyond debate, though, that money has become much more of a driving force in collegiate sports today than when I was coaching. In 1966, our national championship team decided not to attend a bowl game out of concern that an extended season would interfere with players' final exams. Turning down a bowl game today would be incomprehensible, given the money involved.

I support bowl games. Notre Dame used much of its $14.5 million payout from the 2006 Fiesta Bowl to support student financial aid, library acquisitions, and scientific instruments for a new science center on campus. It seems fair to ask, however, as Allen does in this book, whether the increased competition over television dollars has ratcheted up the pressure on coaches to win, and whether they in turn pass the pressure down to the athletes in ways that clash with education.

I, for one, think that it is possible to run an athletics program with an eye toward profit without undermining academic integrity and exploiting athletes. It means recruiting athletes who fit the academic profile of other students on campus, providing academic support for athletes who need it, and insisting on excellence in education as well as on the playing field. Adhering to this formula is not easy, but it can be done. Allen has his doubts. In this book he argues that although a few schools may be able to meet this standard—Notre Dame among them—the gap between big-time college sports and academic values has grown into a giant chasm.

Counterfeit Amateurs looks at the past four decades of collegiate sports from the unique perspective of a Notre Dame football player who came of age politically during the turbulence of the sixties. Many people may be bothered by what he has to say, but his views on sports and education are likely to stimulate a much-needed dialogue on the use and abuse of the term "amateur" in collegiate athletics in the twenty-first century.

Ara Parseghian

Preface

Critics hail Todd Gitlin's book, *The Sixties: Years of Hope, Days of Rage,* as the most comprehensive treatment of the political movements of that decade ever written. Yet the index of this 513-page book contains not a single entry on sports. The index includes names like Frankie Avalon, Patti Page, and the rock group the Moody Blues, but not Muhammad Ali. The author makes several references to Mexico City, in one case as an area where "beats" hung out in the 1950s. The 1968 Mexico City Olympics, and the revolt of black athletes on college campuses it helped to inspire, did not merit a reference. It is astonishing that Gitlin, in his otherwise remarkable book, left the "athletic revolution" of the sixties totally out of history.

My memories of those turbulent years are somewhat different from Gitlin's, in part because of my experiences as a college athlete. In 1966 I played on Notre Dame's national championship football team. Even though football was always on my mind, political upheavals beyond the playing field and outside Notre Dame's rather conservative campus were difficult for me to ignore. In 1963, the year I entered Notre Dame, Martin Luther King delivered his memorable "I have a dream" speech, and the assassination of John F. Kennedy shocked the nation. Over the next couple of years, Klansmen murdered civil rights workers in Mississippi, the United States introduced ground troops in Vietnam, and race riots ripped through major U.S. cities. Although events like these pushed me toward the political left, I had yet to make the connection between sports and politics.

When I entered graduate school at Penn State, I began to read books by sports activists like Dave Meggyesy, Harry Edwards, and Jack Scott. Only then did I realize that the racism, sexism, and other aspects of American culture that were under attack in the sixties were deeply ingrained in American sports. Because athletes were rarely on the political left, I identified strongly with the handful of prominent athletes who spoke out publicly in support of civil and human rights. For me, Muhammad Ali's resistance to the draft, and the symbolic protests against racism by medal winners Tommie Smith and John Carlos during the awards ceremony at the Mexico City Olympics, were among the most memorable events of the sixties. These athletes inspired me to think more critically about the role of sports in all social institutions, including higher education.

The politics of the sixties had a significant influence on my life over the next couple of decades. In 1981 I took a leave of absence from my position as a college professor to serve as the director of the federally funded Center for Athletes' Rights and Education (CARE), an organization cosponsored by the National Football League Players Association and the National Conference of Black Lawyers. CARE took the position that college athletes are employees and therefore should have a right to unionize. Operating out of a community center in the South Bronx, CARE managed to send shock waves from NCAA headquarters in Shawnee Mission, Kansas, to Washington, D.C., where the newly elected Reagan administration's assault on labor unions and on the Department of Education left us struggling to maintain our funding.

CARE hired me as its director in part because of my extensive scholarly research on college sports. My background as a Notre Dame football player was also a plus because it added credibility to progressive ideas that were considered blasphemous at that time. Throughout the 1980s I used my unique experiences as a Notre Dame athlete, sports activist, and college professor to engage in public discourse over issues ranging from whether the NCAA's television plan for football violated antitrust laws—a case I debated with attorneys from the NCAA and the University of Oklahoma on *Good Morning America*—to whether college athletes who suffer catastrophic injuries should receive workers' compensation benefits.

Over the past twenty years I have written extensively on issues and controversies in college sports, generally taking a critical stance toward NCAA policies that have all but eliminated the distinction between amateur college sports and professional entertainment. I remain an activist for college sports reform. In the late 1990s I helped to create the Drake Group, a grassroots organization of faculty and others committed to defending academic integrity in the face of unprecedented commercialism. The focus of my activism is now on defending college classrooms from the encroachments of commercial college sports run amok. Nonetheless, I continue to support efforts by athletes to organize to protect their educational, financial, and medical rights.

Several years ago I had dinner with Murray Sperber, a colleague of mine who has written several fine books on college sports. At some point in our conversation, he asked me if I had ever considered writing a book that incorporated stories about my life as an athlete and activist with my reflections on the dramatic changes that have occurred in college sports since I played in the sixties. In his opinion, my association with one of the most storied football programs in the country would not only attract reader interest but would make it hard to dismiss my views on college sports as just another harangue by a jock-hating intellectual. Before dinner had ended, Sperber had convinced me that a book like the one he was suggesting was worth writing.

Sperber's encouragement helped me to get started on this project. The belief that hypocrisy should not go unchallenged was the impetus to finish. The NCAA claims guardianship of the amateur spirit in college sports. But its season-ending basketball tournament, which generates a $6 billion multiyear TV contract from CBS, has a definite professional feel. Millions rain down from the sale of licensed merchandise, luxury seating, parking, concessions, and other revenue streams. The commercial buzz far exceeds many teams' graduation rates. The true spirit of college sports also shines in bowl games named after corporate sponsors, regular-season football games played on weekday evenings, coaches' salaries that soar into the $4 million range, and conference realignments motivated by the promise of a bigger cut of television revenue.

College sports also shows its true face in NCAA legislation that gives coaches control over athletes similar to that which employers exercise over employees. One-year renewable grants that allow coaches to "fire" athletes who are injured or who turn out to be recruiting mistakes have replaced four-year scholarships like the one I had at Notre Dame. By insisting that big-time college athletes are amateurs, schools can make millions while capping player compensation at room, board, tuition, and fees. Universities have gone to the U.S. Supreme Court to protect their right to market college football to the highest bidder. Athletes who even hint that they deserve a bigger share of the profits are treated like criminals. The amateur myth also understates the academic challenges players must face when an extracurricular activity becomes a form of professional entertainment.

I am an avid fan of big-time college sports, and I support the Fighting Irish as passionately as others support their favorite teams. College sports provides millions of Americans with great entertainment and a point of emotional attachment to the nation's colleges and universities. A winning team can bind a campus community together and attract national attention. Absent the myth that the athletes who fill the stadiums and drive the television ratings are merely amateurs playing games in their free time, I could make peace with commercial college sports and the NCAA. But I fear that the costs of running college sports as honest professional entertainment would be prohibitive, unless big-time programs were spun off as self-supporting businesses. A more practical solution would be a return to a model that embraces the best elements of amateurism, and truly makes athletes an integral part of the student body.

Acknowledgments

M any people have contributed to this book. I would like to thank as many of them as possible. Murray Sperber deserves special thanks for encouraging me to take on this project in the first place. Thanks also to my agent, Neil Salkind, without whom this book might never have seen the light of day, and to Sandy Thatcher and Penn State Press for acquiring the manuscript and providing significant editorial assistance.

I am grateful to Robert and Ceci Berner, Ron Jeziorski, Craig Mortali, Roy and Adam Perry, Jack Salay, Myles Schrag, Chris Siegler, R. J. Siegler Jr., and Ron Villani for reading parts of the manuscript and for providing moral support and critical feedback at various stages in the book's evolution. I am especially indebted to my wife, Gina, who not only provided valuable insight on every chapter but tolerated the countless hours I spent sitting at my computer, pretty much out of touch with day-to-day realities.

Thanks to these people who generously agreed to be interviewed for my book: Robert Sam Anson, James Baugus, Rocky Bleier, Larry Bloom, Brian Boulac, Myles Brand, Ernie Chambers, Michael DeCicco, Jon Ericson, Ed Gebhart, Theodore Hesburgh, Ramogi Huma, Ron Jeziorski, Chris Kvochak, Joel Maturi, Bob Minnix, Mark Naison, Robert Nugent, Alan Page, Ara Parseghian, John Ray, Dan Saracino, Max Segich, Frank Splitt, Roger Valdiserri, and Kent Waldrep. And thanks to many others who provided insights via phone conversations and e-mail.

Two Penn State professors who have had a lasting impact on my thinking are David Westby, whose intellectual curiosity, brilliance, and love for scholarly debate were an inspiration to all who knew him, and Ron Smith, who introduced me to the fascinating world of sports history. The work of my colleagues George Sage, E. Stanley Eitzen, Jay Coakley, and

Ellen Staurowsky has provided an intellectual framework for how I look at sports in society and the role of sports in higher education. Many of their ideas have become part of my intellectual repertoire and are reflected in this book.

I would like to thank all those I met at Sports for the People for helping me grasp the complexities of race, gender, and social class in America. I owe a special debt of gratitude to Mark Naison and Cary Goodman for allowing me to share their dream of using sports as a vehicle for community organizing. I also want to thank members of the Drake Group for identifying the ways that college faculty can "take back their classrooms." Special thanks to current and former Drake members Jon Ericson, Linda Bensel-Meyers, David Ridpath, Jason Latner, Ed Lawry, Rob Benson, William C. Dowling, Ellen Staurowsky, Bruce Svare, Murray Sperber, Andrew Zimbalist, Terry Holland, Richard Southall, Kadie Otto, Jim Reese, Joel Cormier, and Amanda Paul.

I also want to acknowledge Kerry Temple and *Notre Dame Magazine* for publishing several of my articles over the years; my editor, Suzanne Wolk, for her professionalism and attention to detail; the Sabbatical Leave Committee at the University of New Haven for research support while I was just beginning this project; my students at the University of New Haven for forcing me to sharpen the arguments I have presented throughout this book; the Notre Dame archivists who tracked down photos for this book; Michael Morris and Robert Hoffnung for their encouragement; and my sons, Aaron and Ethan, for finding humor in my eccentricities and for their constant support.

PART I

College Football in the Sixties

1

Playing Football in Ara's Era

I played my last football game for Notre Dame in 1966 against Southern California at the Los Angeles Coliseum. Since then, big-time collegiate sports has morphed into a multibillion-dollar industry. Although rampant commercialism jumps out as the most obvious change in college sports since the sixties, changes in NCAA rules that have blurred the distinction between amateurs and professionals have also profoundly altered the college game. Because my personal athletic experiences serve as a point of reference for comparing college sports, past and present, I have decided to begin my story with a description of what it was like to play football for Ara Parseghian in the 1960s, and to be a student during that turbulent decade. As is the case for anyone who engages in highly competitive sports, I had my share of both success and bitter disappointment.

My Fall from Grace

The most disappointing moment of my athletic career occurred in preseason football practice at the beginning of my sophomore year at Notre Dame. The team had already endured two weeks of double sessions in the stifling heat and humidity so common in northern Indiana in the summer. The Darwinian struggle for survival of the fittest had already given players a good idea of where they stood in the football pecking order. I knew that things were not going well for me on the playing field, and that I would probably be at the bottom of the coaches' depth chart. Nonetheless, I was stunned by an announcement made just before our nightly team meeting.

Just after dinner, John Murphy, an assistant coach under Ara Parseghian, called about twenty players aside in a room just outside the main dining hall. He got right to the point. None of the players assembled in that room, he said, would ever dress for a Notre Dame football game. Our job, he said, would be an important one nonetheless. As members of the preparation teams, we would attend practice, run the defenses and offenses of upcoming opponents, and try to simulate real game conditions. I noted that he did not equivocate. He did not say that we would probably not play for Notre Dame. He said that we would not play. I was devastated. I had honestly never realized that some players who receive scholarships never even dress for a game.

To explain my free fall from a highly touted All-State quarterback from Pennsylvania to a defensive end position on what players humorously referred to as the "shit squad," I need to backtrack to the beginning of my freshman year. In 1963 the football program at Notre Dame had fallen on very hard times. Between 1959 and 1962, Joe Kuharich compiled the worst record in Notre Dame history by winning only seventeen of forty games, for a winning percentage of .425. Hugh Devore, who had been freshman coach under Kuharich, replaced him as head coach in 1963, with the understanding that he would serve only as an "interim coach" until a full-time coach could be hired.

Devore recruited a freshman class with depth at every position. I was one of seven quarterbacks in the freshman class, and it seemed to me that many of the players I talked to, regardless of position, had been All-State or even All-American athletes in high school. Alan Page, a high school All-American and future inductee into the National Football League Hall of Fame, left a lasting impression on me by carrying five or six glasses of milk back from the milk machine in the dining hall all at once. He was wearing one of the green tee shirts that had been issued to all of us. His massive forearms, imposing six-foot-five-inch frame, and the air of self-confidence he projected left no doubt in my mind that he was destined for stardom. Many of the other players were equally impressive. This was clearly the big leagues.

Even though freshmen were not eligible for varsity competition back then, we were still expected to be on campus a week or so before other students. No sooner had we arrived than the coaches sent us to the stadium to get equipment we would need for a scrimmage with the varsity the next day. I knew that I had come to Notre Dame to play football, but I had not expected to be playing before my bags were unpacked. The equipment manager, a cantankerous older man with silver-gray hair, called Mac, looked as if he had been around since the Rockne era. Not unlike an army quartermaster dealing with recruits who had just arrived at boot camp, Mac made us feel privileged to have equipment at all, let alone equipment that fit.

We were all given heavy green jerseys, apparel far more conducive to weather in late fall than the dog days of summer. Some of the lucky players received helmets comparable to what they might have worn in high school. Others had to make do with leather models not unlike the ones I had seen in pictures of the Four Horsemen. Mac had no sympathy for players who did not like what they were given, often subjecting them to verbal abuse for questioning his judgment. Joe Smyth, a lineman from the Philadelphia area, ended up with an old leather helmet that earned him the nick name "Big Red" after Red Grange, the legendary University of Illinois football player from the 1920s. I lucked out in the helmet category but ended up with pants that kept sliding down below my hip pads.

Dressed in antiquated equipment and with no idea of what to expect, we marched out to the practice field the next day to be used as defensive cannon fodder for Notre Dame's varsity offense. I am sure that the veteran players saw this as an opportunity to give the freshmen, many of whom had arrived on campus with inflated images of themselves, a much-needed reality check. My first taste of big-time college football came when Bob Meeker, a 240-pound offensive tackle, hit me so hard that I was dazed for a couple of seconds. I was playing safety. I saw a running play developing off tackle, came up to fill the hole, and was pounded by Meeker instead. That was only one of several hard hits I took that day. I survived this rite of passage and left the field feeling confident that I was physically tough enough to compete against players like these.

Throughout the fall, my performance as a freshman quarterback was inconsistent. Some days I felt a little like the cocky young quarterback I had been in high school. A week before the Navy game, I was assigned the task of playing Navy's All-American quarterback and future Heisman Trophy winner, Roger Staubach, on the game preparation team. I did well, getting a few compliments from coaches. For the most part, though, I felt my confidence slowly slipping away. In high school, pass receivers I had thrown to for years had developed an instinctive ability to run under my passes, even when they were not perfectly on target. I missed these players, one of whom had accepted a scholarship to the University of Illinois. Everything was different, from the way the ball was snapped from center to the way I had to plant my feet when throwing a pass. Adjusting to a whole new system, in addition to handling the pressure of being at Notre Dame, was making it difficult for me to do things that had been second nature in high school. My performance suffered.

At the end of the fall I was still viewed as one of the top three freshman quarterbacks. But the fact that freshmen were ineligible for varsity competition, plus Hugh Devore's laid-back approach to freshman player development, made it difficult to evaluate player ability. The athletic demands on freshmen in the Devore era were not excessive, thus making the transition to college life a lot easier from an academic standpoint. However, this lack of systematic attention to the freshman program may also have reflected a certain neglect of the entire football program during this period. Not surprisingly, Devore's team finished the 1963 season with a disappointing 2–7–0 record, one of the worst in Notre Dame history.

Easing into Student Life

My future as a Notre Dame quarterback remained uncertain in the fall of 1963. My life off the playing field, however, was exactly what I'd expected to find in college. Because there were no "jock" dormitories at Notre Dame, I lived in an intellectually exciting environment, surrounded by students, some of them athletes, with a wide variety of academic interests and life experiences. I had grown up in a Lutheran family, but I was skeptical of all religions by the time I arrived at Notre Dame. Thus I constantly debated topics ranging from how Catholics can be so certain that their moral principles are the only valid ones, to broad philosophical questions such as whether God exists and how that can be proved. Over my next four years at Notre Dame, the topics of debate would expand to race, politics, social theory, and war.

I cannot imagine entering college at a time of greater intellectual, social, and political upheaval.[1] In 1962 the nation stood on the brink of nuclear war as President Kennedy took a stand against the Soviet Union in the Cuban missile crisis. In August 1963—when I was working out to get in shape for freshman football at Notre Dame—thousands flocked to Washington, D.C., for an interracial rally at the Lincoln Memorial, where Martin Luther King delivered his memorable "I have a dream" speech. During a geology class at Notre Dame on November 22, 1963, my professor announced that President Kennedy had been shot. The students immediately knelt down with the professor and prayed. In the evening, just after the assassination, I learned the Hail Mary while standing in the rain repeating it with more than a thousand Notre Dame students and others who had gathered at the Grotto to mourn the president's death.

My freshman dormitory, Breen-Phillips Hall, was located across a small roadway from the old field house. In the spring semester, Alabama governor George Wallace, a staunch supporter of racial segregation, gave a talk in that field house. In 1963 Wallace blocked a black student, Vivian Malone, from entering a classroom building at the University of Alabama. My friend Chris Siegler remembers a student from Kentucky who lived in his dormitory proudly parading in the hallway on the day of Wallace's speech, waving a Confederate flag. He also remembers being with students who protested the event by walking out when Wallace began to speak. When the speech was over, Jim Snowden and Richard Arrington, two black players on our team, approached Wallace's limousine, which was parked just outside my dorm. Snowden pounded on the hood while others looked on. This protest was a precursor of the revolt of black athletes that would explode on campuses at the end of the decade.

Raymond Fleming, a black freshman, describes the Wallace visit as one of his most vivid memories during his four years at Notre Dame.[2] Fleming helped plan the demonstration against Wallace. He participated in the march around the building but did not support disrupting Wallace's speech inside the field house. What struck him at the time, and still disturbs him today, were the hostile glares and comments directed at protestors by many of the students entering the field house. "In 1964," says Fleming, "it was difficult to get Notre Dame's highly conservative student body to take a strong public stand in favor of Civil Rights." There were very few political activists on campus at that time. By the end of the decade, however, Notre Dame's president, Reverend Theodore Hesburgh, found himself and his university under siege by student radicals, and made national headlines for the strong position he took in favor of law and order on college campuses.[3]

In 1963 the gap between athletes and other students was not nearly as large as it is today. Average entrance requirements for athletes may have been lower than for other students, but not by much. A comprehensive study comparing the academic performance of athletes and other students over the past four decades was published in 2000. The authors of that study, called *The Game of Life: College Sports and Academic Values,* found that even at the most competitive academic institutions in the country, including Notre Dame, the gap in admissions requirements and other measures of academic performance for athletes and other students has broadened significantly since the late 1950s.[4] In recent years, the gap between female athletes and other female students also appears to be growing, as women have adopted the same commercial and professional model as men.

When I was at Notre Dame, NCAA rules barring freshman football players from varsity competition not only sent a clear message that education was the primary reason for going to college but it also gave athletes a chance to adjust to the academic demands of a fine university. I finished the first semester of my freshman year with a grade point average in the eighty-fifth percentile of the freshman class. The demands of football and my own desire to excel on the playing field diverted my attention from the classroom. At the same time, though, the freshman ineligibility rule was a constant reminder that education had top priority at Notre Dame.

Notre Dame had no courses reserved specifically for athletes in 1963. I would be less than honest, however, if I denied that I sought out professors who had reputations for easy grading. I was a pretty good student, and I was genuinely excited about some of my classes, but I also engaged in behavior on occasion that played into the "dumb jock" stereotype. One course I took in the first semester was taught by a priest who was known among students as "88 Brennan." I did minimal work in his course on logic and language but, not surprisingly, received a B. Jake Kline, my freshman math professor, was known as "99 Kline" because he gave nothing but A's. That I received a B from him says something about my lack of effort in his class. Over the next four years I often took academic shortcuts, doing just what was necessary to get by. Sometimes, though, I actually followed professors back to their offices because I wanted to discuss issues raised in a lecture.

An experience in my freshman composition class highlighted the differences between the lessons learned in sports and those taught in the classroom. Several weeks into the semester, the professor assigned a short essay by E. B. White, a writer for the *New Yorker* who would go on to win a Pulitzer Prize. The professor and I had a major difference of opinion about what White was trying to say, and the professor brought the matter to closure by asserting that I was simply wrong. I am sure that many students have found themselves in this position, especially in humanities classes, where writers' intentions are seldom entirely clear. One advantage I had in this instance was that E. B. White, unlike Shakespeare or Milton, was still alive.

After class I decided to contact E. B. White directly to determine once and for all what he was really trying to say in his essay. I told my classmates what I intended to do and they recommended that I go to the library to find his mailing address. I found it and wrote a letter explaining the situation, never expecting to receive a response. Several weeks later, much to my amazement—and to the surprise of my friends in Breen-Phillips Hall—I found a letter from E. B. White in my mailbox. In his short, typewritten note, replete with strikeover corrections of typos, which gave the letter an air of authenticity, White said he empathized with students in my position and appreciated that I took his work so seriously. He then gave a brief explanation of his essay that came much closer to my understanding than to my professor's. I took the letter to class the next day, and much to my professor's credit, he read it to the entire class. In fact, he complimented me for the effort I had made.

After that episode, I became increasingly aware that I inhabited two very different worlds at Notre Dame. In my academic world, thinking critically was highly regarded and often rewarded. In this arena, students were expected to question, probe, and analyze, rather than to blindly accept what they were told. Although Notre Dame was a conservative place where ideas that challenged the moral authority of the Catholic Church were often suspect, many professors actually enjoyed having students who had strong opinions about issues raised in class and who critically evaluated ideas and beliefs most people seldom question. In time I came to love the give-and-take of intellectual debates, many of which took place in the dormitories with my friends.

In my other world, the world of college football, there was little time or room for intellectual debate. I learned very quickly to keep my mouth shut and never question the authority of the coach. Athletes were expected to be intelligent—I knew no dumb jocks at Notre Dame—but the important lessons of football, such as self-discipline, respect for authority, maintaining poise under pressure, sacrificing for the good of the team, and striving to succeed no matter what the odds, did not require being immersed in the "life of the mind." During my years at Notre Dame, I moved back and forth between the athletic and intellectual subcultures on campus, often feeling too much like a jock to be taken seriously as an intellectual, and too intellectual to feel entirely at home in the Spartan world of athletics.

The Beginning of Ara's Era

Ara Parseghian signed a contract to become Notre Dame's new head football coach in mid-December 1963. When he finally arrived on campus in early January, the excitement was palpable. Notre Dame had finally hired a coach who could possibly return the Irish to their former days of glory. When Ara was introduced between the halves of a basketball game played at home, the students cheered wildly for at least ten minutes. He received a similarly warm reception when he gave a brief talk from the porch of Sorin Hall on the main campus. There was no mistaking that Notre Dame had hired a charismatic coach who could energize a crowd. Whether he could win games remained to be seen.

He certainly had the background and experience necessary to turn things around. He had played college football at Miami of Ohio. He was later drafted by the Cleveland Browns, where he played for several years for Paul Brown, a coach for whom Ara had a great deal of respect. After an injury cut short his professional playing career, Ara returned to Miami of Ohio as an assistant coach under Woody Hayes. When Hayes went to Ohio State as head coach, Ara stepped in as head coach at Miami, compiling an impressive 39–6–1 record over five years. He was then hired by Northwestern to revive a program that had ceased to be competitive in the Big Ten Conference. He quickly returned the Wildcats to respectability. His four straight victories over Notre Dame during the Kuharich era may have been what gave him an edge when vying for the Notre Dame job.

I was not sure how to react to this coaching change. I had never heard of Parseghian and, more important, Northwestern was one of the few schools that had shown no interest in me as a high school recruit. Duffy Daugherty, Michigan State's famous coach, had contacted me a number of times. When I scored my one-thousandth point in basketball during my senior year in high school, he sent me a congratulatory telegram. Coaches from the University of Michigan had offered to fly me to Ann Arbor for a campus visit; I was not interested. Coaches from the University of Illinois, another Big Ten school, visited my high school and took me out to lunch. Yet Ara Parseghian, the man about to take over as Notre Dame's head coach, had not so much as sent me a postcard.

Any misgivings I might have had about Ara Parseghian were quickly dispelled after his first meeting with the team. I had never met a person with Ara's ability to communicate and inspire. It is no exaggeration to say that the players sat spellbound as he laid out his strategy for how we would win the national championship. I have often told people that after that first meeting, Ara could have told us to jump off the top of Notre Dame Stadium, and many players might have seriously considered it. He had a clear vision of where the program was headed and the charisma to make the rest of us believe in it. In the weeks to come, he also demonstrated organizational skills that would have served him well in a military campaign. He left absolutely nothing to chance. Efficiency and time management were the hallmarks of Ara's system. The stopwatch became ubiquitous.

On the first day of spring practice, I witnessed how, under effective leadership, a football team can be transformed into a finely tuned machine. When I walked through the locker-room door, I saw a large felt board on my immediate left to which nametags for every player on the team were affixed. The names were arranged in columns by playing position. The first two columns had gold markers above them, indicating first-team offensive and defensive players. The players assigned to the next two columns, identified with the color blue, were on the second-team offense or defense. The fifth and sixth columns were green and red, respectively, representing players on the offensive and defensive preparation teams. The preparation teams ran the offenses and defenses of upcoming opponents during practice to give the starting teams an idea of what to expect.

Some of my friends and I remarked on how closely the depth chart corresponded to our recorded times in the sprints we had run several weeks earlier in pre-spring workouts. I was disappointed but not surprised to find my name in the column designated for the green preparation team. Several other quarterbacks were also in that column. After locating my name on the depth chart, I proceeded to the printed practice schedule that was taped on the wall just below a bronze plaque inscribed with Rockne's famous "Win one for the Gipper" speech. This daily schedule noted every drill, every scrimmage, and every possible action that would occur in practice broken down into precise time intervals. During my years at Notre Dame, these schedules were followed with clocklike precision.

My next stop after studying the practice schedule was my locker. The assignment of lockers was socially stratified to match the depth chart, with gold teams toward the front of the locker room and prep teams in the back. Having a locker right up front was a sign of prestige. I am sure this was part of Ara's strategy for motivating players by rewarding excellence. When I went to get my equipment, I saw that things had been upgraded substantially since Ara's arrival. Helmets, pads, shoes—everything worn in practice and in games was now state of the art. Equipment managers and trainers in Ara's system were expected to be as efficient and professional as the players and the coaching staff.

In the late nineteenth century, an industrial engineer by the name of Frederick Winslow Taylor developed a system called scientific management to increase worker productivity. Ara must have read his books. Practice always started exactly when the posted schedule said it would. Specialists like kickers, punters, and centers who hiked the ball for them had to be on the field thirty minutes earlier than the rest of us. Ara personally used a stopwatch to time the interval between the snap of the ball and when it was kicked or punted. Every movement was analyzed to eliminate wasted motion. When regular practice started, time continued to be managed efficiently. At intervals perfectly consistent with the schedule posted on the locker-room wall, managers would blast their handheld horns to indicate that it was time to run to another field, another drill, or some other scheduled activity.

Time intervals devoted to conditioning and the kicking game were always scheduled at the beginning of practice. After these, Ara would take his place on a high tower at the center of our practice area to get a better view of practice. He reminded me a little of Napoleon, who would take a position on high ground to watch the progress of a battle. From his perch, Ara could watch players in gold, blue, green, and red jerseys sprinting from one skirmish to another, horns blowing and bodies colliding. No player or coach escaped his gaze. It was not uncommon for Ara to yell down to assistant coaches when players were not doing their job, rather than yell directly at the players. Like loyal lieutenants, the coaches got the troops in order.

After practice, coaches would work late into the evening evaluating player performances on a given day. It was not uncommon for a player who was on the gold team one day to be demoted to the prep team the next. Movement from the bottom up also occurred. Major scrimmages were filmed, and "report cards" rating each player's performance were taped in our lockers the next day. There was no grade inflation on the football field. Ara's system was meritocracy in its purest form. The coaches used to say that it was impossible for any player, even one at the bottom of the chart, to hide during practice. Every player's contribution to the team was closely evaluated. The goal was to use every human and material resource available to maximize efficiency.

In that first spring practice under Ara, my dream of playing quarterback for Notre Dame began to slip away. My lack of speed was part of the problem, but not dealing well with stress was probably what killed me. There is no other way to explain why my tight spirals turned into wounded ducks when Ara was watching, or why on one occasion when he told me to take a snap from center and rifle a pass out to a wide receiver, the ball literally reached the receiver on one bounce. Ara tested me on a number of occasions, giving me every chance to prove myself. I was simply too immature to take the pressure. My quarterbacking career came to an ignominious end one afternoon when Ara totally lost patience with me after I pivoted the wrong way on an off tackle play that I should have had down pat by then. I remember him shouting, "Sack, get off the offensive field and I do not want to see you back here again." As I changed into my red defensive jersey, I figured there was nowhere to go but up.

Fighting to Regain Some Self-Respect

This brings me back to the fateful meeting at the beginning of my sophomore year, when Coach Murphy announced to a group of us that we would never wear a Notre Dame uniform and play in a game. Even after my disastrous spring, I had hoped that I would at least be able to play defensive back. Coach Murphy's announcement dashed all my hopes. Coach Paul Shoults saw no role for me in the defensive backfield, and quarterback was out of the question. I had no strategy for how to deal with this setback. What I did know was that I would refuse to take any abuse on the practice field and that I would do whatever was necessary to preserve my dignity. I refused to be a tackle dummy.

Early in the 1964 season I got a break from one of the coaches who still had some faith in me. During practice one day, Joe Yonto, our defensive line coach, called me over and said he wanted me to try playing defensive end. I was six feet three inches tall and only 193 pounds. Nonetheless I was as fast as, if not faster than, many of the linemen, and the thought of beating up on quarterbacks made me feel a lot better about not being one. I was now a member of the "red raiders," the name we gave to the defensive prep team that wore the red jerseys. And I was in a position where I knew I could improve over time. When Coach Yonto started grabbing me by the face mask and slapping me on the helmet like he did the other linemen, I knew I had found a home.

While I was making my transition to defensive end, the Fighting Irish were returning to glory beyond anyone's expectations. We were seven weeks into the season and still undefeated. Ara's system had made us the number-one-ranked college team in the nation. In a stroke of management genius, Ara had chosen John Huarte, a third-string quarterback on Devore's 1963 team, to be his starting quarterback. Huarte ended up winning the Heisman Trophy. Ara converted running back Jack Snow into a wide receiver, where he developed into a consensus All-American by season's end. The starting defensive line was composed of four sophomores who had come in with my freshman class. Parseghian's rational organization of players and resources was moving Notre Dame into contention for a national championship, just as he had predicted at our first team meeting the previous spring.

As the season progressed, I began to gain confidence in my new defensive end position. As strange as it may sound, some of my best performances during this period were in what players humorously called the "Toilet Bowls." Every Monday, players like me, who did not dress for games, and those who did dress but had not played very much, were required to stay out at practice later than other players to engage in a full-scale scrimmage. The name "Toilet Bowl" derived from the fact that many of the players participating were on the preparation teams, otherwise known as the "shit squads." Although we joked about them, these Toilet Bowls were deadly serious business because they provided the coaches with a mechanism for developing younger players. It was during these scrimmages that I was able to demonstrate that I had the skill and determination to play football at Notre Dame.

I don't know if it was a tackle I made in practice or an exceptional scrimmage I had on a Monday night, but something finally moved the coaches to put me on the list of players dressing for a home game, a nationally televised contest against Michigan State. The experience was one I could never forget. When I arrived at the stadium on game day, my helmet was freshly painted and my uniform was in my locker with the pads already inserted. When I put on the lightweight gold pants and blue jersey bearing the number 88, I actually found myself staring at them, finding it hard to believe that they were actually on my body. I cannot remember much about the actual game. I do remember sitting on the bench late in the fourth quarter and hearing Ara's voice yelling something like, "Sack, where's Sack? He wants to play football." In an instant I had my helmet on and was running onto the field to replace Don Gmitter at left defensive end.

Notre Dame was leading 34–7 with only a minute and thirty seconds left on the clock. On the second or third play after entering the game, I came across the line full steam at the exact moment that the quarterback was rolling out toward my side of the field. I hit him so hard that I am sure the sound of contact could be heard in the stands. The time ran out after that play. When I suddenly realized what had just happened, I was euphoric. I remember going back to my room afterward and lying on my bed, staring at the ceiling and finding it hard to believe that I had just dressed for a Notre Dame game and made a tackle on national television. The following Monday, I ran into a professor I knew as I walked across campus. He congratulated me for playing in the game and added that it was an honor just to wear the uniform. I had to agree.

The last game of the year was an away game against Southern California, so I listened to it on the radio while home for Thanksgiving. Notre Dame was undefeated going into the game and would lock up the national championship with a win over the Trojans. With two minutes left in the game, Notre Dame was leading 17–13. It looked as if Ara was about to finish his first year at Notre Dame undefeated. What happened next was tragic, at least from the perspective of Notre Dame fans. Southern California took possession of the ball on its own forty-yard line. Then two long passes advanced the ball to Notre Dame's three-yard line. With very little time remaining, Southern Cal went in for the score, beating the Irish 20–17. A dream season had ended in bitter disappointment, just seconds short of a national championship.

No sooner had the season ended than I began preparing for the next one. I had to get bigger, faster, and stronger and do it quickly. I understand why steroids are such a temptation for modern-day athletes. In my era, that was not an option. Over the summer I lifted weights and worked out constantly, managing to return in the fall of 1965 weighing 215 pounds. I made the traveling team and started my first game for Notre Dame against the University of Pittsburgh. I broke my jaw in that game, ruining my chances of earning my first varsity letter. Notre Dame, with Bill Zlock as quarterback, ended the season with a respectable 7–2–1 record. The coaches immediately set their sights on 1966, and another run at the national championship.

Finding Time to Be a Student

Although I started only a handful of games while playing for Notre Dame, I often felt totally engulfed by college football. I knew that going to class was important, but my workday really began when I walked through the door at Notre Dame Stadium, checked out the practice schedule, and began putting on my pads. It was possible to cut corners in the classroom, but coaches demanded a total commitment to excellence on the practice and playing fields. From the time I entered the stadium until I arrived back at my dorm, I was part of an athletic system finely tuned for producing a national championship team. Even in the off season (spring and summer), football remained at center stage. For me, it was a challenge to keep much physical or mental energy in reserve to concentrate on schoolwork.

Even with the awesome demands of football, however, I always viewed myself as a student first, and I felt like an integral part of the student body. I did not need the hyphenated term "student-athlete" to remind me why I was in college. In the 1960s there were still NCAA policies in place that served as constant reminders that athletes were students, regardless of the demands of their sport. As noted above, for instance, freshman were not allowed to participate in varsity competition because the university viewed us as students and wanted us to have time to adjust to the demands of academic life. Many athletes did not like the rule, and many coaches, including Ara, opposed it. Nonetheless, the message it conveyed was clear. Education came first.

Freshman ineligibility worked for me. When I began my struggle for athletic respectability, the time and attention I gave to coursework decreased significantly. When I finally got my priorities straight in my senior year, it was my solid classroom performance as a freshman that allowed me to make an academic comeback. Today's freshman football players, many of whom are far less prepared for college-level work than I was, are allowed to play their first game on national television before they have even attended a class. I am not alone in supporting freshman ineligibility. Some of the finest coaches in collegiate sports history, including former basketball coaches Dean Smith, John Wooden, and Terry Holland, bemoan the fact that the NCAA abandoned this policy in the 1970s.

Another NCAA policy that made it clear that athletes were students first was the rule that allowed four-year scholarships that could not be taken away because of injury or poor athletic performance, instead of the one-year scholarships that are awarded today. When I was being recruited in high school, coaches were able to assure my parents and me that only through failure to maintain satisfactory progress in the classroom could I lose my financial aid. Again the message came through loud and clear that athletes were valued as students, not merely because they could put money in the coffers of the athletic department. When I played, athletic scholarships were educational grants, not contracts for hire.

I am certain that Ara and his staff had serious doubts about my ever playing football for Notre Dame. My freshman year had been a disaster. Yet because they were stuck with me for four years, they had to use their coaching skills to help me realize my full potential. Ara was a strong supporter of four-year scholarships. "My position," says Ara, "was that it was a four-year deal and it wasn't anything other than that, even though the rules changed in 1973. I have seen kids come in as freshmen who are awkward, but by the time they are seniors they look like Greek gods. Maturity is important, and even if you think the kid may be a mistake, they may end up being far better than you expected."[5] Ara also feels that conditioning the renewal of athletic grants on performance damages the image of universities as educational institutions.

When Coach Murphy called the small group of ballplayers together to inform us that we would never dress for a Notre Dame game, I felt like I had been punched in the stomach. I also felt that I had let down the people in my hometown who wanted so much for me to succeed. But the thought of transferring out of Notre Dame to play football elsewhere never entered my mind. Coaches did not pressure me to transfer to another institution, as often happens today. My scholarship was secure, and the coaching staff was committed to making me as good an athlete as I could possibly be. College football was extremely important to me, but unlike so many of today's players, I was not in college primarily to play football.

Compared with corporate-driven college sports in the new millennium, my early experiences at Notre Dame seem quaint. We played a ten-game schedule and did not attend bowl games. Playing games on weekdays was incomprehensible, and education had not yet been reduced to an exercise in maintaining athletic eligibility. The lessons and values of the gridiron were often quite different from those associated with critical inquiry and intellectual growth. Yet athletes had not yet been transformed into skilled specialists, cut off from mainstream college life and receiving spoon-fed lessons in elaborate, athletically controlled counseling centers. There was still a clear line between collegiate and professional sports. Although big-time college sports in that era had its share of scandals, the NCAA was holding on, albeit tenuously, to the amateur traditions it had espoused since its founding in 1905.

2

Scholastic Sports as a Pipeline to the Pros

Several years ago I was required to take a very close look at my athletic background, from childhood on, when I served as an expert witness in a case involving the Tennessee Secondary School Athletic Association (TSSAA) and Brentwood Academy, a private school in Nashville, Tennessee.[1] At issue was whether TSSAA recruiting rules violated the First Amendment rights of a Brentwood Academy football coach by limiting his contact with prospective athletes from area junior high schools. This case had already gone to the U.S. Supreme Court, where it was decided that the TSSAA should be treated, like any other arm of government, as a public agency bound by the Constitution. The case was then sent back to the U.S. District Court in Nashville to examine whether TSSAA rules actually violated the coach's right to free expression.

I was hired by the attorneys for the TSSAA to discuss the negative educational consequences of recruiting seventh- and eighth-grade students on the basis of athletic ability. I seemed like a good candidate for the job. In the attorneys' opinion, my background as a former Notre Dame football player was a definite plus, as was the research I had done on how recruitment and subsidization of high school athletes have historically undermined academic integrity. My direct experience with high-pressure recruiting while in high school was also something that could help the TSSAA's case. My one area of vulnerability, and one the attorneys for Brentwood Academy skillfully exploited, was that my experiences as a high school recruit were in some ways quite positive. During my eight-hour deposition, Brentwood's attorney, Lee Barfield, delved into areas of my past that I had not thought about for years.

Emerging from the Sandlots

My first memories of playing sports go back to summer days when my friends and I would go from house to house trying to coax others out into the heat to play sandlot baseball. Getting a critical mass of six to eight players was only part of the challenge. Next we had to find someone with a bat and ball. The bats we found were often broken near the handle and had to be repaired with nails and black electrician's tape. We also used the tape to wrap balls that were literally coming apart at the seams. We were only eight or nine years old and had no adult supervision. Yet somehow we managed to choose sides that were competitively balanced; we often made up rules as we went along. When we were tired we went home and listened to the Philadelphia Phillies on the radio and dreamed of becoming professional baseball players. If there is such a thing as pure play, this was probably it.

I was born in the suburbs of Philadelphia in 1945, a few months before the atomic bomb was dropped on Hiroshima. My parents and my three-year-old brother, Nelson, had moved to this area from Scranton, Pennsylvania, during the war because my father had found a job in the shipyards in Wilmington, Delaware. By the time I was born, they had saved enough money for a mortgage on a $2,000 house in Boothwyn, Pennsylvania, a small town not far from the steel mills, oil refineries, and factories that crowded the west bank of the Delaware River running south from Philadelphia to the towns of Chester and Marcus Hook. Boothwyn was a rural community back then, but it was close enough to the river that the torches that burned off the impurities from the Marcus Hook refineries lit up the sky at night. The smell of chemicals often filled the air.

My father had only an eighth-grade education. During the Depression he avoided the soup lines in Scranton by working in the newly created Civilian Conservation Corps. He then joined his father and brothers in the Pennsylvania coal mines, where he loaded coal cars and inhaled coal dust that permanently damaged his lungs. In the shipyards of Wilmington he worked as an electrician during a period when asbestos insulation was blown out of hoses, filling the air that workers breathed with deadly fibers. His exposure to asbestos continued when he later worked in steel mills as an electrical repair foreman. He died of asbestosis and lung cancer not long after his retirement. While on his deathbed, he told my brother and me that he was happy to have had jobs that allowed him to support his family.

Both of my parents encouraged my brother and me to be involved in sports and spent time teaching us the basics. It was my parents who instilled in me an indefatigable work ethic that was a necessary condition for success in sports. My brother, three years my senior, also played a cru-cial role in my sports career. When I was in junior high school he let me tag along with him to basketball courts where all of the players were much older than I. I would wait patiently at courtside until a team was desperate for another player. From those early pickup games I developed into a very good basketball player. In junior high school, basketball was my first love. I played for the sheer joy of it. There were no specialized sports camps back then, and the thought that playing sports would someday earn me a scholarship never entered my mind.

Our junior high school basketball coach, Robert Nugent, would occasionally pile players into his car after practice and take us to the Palestra in Philadelphia to watch St. Joseph's, Temple, La Salle, Penn, and Villanova battle it out for bragging rights in what was called the "City Series." The Palestra was a compactly designed gym at the University of Pennsylvania that put fans, many of whom were college students, so near the floor that they could almost touch the players. The Palestra's seating capacity of around eight thousand made it the largest sports arena I had ever seen. The deafening noise of the crowd and the excitement and pageantry associated with that classic round-robin series made a lasting impression on young athletes like me. These games were my first direct exposure to college sports, and they had an impact that far exceeded watching games on television or listening to them on the radio.

By the time I reached adolescence I had been swept up by the sports enthusiasm that pervaded Boothwyn and the surrounding towns. Although I was still in junior high school, I sensed that school sports, especially high school football, were an important focus of community pride. On Saturday mornings in the autumn, the topic of discussion in the grocery stores and other local establishments was the upcoming football game. And later in the day, whether people were working in their yards or hunting small game in the fields and woods near my house, there was no escaping the Saturday afternoon ritual. When the wind was right, the sound of beating drums and cowbells clanging after a touchdown could be heard in the distance. After a big victory, the band, followed by jubilant fans, literally took over the streets. High school football players were heroes.

I began playing football in eighth grade. Although I preferred basket-ball, football was valued so highly in my community that playing the game was a badge of honor. For young men going through the often socially awk-ward years of adolescence, playing football provided a significant source of self-esteem and peer-group support. I played quarterback in eighth grade and started at that position throughout high school. By the time I was a senior I had been named first-team quarterback on several all-county and all-regional Philadelphia football teams. I was also third-team All-State in football and little All-State in basketball. Other honors kept rolling in, and press coverage began to expand beyond the local papers to the Greater Philadelphia area. One article, entitled "Statistics Don't Lie About Allen Sack," called me a six-three 207-pound quarterback (I actually weighed closer to 193 pounds) and said I had rushed for 934 yards in seven games (I think half that would be more accurate). With that kind of press coverage, it was little wonder that college recruiters began to beat a path to my door.

Recruiting from the Cradle

During my deposition in the *TSSAA v. Brentwood Academy* case, I tried hard to respond to questions with yes, no, or don't-know answers whenever possible. If a longer answer was required, I tried to be honest. One of the first questions Brentwood attorney Lee Barfield asked me, after he had finished delving into my childhood and early involvement with sports, was whether I had ever been recruited by a high school coach while still in junior high school. To this I responded "no." It was taken for granted that students from Chichester Junior High School would advance to Chichester Senior High School, the former being the "feeder school" for the latter. The high school coach did not have to recruit me; I just followed the feeder pattern.

The next question was whether I had ever been recruited by another high school on the basis of athletic ability while still in high school. Barfield knew the answer to this question was yes because he had obviously read a *New York Times* column I had written in which I had briefly mentioned such a recruiting experience. The school I had mentioned was the Hill School, a prestigious private boarding school in Pottstown, Pennsylvania, founded in 1851. If Barfield could establish that I had actually benefited from the Hill School's efforts to recruit me, it would strengthen his argument that athletic recruiting by high schools such as his client, Brentwood Academy, could benefit young athletes trying to make informed choices about the kind of high school they wished to attend.

Barfield grilled me for at least two hours on my contacts with the Hill School. Because the contact had occurred more than forty years earlier, I was a little vague on the details. I did find out later, when I did a little research after the fact, that the gentleman who had contacted me was from Wayne, Pennsylvania, a town on Philadelphia's Main Line. His name was David Schaff, an investment banker who had graduated from the Hill School in 1920. He does not appear to have been a formal representative of the school or its athletic department. My guess is that he liked to help promising young athletes from the area get the advantages of a Hill School education, while at the same time enhancing the school's athletic prestige.

Schaff invited my parents and me to visit the school. It was a cold, dreary day, probably in late winter. It rained continuously, making it difficult to fully appreciate the beauty of the school's buildings and surrounding athletic fields. Students must have been on some sort of break, because there was almost no one on campus. I must admit that I was intimidated by the strange surroundings and a curriculum that seemed very different from the one to which I was accustomed. More important, the thought of leaving my family and friends to board there full time seemed unnatural. I sensed that although my parents were having similar feelings, they were feigning enthusiasm so as not to discourage me.

Schaff said the annual cost of attending the Hill School was about $3,000. He was confident that a need-based scholarship would cover most of that in my case. Schaff pointed out in a letter sometime after our visit that the Hill had produced dozens of influential graduates—the presidents of Westinghouse, Union Carbide, General Dynamics, and Pan-American Airlines, to name just a few from the corporate world. When my high school played football against teams from the upscale Philadelphia Main Line area, our coach, himself a product of the Pennsylvania coal country, used to psych us up by telling us that the fathers of the players on these teams were our fathers' bosses. This was not far from the truth. The question was whether I wanted to be a part of that world. I ultimately decided that I was not yet ready to break away from my family, friends, and community.

A question Barfield asked me over and over again, often leading in with long hypothetical scenarios that drove my attorneys crazy, was whether I had been emotionally or otherwise harmed by the Hill School recruiting experience. I had been hired by the TSSAA to testify that recruiting students on the basis of athletic ability was apt to distort a young student's priorities by sending the message that sports rather than education is what matters most. Yet in this case, argued Barfield, was it not true that the recruiting experience actually broadened my horizons, presenting me with opportunities for advancement that I previously had not known existed? Wasn't Schaff as interested in my education as he was in my skills as an athlete?

I had to be honest. The Hill School experience had been a very positive one for the reasons cited by the Brentwood attorney. Most important, it had forced me outside my comfort zone, and had made me consider options that could radically alter my life. I added, however, that if scores of high school coaches had descended on me in junior high school, competing for my athletic services and stroking my ego in the process, I had no doubt that I would have started acting like an overindulged jock much earlier in my life than I did. And I would have begun to exaggerate the role of sports to the detriment of academic achievement. I am also fairly sure that unleashing recruiters on me in junior high school would have robbed me of some of the most enjoyable athletic experiences of my youth.

One of the major differences between the Hill School's attempt to recruit me and many of the recruiting problems encountered by high school athletic associations today is that the Hill School did not compete with public schools like those in my athletic conference for state championships. If it had, its ability to recruit and subsidize athletes from a wide area would have given Hill School athletic teams an unfair competitive advantage. The central issue in the Brentwood Academy case, by contrast, was whether Brentwood, a private high school that competed head to head with public schools for championships, was using undue influence to funnel talented eighth-grade football players from the public schools into its powerhouse football program.

My encounter with the Hill School also differed from what athletes often experience today in that had I transferred to the Hill School, the major advantage would have been educational rather than athletic. What Schaff offered me was exposure to a rigorous curriculum and a pipeline to the Ivy League, not preparation for big-time college football and the pros. By contrast, I sense that many athletes who hop from one high school to another today are seeking more playing time, skill development at a given position, or the opportunity to play in a high-profile program that will make them more marketable to college recruiters. In other words, many athletes are using the school system primarily to hone their athletic skills, and high schools, especially private schools that have no clear-cut feeder system, are more than happy to market themselves to middle and high school athletes who make themselves free agents.

I am not alone in thinking that many high schools have begun to mimic practices long associated with college sports. As the 2001 report of the Knight Foundation Commission on Intercollegiate Athletics put it, "we sense that some secondary schools now emulate the worst features of too many collegiate programs: recruiting players and pursuing television exposure and national rankings with the same passion as universities."[2] Under the influence of television and the mass media, the professional model has filtered down to the level of youth sports. High school coaches have always been under pressure to win. Television exposure and other commercial pressures have raised the stakes, increasing the likelihood that coaches will bend the rules to attract marquee athletes to their schools.

Multimillion-dollar investments in stadiums, skyboxes, and other sports facilities also ratchet up the pressure on high schools to recruit athletes who can get paying fans in the seats and attract corporate sponsors. Jesuit High School in Portland, Oregon, for instance, recently spent $850,000 on a new press box with its own elevator. A new scoreboard updates fans with results from around the state. The school has a promotional deal with Nike, which is located nearby. Lafayette High School in Indiana recently built an $8 million, 6,500-seat stadium that has a seven-story press box with a hospitality area. A local real estate developer donated $4 million for the stadium.[3] I played high school sports in an era when mothers of team members sold baked goods to raise money for athletics. Scholastic sports in increasing numbers of high schools today have the feel of professional entertainment.

In an effort to minimize the number of athletes who move from school to school strictly to play sports, high school athletic associations throughout the country have been revising eligibility rules for transfer students. The Public School Athletic League (PSAL) in New York City now requires that athletes who transfer from one public school to another sit out one year unless they can demonstrate a change in residence by the athlete's parents or legal guardian. This rule change followed nearly two years of controversial transfers. In one high-profile case, a high school basketball player in Brooklyn left one high school in Brooklyn for another located only several blocks away, making stops at two Queens schools while en route. Before this rule change, the PSAL had no way to stop this kind of maneuvering by players.[4]

Not everyone supports legislation that restricts the movement of students from one high school to another for athletic reasons. In Florida, for instance, opponents of such legislation argue that transfers solely for athletic reasons should be allowed because for some students athletics is a key to success. Bob and Pam Tebow, the parents of Tim Tebow, a star quarterback who signed with the University of Florida's football team in 2006, acknowledge that they "shopped" for a program where their son, a defensive back in his original school, could play quarterback, even though this meant renting an apartment in another county.[5] For increasing numbers of Americans, success in school sports is viewed as a ticket to an athletic scholarship and a shot at a professional sports career, even though chances of attaining either of these goals are remote.

In 2005 an investigative reporter from the *New York Times* revealed that high school athletes whose grade point average did not meet NCAA requirements for eligibility to play college sports were transferring to high school diploma mills during their senior year to raise their averages quickly.[6] Since then the NCAA has launched an investigation of scores of "storefront high schools" whose only reason for existence is to provide athletes with an academic makeover. Athletes at these schools attend no classes and do little or no work. They merely receive a diploma and the necessary grade point average for a fee. The most distressing part of this story, in my opinion, is that many of the athletes who attend these phony high schools end up playing Division I football at reputable schools like Florida State, Auburn, Rutgers, Tennessee, and the University of Florida, adding credence to the argument that, poor grades aside, athletics is the ticket to college.

College Recruiting

A quick scan of the recruiting letters that have survived in my attic reveals that almost all of them were sent during my senior year. That is when the recruiting process really began in earnest. Overall, about one hundred colleges and universities contacted me, either by phone, through the mail, on visits to my home or school, or at dinners, luncheons, or other social events. The phone rang constantly. I often missed class in order to meet with a visiting coach at my high school. I received complimentary tickets to games, was taken out to lunch, had recruiters attend my games and practices, and received congratulatory telegrams from famous coaches upon reaching milestones in my young athletic career. I was treated like a celebrity by adults who were famous in their own right. It seems impossible to me that young students can go through this process without developing a feeling of entitlement and a false sense of the importance of athletics in their long-term future.

One of my top three choices from the schools that recruited me was Brown University. Stan Ward, the head basketball coach at Brown, began sending me letters, many of them handwritten, in early September, and continued until I made my final decision in the spring. I went out to dinner with him. He met my mother and father. He was a decent man who obviously loved Brown University. In one letter he expressed chagrin at what he perceived as my lukewarm reaction to Brown. "I have the feeling at times," he wrote, "that you underrate a school that I love very dearly." He went on to discuss Brown's record in placing people in graduate school and the significant number of students who received fellowships and grants there. Only toward the end of the letter did he talk about how the basketball team was doing. The head football coach, John McLaughry, also wrote to me.

Brown University was the first school I visited. It was also the first time I flew on an airplane. The campus was impressive. On Saturday afternoon I attended a picnic with Brown athletes, coaches, and several other recruits. I was introduced to skeet shooting, long an aristocratic pastime. Later that night I went drinking with one of the players on the football team, who was acting as my host. I attended my first toga party. Guys in togas were actually carrying women around on their shoulders. After a couple of drinks, my host opened up and told me what he really thought of Brown. Much of what he said was very positive. His only criticism was that he thought many students treated football players like "dumb jocks." He was very sensitive to what he perceived as class distinctions in the student body.

I was very serious about Princeton, a school not far from my hometown in Pennsylvania. Both the football and the basketball coaches contacted me. I had always viewed Princeton's All-American basketball player, Bill Bradley, later a U.S. senator, as a role model. Bob Nugent had taken us to see him play at the Palestra in Philadelphia. It was not until November that I expressed an interest in Princeton to some Princeton graduates who lived in Delaware County. I had some contact with the football coach over the next couple of months. What really sold me on Princeton was a visit Bill Bradley and head basketball coach Butch Van Breda Kolff made to my house.

One night, Coach Van Breda Kolff was supposed to come to my house to speak with my parents and me about Princeton. Because Princeton was playing in Philadelphia that evening, he decided to bring Bradley along with him. We talked in the living room and later moved to the kitchen for coffee and desert. Afterward, Bradley, an All-American soon to be a Rhodes Scholar and later a U.S. senator, helped my mother clean off the table and pile dishes in the sink. My mother never got over that. At about this time I made a campus visit to Princeton. I loved it. The only problem I had with Princeton was that it played a single-wing offense, rather than an offense better suited to my drop-back passing style. The fact that the nature of Princeton's offense played a role in my decision still amazes me today.

Wining and Dining with Leonard Tose

Notre Dame entered the recruiting picture in the late fall when its coaches arranged a meeting with my parents and me. On the evening of the visit, a man who I assumed was the head football coach knocked on our front door. He was built like a football player and appeared to be in his midthirties. He was accompanied by an older gentleman who looked as if he might have played for Knute Rockne, or maybe even coached him. The imposing figure turned out to be Gus Cifelli, an assistant coach and former tackle at Notre Dame. The older man was Hughie Devore, the person who was about to take over as Notre Dame's head coach. Devore had extensive coaching experience at the collegiate level and had been head coach of the Philadelphia Eagles.

Their message was honest and to the point. The Irish had gone through some hard times during the just completed Joe Kuharich years, and they needed a quarterback. I was six foot three and weighed 193 pounds. I could throw a football close to sixty yards. They had seen the game films my coach had sent them, and in their opinion I could play at Notre Dame. They talked with my parents and me for a while. There was no pressure, no hype. They did not follow up with a lot of written material and letters, as many of the other recruiters did; at least I cannot find any in my files. All I have is the letter of acceptance from the admissions office.

A month or so later, Cifelli took me out to dinner in Philadelphia. He was one of the nicest men I met during the recruiting process. He told me about the awesome physical and emotional demands of playing at Notre Dame. He also made me aware of the potential rewards. He had been through all of this himself. Being with him was like a crash course on how to survive the recruiting process. As we left the restaurant, he gave me a piece of paper with a name and phone number on it. The name was Leonard Tose. Cifelli said this was someone I should meet and that Tose was expecting my call.

Leonard Tose, as I later found out, owned a multimillion-dollar trucking firm that had been started by his immigrant father. Tose had graduated in 1937 from Notre Dame, where he had played on the freshman football team. Later in his life, he bought the Philadelphia Eagles. He was a compulsive gambler. By his own estimate, he lost more than $20 million at Resorts International and more than $14 million at the Sands. He ultimately had to sell the Eagles as well as his trucking firm to pay off his gambling debts. When he died, in 2003, he was living modestly in the Warwick Hotel in Philadelphia's Center City, the same hotel where I first met him in 1963 after I followed Gus Cifelli's advice and gave him a call.

I took a train into the city to meet Tose. When I met him in the lobby of the Warwick Hotel, he said he was taking a break from negotiations with the Teamsters Union to have dinner with me. He was impeccably dressed in a dark suit and what could be called a power tie. He was tanned, perhaps from a trip to the islands. I had borrowed my brother's green blazer for the occasion. Tose remarked that it made me look like I belonged at Notre Dame.

When we walked into the dining room, a string ensemble was playing light classical music off to the side. Tose seemed right at home in these elegant surroundings. The maitre d' knew him by name and the waiters treated him with deference. I had never been in a place like this before. I must have looked perplexed as I stared at the menu, because Tose suggested that I try the filet mignon. I did not know what that was, but I ordered it anyway to avoid embarrassment. When I tasted my salad I splattered salad dressing on my brother's blazer; Tose politely reached over and used his napkin to help me wipe it off.

I was off to a shaky start, but things improved as the evening progressed. For a while we talked about my family. I told him my dad worked in a steel mill and my mom in the high school cafeteria. I told him about the other colleges that had contacted me and that I had narrowed my choices to Brown, Princeton, and Notre Dame. He asked what it would take for me to make up my mind. I was not sure what he meant, so he had to be a little more direct. Out on the bargaining table came travel expenses back and forth to Notre Dame during the school year, a summer job, and the payment of other expenses I might incur beyond room, board, and tuition. I often wonder if I could have asked for more—like a car and membership in the Chicago Playboy Club—but Mr. Tose focused on basic living expenses and the benefits of attending Notre Dame.

I saw nothing particularly unusual about these offers. After all, several universities had already paid my travel expenses to visit their campuses. I was invited to lunch at the Yale Club of Philadelphia, and to dinner with Dartmouth recruits at a Valley Forge estate. I received congressional nominations to two of the military academies before I had even applied. Special treatment seemed like a regular part of the recruiting process. When I told my high school football coach about Tose's offer, he thought it sounded very reasonable. It was just a normal part of the recruiting game. As long as the payments were for regular expenses related to going to college, he saw no problem, even though they were a violation of NCAA rules.[7]

My attraction to Notre Dame went well beyond the financial support from Tose. First, there was a perception among people I respected, such as teachers and guidance counselors, that Notre Dame had a tradition of both academic and athletic excellence that set it apart from the Ivy League schools, where athletics was deemphasized. This undoubtedly influenced my thinking. I also thought the campus was right up there with Princeton's aesthetically. The day I arrived in South Bend for my visit to Notre Dame, it was snowing. Though I am not a Catholic, walking past the Grotto on a snowy afternoon made a lasting impression. Ice-covered lakes, a beautiful Gothic church, dormitories with slate roofs bordering expansive quadrangles—these things worked a spell on me.

Most of the people in my hometown were rooting for me to choose Notre Dame. According to Ed Gebhart, a former *Delaware County Daily Times* reporter, "It was a big story if a kid went to Notre Dame. There were so many Notre Dame fans around here that it attracted more media attention than if a kid went to Michigan or a school like that."[8] In the 1950s and 1960s, my community had a very large Catholic population, many of whom were the offspring of first- or second-generation European immigrants. For them, Notre Dame was a rallying point for ethnic and religious pride. A Notre Dame victory over Northwestern or some other elite university in football could be viewed as a victory for steel workers, pipe fitters, stone masons, and other blue-collar workers over their Protestant bosses. If I chose to attend a school like Princeton or Brown, I risked being accused of fraternizing with the enemy.

The recruiting experience had given me opportunities available to few seventeen- or eighteen-year-olds from my social class. I was in the enviable position of being able to turn down offers from schools to which students with better academic credentials than mine could not gain admission or could not afford. Even Yale, one of the most academically competitive institutions in the country, did not simply turn me away. In his rejection letter, the director of admissions said that his committee urged me to consider a postgraduate year of secondary school at one of the "strong preparatory schools" with which they were familiar. He said he would be glad to help me with this. One of the schools he clearly had in mind was the Hill School.

In the spring I had received a six-page, single-spaced typewritten letter from David Schaff, the Hill School graduate who had contacted me two years earlier. Schaff pointed out that a postgraduate year at the Hill could get me into a school like Yale. He mentioned Yale specifically and the Yale coach who had recruited me. He assured me that financial aid would not be a problem. He also talked in glowing terms about Yale's football program and suggested that I talk to one of his friends on Yale's board of trustees. I realize that these offers were being made in large part because I was a fine athlete. But there is no denying that contacts like these were providing me with tremendous opportunities for personal and academic growth.

Some Final Thoughts on Recruiting Then and Now

The recruiting experience gave me some once-in-a-lifetime opportunities. There was also a downside. During my senior year, the special treatment I received as an athlete began to skew my priorities away from education. High school teachers let me cut classes to meet with recruiters. I traveled around the country visiting colleges, often missing classes to do so. I began to feel entitled to this kind of special treatment. Before my trip to Notre Dame, I failed to inform my Latin teacher that I was going to miss her exam. She refused to give me a makeup and gave me the only F I ever received on a report card. That was the only reality check I can recall during the entire recruiting year. The dominant message was that academic compromises could be made for athletes.

In college I continued to play a role that many people associate with being a "dumb jock." I cut more than my share of classes, took advantage of "friendly faculty" when I could find them, and continued to feel that the rules that applied to other students did not apply to me. The recruiting experience left me with a feeling of entitlement that is the root cause of some of the most boorish forms of jock behavior. What saved me from academic disaster was that I arrived in college with the basic skills needed for academic survival. I think it is important to ask what would have happened to me had the media exposure and aggressive recruiting begun in junior high school or earlier. What would have happened if I had gotten the message much earlier that sports rather than education is the real key to success?

The increased commercialism and professionalism of collegiate sports over the past forty years have generated a no-holds-barred struggle for talented athletes of all ages. Recruiting as I experienced it seems primitive by comparison. A quick search of the Internet yields dozens of athletic recruiting services whose business is to help prospective college athletes get athletic scholarships. One of these companies, the National Scouting Report (NSR), employs twenty full-time people and has hundreds of field scouts who make personal calls on high school coaches throughout the country to gather information on potential clients. NSR's annual gross revenues in 2004 were between $3 and $5 million. Its Web site receives more than two million hits per month, many from college coaches who use the site for updated prospect information.[9]

Recruiting companies send out information on their clients' athletic achievements, awards, and vital statistics, such as speed in the forty-yard dash and vertical jump, to coaches and recruiting departments at colleges. The more expensive programs may include the placement of a highlight video provided by the athlete on a "mini CD," which also contains the prospect's profile. NSR furnishes free copies of prospect videos to coaches from its extensive video library. It also has a video room at its home office where coaches can come to evaluate tapes of hundreds of prospects for free. In my era, alumni did much of the legwork of locating talented athletes for college coaches. Scouting services of various types and quality now scour the United States and other countries for information on top prospects.

In the sport of basketball, tournaments run by the Amateur Athletics Union (AAU) in the spring, summer, and fall bring top school-age basketball players together, where they are viewed by college coaches from across the country. Some AAU teams play close to a hundred games a year, traveling from one town or state to another. The tournaments, sponsored by major sneaker companies, provide one-stop shopping for college recruiters, who can watch athletes perform and pick the ones they want to recruit. According to my friend Bruce Svare, a former AAU coach and current director of the National Institute for Sports Reform, this system especially exploits African Americans, whose attention is diverted from the classroom by the remote possibility that they may catch the eye of a college or professional scout.[10] Education cannot compete in terms of the glamour associated with these corporate-sponsored recruiting events.

Football camps and combines where high school athletes can put their talent on display for college recruiters have proliferated in recent years. Camps (where players work to improve their skills) and combines (where players are tested and evaluated) have sometimes been sponsored by companies like Nike. Before the passage of restrictive legislation in 2006, some of these combines attracted large numbers of Division I coaches to a variety of locations—some on college campuses—to evaluate potential recruits. NCAA legislation now prohibits coaches from attending these combines, but it does allow athletes to attend football camps sponsored by individual universities and staffed by their coaches. Independent combines still serve as part of the recruiting process by disseminating information on athletic performance to the college programs.

Internet recruiting networks such as Rivals.com and Scout.com target the growing number of fans who passionately follow the college recruiting process. Sites like these report news and provide rankings on top high school teams and players. Rivals.com provides national player rankings, online video highlights, player cards and a searchable player database, official visit lists, text alerts to cell phones, and message boards and community tools that increase fan knowledge and involvement. Both Scout. Com and Rival.Com act as integrated sports publishing companies that provide not only player databases but specific sports coverage in online sports magazines and other publications. College scouts as well as high school and college sports fans are important target markets for these multimillion-dollar businesses.

In 2006 the Rutgers University football team stunned the nation by cat-apulting from its usual position in the cellar of the Big East Conference to number 6 in the Bowl Championship Series rankings. A novel recruiting strategy contributed to this incredible turnaround. In December 2001, the peak of recruiting season, the new Rutgers coach, Greg Schiano, per-suaded the Athletic Department to buy advertising space on billboards near powerhouse football high schools in south Florida featuring pictures of Schiano surrounded by every Rutgers player from Florida. In addition to yearly billboards, Rutgers also paid for Schiano's weekly television show on Sun Sports, a Florida cable channel, and allowed him to hold summer camps in the area. As a result, the number of players from Florida on the Rutgers roster rose from four to twenty-one between 2000 and 2006.[11]

The recruiting year in college football culminates on February 2 with national signing day, the first day on which high school seniors can offi-cially submit their college letters of intent. In the 1960s, newspapers often gave some coverage to a highly recruited athlete's decision to attend one school or another. But the current media hype surrounding national sign-ing day would have been inconceivable. In recent years College Sports Television (CSTV) has presented a two-hour prime-time special dedi-cated solely to football's national signing day. The show, called *Crystal Ball*, features player and college coach press conferences and analysis from recruiting gurus such as Tom Lemming of ESPN. The network also scans the nation that day, covering exclusive high school player signings and press conferences with college coaches, who announce their signing classes. National signing day has become a major media event, not unlike the NFL draft.

There has always been a symbiotic relationship between high school sports and the media. In the 1950s the media promoted Wilt Chamber-lain, a basketball sensation at Overbrook High School in Philadelphia, and Wilt sold a lot of papers in return. But the media attention received by high school athletes in that period pales in comparison with today. This is in part the result of a technological revolution in sports broadcast-ing and the growth of sports into a $213 billion industry. High school phe-nomenon Lebron James, who skipped college to go directly into the NBA, had his high school games air on local pay-per-view TV, then national cable. According to *Minneapolis Star* sports columnist Jay Weiner, James sent out press releases for the rollout of his own Web site. He signed a $90 million advertising contract with Nike.[12]

High school athletes headed for college are also more sophisticated than ever in the art of using the media for self-promotion. For instance, quarterback Jimmy Clausen, rated one of the top football players in the country, recently rolled into South Bend, Indiana, in a white Hummer stretch limousine to announce his decision to attend Notre Dame. Clausen—who was only a junior in high school at the time—and his family had hired a public relations firm to orchestrate the press conference, which was held at the College Football Hall of Fame in South Bend. ESPN jumped on the story, as did just about every other media outlet in the country. In an era when celebrity college coaches routinely sell themselves to sneaker companies and the NCAA extols the virtues of brand management, self-promotion by athletes seems perfectly natural.

Clausen admitted at the press conference that he had not given much thought to what his academic major might be, but he laid out his athletic game plan with precision. He chose Notre Dame over USC in order to sharpen his quarterback skills. Charlie Weis, the former New England Patriots' offensive coordinator, who had just accepted the head coaching job at Notre Dame, would be his mentor. He had also decided to graduate from high school in December of his senior year. By enrolling early at Notre Dame, he could attend spring practice, thus getting a jump on learning Weis's system and improving his chances of playing football in the fall of his freshman year. Though only a junior in high school, Clausen had arrived in South Bend with a plan for marketing himself to the media and for using the educational system as a pipeline to the pros.

College sports as a popular form of commercial entertainment was deeply embedded in American culture even when I played, and there have always been high school heroes. Over the past couple of decades, however, commercialism has swamped academic values, and the dominant spirit of college sports has become unmistakably professional. As this professional model has filtered down into the secondary schools, priorities have shifted toward producing athletes rather than well-educated citizens whose lives are enriched by competitive sports. The enormous emphasis that American universities place on mass spectator sports has created a class of highly skilled athletic specialists, especially in high-profile sports like football and basketball, who are often isolated from mainstream academic life.

The trend toward greater specialization in sports at all levels has all but eliminated the play component from modern games. One of the most striking revelations for me in the *TSSAA v. Brentwood Academy* case was not that coaches were violating recruiting rules by contacting eighth graders about spring football practice but that high schools had spring football practice to begin with. When I was in eighth grade I played football, basketball, and baseball and still had time to wander the fields and explore the streams and woodlands that surrounded my small town. I was passionate about sports, but it was an avocation, not a year-round quest for an athletic scholarship. In the 1960s, amateurism was alive and well, at least for eighth graders.

The United States is the only nation in the world where schools and universities have become training grounds for professional sports. Most countries have club systems that are totally unrelated to their schools to oversee sports from the recreational level to the highest levels of international competition. In nations like Japan, Germany, France, and South Korea—countries where students consistently outperform American students in science and math—the primacy of education and academic achievement is absolutely clear.[13] This same commitment to education in the schools can also be found in other countries with which the United States must compete in the global economy. Yet, despite the well-documented fact that our nation is losing its global advantage in educational preparedness, universities continue to send the message to Americans of all ages that sports, rather than education, is the main attraction.

3

The Game of the Century

On the first day of preseason practice in 1966, one of the coaches stood close by to make sure that players weighed in and recorded their weight accurately. Much to the coaching staff's surprise, I weighed in at 230 pounds. Over the summer I had worked at the British Petroleum oil refinery in Marcus Hook, Pennsylvania. As in previous years, Leonard Tose kept his promise and helped me find employment. My job was to load large oil drums onto trucks manually, an operation that required considerable strength. During the thirty-minute lunch break I would eat and have a couple bottles of beer at a waterfront bar with old-timers who had been working on the loading dock for years. We would then return to work and continue loading trucks in temperatures seldom lower than 90 degrees. After work I did my serious workouts. By the end of the summer I was bench pressing close to three hundred pounds and lifting oil drums during work breaks just for the fun of it.

The hard work paid off. During the two weeks of double sessions, I worked my way into the starting defensive end position. Tom Rhoads, my main competitor, had come back overweight and a little out of shape. I am sure that he had spent far more time at the beach than in the gym during his summer break. Just a week or so before the opening game against Purdue, I was in the starting lineup, which meant that for the first time at Notre Dame I had actually earned the right to wear a gold jersey in practice. But as Johnny Ray, our defensive coordinator, never tired of saying, "It is much easier to get to the top than it is to stay there." It remained to be seen whether I had the physical and emotional maturity to handle the stress of wearing the gold.

The real test for me came during the final scrimmage before the Purdue game. We had been practicing hard for about two weeks and I, like everyone else, was bruised and totally exhausted. On a Friday evening at dinner, a major scrimmage was announced for eight o'clock the next morning. I knew that a scrimmage was likely, but not at eight o'clock in the morning. When I walked over to the stadium a little after seven, it was already hot and muggy, with no hint of a breeze. I knew it would only get worse. Between exhaustion and the heat, I simply could not get my body interested in playing football. To paraphrase a comment by Michael Oriard, a former Notre Dame football player, my bones were moving, but my flesh simply did not want to follow.[1]

Early in the scrimmage I came across the line, shed a block thrown by a running back, and had a clear shot at the quarterback, who was dropping back to pass. Somehow, and I really do not know how this happened, Jim Lynch, the outside linebacker, and I tripped over each other when we were about to make the tackle, allowing the quarterback to run for fairly significant yardage. I might well have been at fault. Regardless, John Ray pulled me out of the scrimmage and sent Tom Rhoads in. Tom performed brilliantly in the scrimmage and managed to win back his starting position. He started against Purdue the next Saturday and had what I think was the best game of his life. He was awarded the game ball by the coaches. He had certainly earned it.

Notre Dame had come into the Purdue game ranked sixth in the nation. Purdue, with its great All-American quarterback Bob Griese, was ranked eighth. It was in the Purdue game that Notre Dame's sophomore sensations, quarterback Terry Hanratty and wide receiver Jim Seymour, established themselves as the finest passing combination in the country. Hanratty completed sixteen of twenty-four passes for 304 yards. Seymour had thirteen pass receptions for 276 yards, breaking records held by Notre Dame's greatest pass receivers going back to Knute Rochne. Notre Dame won the game 26–14, getting off to a great start against a very good team.

After Purdue, we went on to beat Northwestern and Army easily, rising in the national rankings to number two. Because Tom Rhoads was injured in the Army game, I started against North Carolina and then again against the University of Oklahoma. We won both games by large margins, even though Oklahoma was ranked tenth in the country. The Oklahoma game was my high-water mark as a college athlete. I never felt better before a game in my life. I was healthy and extremely well prepared after a terrific week in practice. Early in the game, however, I injured my ankle and

Achilles tendon and had to limp off to the training room. Rhoads was able to fill in for me, and he played a great game even though his shoulder was still hurting.

We beat Oklahoma 38–0, the worst Oklahoma defeat in twenty-one years. Notre Dame had come into the Oklahoma game ranked number one and had no trouble staying at the top of the rankings for the next three weeks. I missed most of the Navy game because of my injury. We won 31–7. We cruised past Pittsburgh 40–0 and annihilated Duke 64–0. Against Duke, everyone who dressed for the game played. These teams simply did not have the depth that Notre Dame did. Even Notre Dame's second unit would most probably have clobbered Pittsburgh and Duke. Ara actually tried not to run up scores against these teams, but even massive substitutions and keeping the ball on the ground could not stop the scoring. The next game, against Michigan State, was a totally different story.

The Biggest Game of Them All

Michigan State was by far the toughest team on our 1966 schedule. Eleven Michigan State players were named to All-American teams at season's end, including the likes of Bubba Smith, George Webster, and Gene Washington. Notre Dame students held rallies throughout the week and the media swarmed all over campus, even though the game was to be played in East Lansing. A major challenge for the team was not to get so pumped up early in the week that we would go into the game emotionally flat. The Michigan State game was noteworthy in terms of the media attention it garnered, the controversy it generated, and the pivotal role it played in ushering in a new era in collegiate sports. The Michigan State game is arguably the most talked-about and debated game in Notre Dame history.

Notre Dame and Michigan State came into this game ranked as the number-one and number-two teams in the nation, respectively. Because the game was played so late in the season and both teams were undefeated, the winner was most likely to be the national champion. Unlike today, the national championship team was announced before the bowl games. In fact, neither team was able to play in a bowl game. In Notre Dame's case, bowl games were against university policy. Michigan State was excluded because Rose Bowl policy prevented participation two years in a row. Given these circumstances, the game took on qualities not unlike those of a major bowl game. It has even been compared to the Super Bowl in terms of the attention it attracted.

The controversy that has kept the 1966 season in the public conscious-ness over the decades has to do with decisions Ara Parseghian made in the closing minute and a half of the game. The score was tied 10–10. Notre Dame had the ball deep in its own territory. Instead of using his passing game to score before the clock ran out, Ara chose to keep the ball on the ground for much of Notre Dame's final possession, giving the appear-ance that Notre Dame was willing to settle for a tie. The situation was far more complicated than that. Notre Dame started the game without its All-American halfback, Nick Eddy, who had re-injured his shoulder get-ting off the train when the team arrived in East Lansing. His backup, Bob Gladieux, had not started a game all year.

Early in the game, our starting quarterback and center were injured. Then Gladieux bruised his thigh and was replaced by a third-string run-ning back. As a result of attrition, Notre Dame had several inexperienced players in key positions as the clock was running out. Given the brisk wind blowing in Notre Dame's face and the fact that Michigan State had one of the finest field goal kickers in the nation, a turnover would have ended Notre Dame's quest for the national championship. I believed at the time, and still do today, that Ara did the right thing by keeping the ball on the ground for several plays before finally calling a pass play to get into field goal range. Because that strategy looked a lot like running out the clock instead of going for a win, Ara has been relentlessly, and sometimes sav-agely, criticized over the decades for allegedly "tying one for the Gipper."

In the midst of all of the controversy, one thing was certain. By not losing to Michigan State, Notre Dame found itself in an excellent position to win the national championship. Unlike Michigan State, whose season was over, Notre Dame had an opportunity to redeem itself the next week in a game against tenth-ranked Southern California. While the rest of the student body was home for Thanksgiving, we flew to California for what was undoubtedly the most exciting road trip I ever made as a Notre Dame athlete. The night before the game, the team privately previewed a film about to be released by Paramount Pictures in Los Angeles called *El Dorado*. We watched the movie in a private screening room at Paramount, sitting in plush black leather chairs and joking with Robert Mitchum, one of the stars of the film. He seemed to be having as much fun as we were.

The next day we trounced the Trojans 51–0 before about ninety thou-sand fans in the Los Angeles coliseum. Although this was the only game in my life in which I took two shots to the groin within fifteen minutes, I actually had fun. On one kickoff, I came downfield as fast as I could sprint and hit the ball carrier at the exact moment that he made a sharp cut in my direction. The collision brought the kind of groan from the packed stadium that defensive players dream about. Maybe it was because this was my last game and I had nothing to lose—whatever the reason, I felt fast and under control. Once the game was pretty much decided, Tom Rhoads and I began taking turns going in and out of the game, without even consulting the coaches. The feeling of freedom was exhilarating.

After the game, Hollywood celebrities made their way through our locker room while we were celebrating our victory. The team was invited to dinner at a huge house owned by a Hollywood attorney. I had never been to a house that had servants and its own pipe organ. While standing in the dessert line, I noticed a small man in front of me who had just arrived. When he turned around and said hello, I saw that it was Jimmy Durante. We had a chance to talk a little bit over dessert. Later in the evening Durante sat down at the piano and serenaded the team with songs he had made famous. Players joined him at the piano, arms around each other and around Durante.

On the night before we flew back to South Bend, Tom Rhoads and I visited as many bars and nightclubs in Los Angeles as possible, and after staying up all night we almost missed the flight back to Indiana. We slept all the way to Chicago, where our flight had been diverted from O'Hare to Midway Airport because of a snowstorm. When Tom and I finally got off the plane, the team was posing for a group photo with their fingers in the air, shouting, "We're number one!" As Ara predicated, our victory over USC had led both the UPI and AP polls to vote Notre Dame number one and Michigan State number two, thus making Notre Dame the 1966 national champions. We then returned to South Bend and took buses back to campus. On the way home, people lined both sides of Notre Dame Avenue, and the team was greeted at the entrance to campus by a student body gone wild.

As the years have passed, the Michigan State game, rather than detracting from our national championship season, has actually enhanced it. Very often when people hear that I played on the 1966 national championship team, they immediately ask me about the Michigan State game. They want to know my opinion of Ara's decision to play conservatively, and I enjoy giving my play-by-play account of the game and my description of the atmosphere on the sidelines, where I stood watching Ara and the other coaches making decisions under extreme pressure. Although the stress did not compare to what Eisenhower faced when trying to decide whether or not to launch Operation Overlord, there was certainly a hint of that kind of tension in the air. When the game ended, the stadium went eerily silent.

Notre Dame–Michigan State was what author Mike Celizic has called the "the first mega-game of the modern television era."[2] The game was one of the first to reveal the incredible potential of televised college sports as a form of mass commercial entertainment. This game, which I think deserves to be called "the game of the century," had a Nielsen rating of 22.5, the highest ever recorded for a regular-season game up to that time. The game was broadcast to soldiers in Vietnam and to fans in Hawaii via satellite. With these kinds of ratings, college football demonstrated its ability to reach target markets that advertisers dream about. After 1966, college sports turned the corner into becoming a major marketing platform for corporate America, with television leading the way.

When I watch the highlight films from the 1966 season, I am struck by how unaware the players appear to be that they are on television. When I was on the field, my major concern was the game films that I knew would be played and replayed at our Sunday night team meetings, highlighting every missed tackle and blown assignment. Hamming it up for a television audience never entered my mind. Today's collegiate athletes are much more media savvy and aware that part of their job is to entertain the general public. Notre Dame pep rallies in the 1960s were raucous affairs, played out in a crowded field house packed with several thousand sweaty students on the verge of breaking into a riot. Pep rallies today seem choreographed by comparison, as if being staged for TV.

The Notre Dame–Michigan State game was also significant in terms of what it said about changing race relations in collegiate sports. In the mid-to late 1960s there were relatively few African American college athletes. In the Southeast Conference there were none. Michigan State, by contrast, fielded a football team in 1966 that was primarily African American. By the early 1970s, even the Southeast Conference was recruiting African Americans heavily. This may indicate progress toward eliminating racial bigotry. But the absence of a similar explosive increase in the percentage of African Americans among regular college students suggests that what colleges had discovered is that African Americans can win games and increase television exposure. Whether this has led to increased educational opportunities for African American children is a question that continues to be hotly debated.

In 2004 African Americans made up about 10 percent of all students at Division I universities. However, 53 percent of athletes with football scholarships and 60 percent of male basketball players with basketball scholarships at these schools were African American. About 82 percent of all African American athletes played in two sports—football and basketball—the only sports that produce revenues and the sports with the lowest graduation rates.[3] Some of these athletes have undoubtedly benefited from college sports. But many others whose labor has generated millions of dollars in revenue—some of it earmarked for scholarships in sports in which most participants are white and relatively privileged—have received a watered-down education at best. I focus on the ethics of this arrangement in later chapters.

Trying to Be an Intellectual?

After the euphoria of winning the national championship began to wear off, I realized that my daily life at Notre Dame was about to change significantly. I immediately crossed spring practice off my list of things to do, along with pre-spring practice, sprinting up stadium stairs, trips to Father Lange's weight room—unless I had the urge to work out—and all of the other football-related rituals that had been so important to my life in college. I was taking some time off to see what it was like to be a regular student and sociology major. I attended all of my classes, did reading assignments, made the dean's list, and still had time for a social life. The pressure to take academic shortcuts suddenly lifted, and I had no desire or need to miss my 8:00 A.M. classes. I had never known that going to college could be so much fun.

A couple of weeks into the spring semester, Ara called a team meeting to discuss odds and ends left over from the fall. When the meeting ended, Tom Pagna, our offensive backfield coach, walked up behind me and gave my hair, which had grown just long enough to touch the collar of my shirt, a little tug. "What are you trying to do, Sack, be an intellectual?" he asked. I know that he was just kidding around, but there was a hint of sarcasm in his voice, as if the term "intellectual" was derogatory. I found this fleeting encounter a little peculiar because I had naively assumed that intellectuals were held in high esteem in American culture, especially in universities.

Not long after that meeting, I read a Pulitzer Prize–winning book by Richard Hofstadter entitled *Anti-Intellectualism in American Life,* which argues that while intelligence is a quality of mind that many Americans readily embrace, intellect is somewhat more suspect. Intelligent people, according to Hofstadter, are practical problem solvers who have little interest in abstract ideas that do not help to achieve clearly defined goals. They are not particularly interested in scratching below the surface to discover the ultimate meaning of things. Raw intelligence, says Hofstadter, has long been associated in the public mind with successful entrepreneurs or captains of industry, people who have built fortunes through hard work and common sense.[4]

Intellectuals, by contrast, are likely to see intrinsic value in pursuing knowledge and ideas simply for the sake of expanding human understanding. According to Hofstadter, intellectuals refuse to limit their thinking to the accomplishment of narrowly defined objectives such as maximizing profits or realizing a return on investment. They also raise questions about ethics and the human condition that often have no clear answers. Intellectuals constantly question, probe, and challenge authority rather than accepting its dictates uncritically. If I understand Hofstadter correctly, intellectuals are subversive almost by definition, because there is nothing they will not criticize or throw into question.

After reading Hofstadter's book, I realized that Pagna was right. During my four years at Notre Dame I had drifted to the intellectual side of the academic spectrum. I was excited about ideas. When I took off my pads and limped back to my dormitory, I entered a world that for me was refreshingly subversive. I could literally walk down the hallway and find students more than willing to debate issues ranging from race relations to the existentialism of Jean-Paul Sartre. Some of the students were active in civil rights initiatives, antipoverty programs, and other progressive causes. Many others were fairly conservative, which made the intellectual dialogue even more exciting. Slowly but surely, my hair probably did begin to get a little longer, as I began to experiment with new ways of thinking and challenging convention.

By the time I reached my senior year at Notre Dame, I had majored in sociology and become a staunch supporter of the civil rights movement. In high school, our athletic director gave me his copy of a book entitled *The Conscience of a Conservative*. This book, written by Republican senator Barry Goldwater, presented a picture of America as a meritocracy where everyone had ample opportunities for advancement if only they would take advantage of them. The book's emphasis on individualism, free enterprise, and the rewards of hard work and sacrifice resonated with my experiences in sports and with my family's Polish immigrant values. Goldwater's emphasis on people's need to "pull themselves up by their bootstraps" made a lot of sense to me then and continues to influence my thinking today.

But life in America in the 1960s simply did not fit the model presented by Goldwater. The most glaring contradiction in the meritocratic model—gender and other types of inequality were just entering my radar screen—was in the area of race relations. How could anyone possibly talk about equal opportunity when African Americans in Greensboro, North Carolina, could shop in a department store such as Woolworth's but not eat at its lunch counter? Throughout the South, Jim Crow laws supported a system of apartheid that denied African Americans equal access to schools, restaurants, hotels, theaters, public transportation, and just about every other kind of public service or facility. African Americans were lynched because of racial hatred and denied jobs because of the color of their skin. Racial discrimination was also the norm in the North.

I found it difficult to ignore racial prejudice and class differences in opportunity as factors that influence where people are likely to end up in society's pecking order. I was well aware that some people claw their way to the top even though born into humble circumstances. But I found the sociological argument that social class and race can have a profound effect on a person's life chances very compelling. As my focus began to shift from flaws in individual people to flaws in the larger social system, my politics became more liberal. My drift to the political left was reinforced by the political turmoil of the times. In 1966 Martin Luther King brought the civil rights campaign to Chicago, and Notre Dame students staged their first antiwar protest on campus. Some students were beginning to ask why Notre Dame did not admit women.

After reading Hofstadter's book, I began to understand more deeply the tension that often exists between the culture of big-time college sports and the core intellectual values and priorities of academe. Big-time college athletes, and those who rally around them, tend to be practical and intelligent rather than intellectual, and consider the lessons learned from college sports—fierce competitiveness, teamwork, respect for authority, and discipline—as important as, if not more important than, what is learned in a classroom. The intellectual's emphasis on questioning and critical analysis also clashes with a culture that makes obedience to authority its centerpiece. For many big-time college athletes, sports is training for a professional career, be it in sports or business. Intellectuals view college sports as an extracurricular activity that should complement, not overwhelm, traditional academic values.

Some Observations on College Football Then and Now

Although it was often difficult to reconcile the demands of football with the demands of being a college student in the 1960s, I feel extremely lucky to have played at a time when universities and the NCAA still treated athletes as students rather than as professional entertainers. The freshman ineligibility rule helped me get off to a good start academically and drove home the point that universities were institutions of higher learning, not specialized training camps for the pros. That Notre Dame had made a four-year financial commitment to me, even if I fell short of coaches' expectations on the playing field, reinforced my awareness that the school was committed to me as a student. Athletes lived in the same dorms and attended the same classes that other students did.

In the 1960s, playing college football did not require that athletes be cut off from the general student body, including that segment that placed a high value on what Hofstadter referred to as the "life of the mind." In recent years, however, college education for athletes has been redefined in narrow vocational terms. What passes for education in some athletic programs is being dragged half-asleep from class to class by an army of academic counselors whose job it is to keep athletes eligible. Athletes attend mandatory study hall, often take classes that have little academic substance, and study in athletic counseling centers that are segregated from the rest of the student body. Academic life for athletes has become as regimented as their life on the playing field, making it difficult for them to explore new ideas or take advantage of opportunities for personal growth.

Not long ago I visited an academically prestigious university in Connecticut that provides quite a bit of counseling support for athletes. I was somewhat taken aback, however, to hear that all varsity athletes, regardless of grade point average, had to attend mandatory study hall in a facility housed in the very center of the athletic complex. "What about highly motivated students who would prefer to study in the library, or with friends, or at Starbucks with their laptops and a chai tea?" I asked. I was told that the athletic learning center had computer and other resources that were comparable to if not better than those in the library or elsewhere on campus. The notion that some athletes might prefer to study in solitude or with other students did not seem to be popular among athletic staff, for whom academic life, like everything else in the game plan, has to be managed closely if teams are going to win.

The Notre Dame–Michigan State game during my senior year was a harbinger of the rampant commercialism that was about to invade college campuses and collegiate athletic programs. Yet, compared with today, college football in the 1960s was still tethered, albeit tenuously, to its amateur moorings. Universities had not yet sold their athletic programs to companies like Nike and Reebok to be used as marketing platforms. Ara and the other coaches had some business deals on the side, but they were modest ventures compared to those of today's celebrity coaches. Televised football games on weeknights were still unthinkable, as were multibillion-dollar rights fees for basketball. Even on the weekends, the only nationally televised college football game was the NCAA "Game of the Week." There was no Bowl Championship Series, and the bowls were not yet named after corporate sponsors.

Since 1966 Notre Dame has built a college football television empire. NBC Sports pays millions of dollars to televise all of Notre Dame's home games nationally and recently renewed the contract, worth $9 million a year, through 2010. The away games are shown by ABC, CBS, and ESPN. As a member of the Big Ten, Michigan State football has also become a media giant. In 2006 the Big Ten Conference announced the creation of its own television network, which involves a twenty-year deal with the Fox network. The establishment of the Big Ten Channel in 2007 was inspired by the growth of regional networks like YES, which is owned by the New York Yankees. The Big Ten also has a contract with ESPN worth about $100 million a year for football and basketball and adds offerings to ESPN's broadband, cell phone, Internet, and video-on-demand business.[5]

John Huarte, the quarterback of Notre Dame's 1964 football team, won the Heisman Trophy. I remember congratulating him and shaking his hand in the locker room when the decision was announced. This was a really big thing. But the thought of promoting his Heisman Trophy candidacy by investing $250,000 in a gigantic billboard in New York's Times Square had not yet occurred to anyone. In 2001 the University of Oregon did just that when it paid for a billboard that was a hundred feet tall and eighty feet wide to promote quarterback Joey Harrington for the Heisman. The billboard, which was ten stories high, displayed a likeness of Harrington with his last name crossed out, graffiti style, so that the name appeared as "Joey Heisman." Huarte was a celebrity and he attracted a great deal of attention. But in 1966, universities still showed some restraint when it came to marketing athletes as commercial properties.

Along with unbridled commercialism has come an assault on academic standards. The gap in admissions standards between athletes and regular students has grown substantially since I left Notre Dame. In their groundbreaking study *The Game of Life: College Sports and Educational Values,* James Shulman and William Bowen focused on ninety thousand undergraduate students—athletes and others—who entered a total of thirty academically selective colleges and universities, including Notre Dame, at three points in time: the fall semesters of 1951, 1976, and 1989.[6] They found that the gap in admissions standards and academic performance between athletes and nonathletes has been broadening at Division I institutions. At Ivy League and selective liberal arts colleges, athletes must still meet high academic standards, but even there the gap between students and athletes is increasing.

When universities sell their athletic programs to corporate sponsors and television networks, attracting marquee athletes who can fill stadiums and increase television ratings often takes priority over whether an athlete actually belongs in college. Several years ago the president of St. Bonaventure overruled his admissions staff to declare a basketball player eligible to compete, even though the athlete had received a degree in welding rather than an associate's degree. The scandal eventually led to the suicide of the chairman of St. Bonaventure's board of trustees. This is an extreme case of how the pressure to win can distort academic priorities and lead to tragic consequences for a fine university and its constituents. It also suggests that market values are beginning to undermine the core intellectual and moral values that have traditionally been the bedrock of higher learning.

Faculty members also feel the pressure. The *New York Times* reported recently that an Auburn football player had been honored as a scholar-athlete for his work in sociology. When the chairman of the Auburn Sociology Department—who had never heard of the student or had him in class—checked his file, however, he found that this football player and seventeen others had received high grades from a professor who required no classroom attendance and little work. As a result of this fraudulent grade inflation, several Auburn players who were academically at risk were able to compete on a team that went undefeated and finished number two in the nation in 2004.[7] Athlete-friendly faculty are nothing new. Their numbers appear to be increasing, however, as they have become the primary release valve for the pressure-cooker world of corporate college sports.

In the first decade of the twenty-first century, many universities are adopting standard business practices to ensure their financial viability. Students have become customers, academic programs are now referred to as products, and academic departments are increasingly being evaluated in terms of their contribution to the bottom line. In this new entrepreneurial environment, commercialized college sports, with its emphasis on marketing, promotion, and revenue generation, seems more in line with the direction of higher education than with the traditional view of a university as a community of scholars insulated from the contaminating influence of external pressures. In this era of academic capitalism, high-profile athletic teams are presumed to give universities an edge in attracting new students, creating revenue streams, and generally enhancing a university's brand name. Academic compromises for athletes are tolerated as long as they don't dilute the brand.

Dodging the NFL Draft

Eight players from the 1966 national championship team were drafted by NFL teams in 1967. Much to my surprise, I was one of them. Alan Page and Tom Rhoads, the other two defensive ends, went in rounds one and four, respectively. I was drafted in round sixteen (in the 1960s there were seventeen rounds). Coincidentally, Notre Dame legend Paul Hornung was also drafted in round sixteen by New Orleans as part of the expansion draft. Hornung, who had been a first-round choice of the Green Bay Packers in 1957, was just getting back into football after a suspension for gambling. Rocky Bleier, who went on to greatness with the Pittsburgh Steelers, was drafted in the sixteenth round in 1968. That Rocky and I were drafted in the same round convinced me that the NFL draft was far from an exact science.

Several weeks after the 1967 draft choices were announced, Art Dobson, a friend who lived across the hall from me, came to my room to say that Elroy "Crazy Legs" Hirsch from the Los Angeles Rams wanted to talk with me on the phone. Hirsch, a member of the National Football League Hall of Fame, had been one of my heroes when I was a kid. At first I thought Art was kidding. A few weeks earlier a friend had called the dorm, disguising his voice, to tell me that he was from the Scranton (Pennsylvania) Miners and that I was their first-round draft pick. I had actually believed him for a minute or so. The call from Crazy Legs was for real, however, and he wanted to talk about what the Rams were willing to offer. As I recall, it was not much more than living expenses. I told him I would have to think about it and get back to him.

People often ask me why I decided not to take the Rams up on their offer. My usual response is that I was drafted as a linebacker, and that I knew that I did not have the speed and lateral movement to handle pass coverage in the NFL. I also point out that I was too small to play defensive end. Deacon Jones, a very fine defensive end, was playing for the Rams back then. I saw no future for myself at that position. Most important, I think I was suffering from college football burnout. Football had been good to me. It had made it possible for me to attend a great university where I was able to grow intellectually and to expand my horizons. But football had become more of a job than something I did for the fun of it. When I was accepted at graduate school in sociology at Penn State, I was thrilled by the prospect of taking on a new challenge. I had been playing football every year since junior high school. I was ready for a change.

PART II

Linking Sports and Politics

4

Politics, Protest, and the Athletic Revolution

Radical Student Politics 101

Pennsylvania State University is located in the geographical center of Pennsylvania, about two hundred miles from major population areas such as Philadelphia and New York City. It is in an area of considerable natural beauty. The campus is surrounded by rolling farmland that stretches out to the forested ridges of the Appalachian Mountains. Despite its relative isolation, Penn State's large undergraduate student body, substantial number of graduate students, and thousands of faculty, staff, and others who in some way make a living from the university give the small town of State College an air of urban sophistication. Joe Paterno's winning football teams have also helped to open up State College to the outside world.

During my first week of graduate classes in the fall of 1967, it became immediately apparent why Penn State and its surroundings are often referred to as "the happy valley." In addition to its natural beauty, the area had more than its share of college bars, nice restaurants, and fraternity and sorority life. At Notre Dame, which was still an all-male institution at the time, students would often whistle and shout out of dorm windows when a woman was spotted walking across campus. At Penn State women were everywhere, and their presence was a normal part of campus life. Penn State had many of the amenities of an urban environment, but from what I could tell there was no poverty and very little crime.

Given Penn State's reputation as a fairly conservative party school, I was somewhat surprised to find that the student movement had already made significant inroads there. On my first day of classes I passed students at a main entrance to campus distributing antiwar leaflets and other literature for organizations such as Students for a Democratic Society (SDS) and the Progressive Labor Party (PLP). I was clueless as to what these organizations stood for. Not far from where young radicals were handing out political pamphlets, students were sitting on a wall that was a gathering place for Penn State's counterculture. Many of the guys were dressed in ripped and faded bell-bottomed blue jeans and blue work shirts. Army-Navy stores had become the retail outlet of choice. Women also wore jeans or long dresses with flowery designs. Their hair was long and stringy, or disheveled and naturally wavy. Some students were wearing headbands and granny glasses; others were openly smoking marijuana. The guys had hair that was long enough to be tied back into pony tails. Peace signs were ubiquitous. I had never seen anything like this at Notre Dame. I was in culture shock.

The Nittany News, a magazine store close to where I often had lunch, sold the *Village Voice, Ramparts,* the *Berkeley Barb, I. F. Stone's Weekly,* the *Daily World,* and other newspapers and magazines with a liberal or radical slant. The *National Review* and other conservative magazines were also on the shelves. Student radicals constituted only a small minority of Penn State students, but they were a very visible and vocal minority. During my senior year at Notre Dame, a major issue in the campaign for student body president was whether students should have to wear sport coats to dinner in the dining halls. Suddenly I found myself in an environment where debates about war, poverty, gender relations, and race were fairly common on campus and in the streets. These were tumultuous times, and at Penn State this was difficult to ignore.

During my first semester at Penn State, I married Gina Rapposelli, a woman I had been dating since high school. In January 1968 we moved into an apartment in State College to begin our life together. Little did we know that the coming year would be the most turbulent one in a decade already marked by significant social upheaval. No sooner had we plugged in the television than the news reported that Vietnamese rebels loyal to Ho Chi Minh had launched a major offensive during the Tet, the Lunar New Year holiday, against scores of cities, provincial and district capitals, and hamlets in South Vietnam. The attack, which took U.S. and South Vietnamese forces totally by surprise, was eventually repelled after very heavy losses were inflicted on the Viet Cong. Nonetheless, the Tet Offensive demonstrated that the U.S. military, which already had 500,000 troops in Vietnam, might have underestimated the enemy's resolve and that the war was likely to be long and costly.

In March 1968 American troops opened fire on women, children, and old men who inhabited the village of My Lai in Vietnam, even though they had received no fire and no enemy combatants had been sighted. More than five hundred Vietnamese were killed. This massacre did not become public news until 1970, but opposition to the war had become so great by the spring that Lyndon Johnson decided not to run for re-election. Martin Luther King was assassinated in April 1968. In June, Sirhan Sirhan, a Palestinian sympathizer, assassinated Senator Robert Kennedy just after Kennedy had won the California Democratic presidential primary. Hubert Humphrey and Eugene McCarthy were left to fight it out for the Democratic Party's nomination.

The Olympics were held in Mexico City that summer. During an awards ceremony, U.S. Olympic runners Tommie Smith and John Carlos raised their fists high in the air in a black power protest against racial discrimination in America. The Olympics were followed in August by the riotous Democratic National Convention in Chicago. As the whole world watched on television, radicals and others who had come to Chicago to show their dissatisfaction with the Democratic Party fought pitched battles in the streets against police and the National Guard. Just after Chicago, supporters of the women's liberation movement picketed the Miss America Pageant, accusing it of perpetuating sexism. The year ended with the election of Richard Nixon, a conservative Republican and supporter of the Vietnam War, as president.

These events shocked all thinking Americans, but the tremors were strongest on college campuses, where, as Notre Dame's Father Hesburgh has astutely pointed out, students "had time to read, to think, to discuss, to question, and to criticize."[1] In 1968 student radicals at Columbia University occupied buildings and administrative offices, signaling a trend toward more disruptive and, in some instances, violent protests. At Notre Dame, students staged angry protests when Dow Chemical Corporation, the manufacturer of napalm—a substance used in jelling gasoline so that it could be used in incendiary bombs—attempted to recruit on campus. As the war escalated, Vietnamese civilians who happened to live in areas where enemy troops were concentrated were incinerated. Huge areas of Vietnam were defoliated by American herbicides and remained barren for years after the war. Many young activists were questioning whether the war's objectives justified the massive death and destruction. Could this war be justified on moral grounds?

The events of 1968 substantially altered the way I viewed the world, in part because I experienced them while immersed in the intellectually supercharged environment of a major university. As a graduate student,

I struggled to develop an intellectual framework for making sense of the events that were so rapidly unfolding around me. David Westby, a sociology professor who had become my academic advisor, was interested in social movements and asked if I wanted to write my master's thesis on a topic related to radical student politics. I jumped at the opportunity, if for no other reason than that it would help me better understand events that dominated the news every day. Taking on this project was a crash course in the politics of the 1960s. In addition to what I was reading in my regular classes, I began reviewing the literature on the student movement, as well as the political traditions from which it took its inspiration.

During this period I studied the differences between the socialist movements of the 1930s (the so-called Old Left) and the New Left that was so closely identified with protests against the Vietnam War and other campus uprisings in the 1960s. The first graduate assistantship I had at Penn State was in the Labor Studies Program. While helping to organize a voluminous collection of documents and correspondence donated to Penn State by the United Steelworkers of America, I learned quite a bit about the role of the Communist Party in the American labor movement and how communists were purged from unions during the cold war. When I was very young, my father, a member of the Steelworkers Union, once took me along to walk a picket line when the union was on strike. Reading about those strikes in original labor union correspondence gave me new insights into my working-class background.

Jack Newfield's *The Prophetic Minority* was my introduction to organizations such as Students for a Democratic Society, the Student Nonviolent Coordinating Committee, the Progressive Labor Party, and the Young Socialist Alliance. Books by Michael Harrington and C. Wright Mills changed the way I looked at poverty and the distribution of power in America. I also followed the evolution of the black power movement and its gradual abandonment of the nonviolent tactics of Martin Luther King Jr. It did not take me long to realize that what was often referred to as "the movement" was composed of many diverse factions whose motives ranged from serious opposition to war and inequality to generational rebellion against all authority. Some people were attracted to the movement because they had clear-cut political agendas; others were looking for an alternative lifestyle based on sex, drugs, and rock 'n' roll.

As I read about and researched these issues, I found myself becoming increasingly radicalized. I had arrived at Penn State a political liberal, meaning that I supported capitalism but believed it needed some fine tuning to make it more responsive to the needs of minorities, women, and the poor. Like most liberals, I supported the Democratic Party, the civil rights movement, and federal spending to eliminate poverty and other social problems. In the late 1960s and early 1970s I moved further left, becoming increasingly convinced that capitalism, with its concentration of power in the hands of a small corporate elite, might be beyond reform and that only some form of democratic socialism could create a more humane and just society. How this would work, I was not exactly sure.

My first direct contacts with radical organizations were related to my master's thesis research. One night, for instance, I attended a meeting of the Progressive Labor Party just to see what kinds of people it attracted. The PLP was a doctrinaire Marxist organization. The members eschewed long hair and other trappings of the 1960s counterculture, preferring to present themselves as serious revolutionaries. One of the members gave a fairly lengthy presentation in which he tried to explain the Vietnam War in terms of Marx's labor theory of value and dialectical materialism. There was no room for debate. *Das Kapital* was the Bible. I found the parallels between the PLP and fundamentalist Christianity absolutely frightening. I also attended SDS meetings. Although I never joined SDS, I found its New Left ideology more consistent with my left-liberal politics.

My first involvement in protest demonstrations was also related to my academic research. I wanted to better understand why some people get directly involved in protests while others with similar political outlooks do not. So I attended some demonstrations as a participant-observer. As time went on, however, I became more of a participant than a detached observer. As Gina and I met friends who were activists and shared our political outlook, we found it a lot easier to face the abuse often heaped on protestors by the general public. Gina and I attended antiwar protests and other marches and vigils, several in Washington, D.C. At one demonstration a cloud of tear gas enveloped us as the National Guard reacted to a disturbance several blocks away. The experience of running in a panic-stricken crowd, trying to escape the burning and suffocating effects of tear gas, drove home the point that challenging authority can be very risky business.

Vietnam and the Draft

The more I read about the war in Vietnam, the more I opposed it. A book by Bernard Fall, a French scholar and historian, left a lasting impression on me. In *The Two Vietnams* Fall argued that the Vietnam War was an extension of Vietnam's struggle over many centuries to free itself from foreign invaders.[2] I understood how Soviet aggression in Eastern Europe and the U.S. conflict with China in North Korea fueled the cold war pre-occupation with containing communism—but this cold war logic tended to ignore Vietnam's unique history and aspirations. After reading Fall's book, I began to doubt that Ho Chi Minh, though a communist, was a pliable tool of China and the Soviet Union. Throughout his life he had been an ardent Vietnamese nationalist. His goal, it seemed to me, was the creation of an independent Vietnam, not a Soviet or Chinese satellite state.

In the late 1960s my views on Vietnam were not very popular, especially among college athletes, whose views on politics often reflected militaristic values such as strict discipline, physical aggressiveness, and blind obedience to authority figures. A striking exception to this "jock" stereotype was Muhammad Ali. Ali stands out in my mind as a major cultural icon of the sixties who opposed racism and the war in Vietnam and put his career on the line to do it. As heavyweight boxing champion of the world, he was brashly outspoken about racial issues, often enraging Americans who expected black athletes, even the very greatest ones, to show obsequious deference to the white establishment. Ali symbolized black pride and became a hero for both black and white activists because he stood up for principles and refused to back down in the face of threats from those in authority.

For many young Americans, including me, Ali's opposition to the war and his refusal, in 1967, to be inducted into the army helped connect racism in the United States and colonial exploitation in other parts of the world. When Ali said, "I ain't got no quarrel with the Vietcong," I took him to mean that from his perspective, the subjugation of the Vietnamese by various colonial regimes was not unlike the subjugation of blacks in America. Opposing the war, in other words, was a way of supporting people of color in another nation who had toiled on plantations and been oppressed and degraded, much as African slaves had in America. Ali was stripped of his title and sentenced to prison for refusing to fight in Vietnam. His conviction was later overturned, and he became an inspiration for oppressed people throughout the world. I identified with him because he was both an athlete and a radical.

I spent a great deal of time thinking about the war because I figured that it was very likely I would end up fighting in it. Although I opposed the war and took part in antiwar protests at Penn State, I ultimately concluded that I had a responsibility to fight if called. I felt I had little choice. Unlike Muhammad Ali, I was not a pacifist. If I had been, I would have opposed all wars, not just this one. Nor was I willing to give up my American citizenship, which was another alternative. Thus when I received a notice ordering me to report for a physical exam in 1968, I made the trip to Philadelphia and passed my physical with flying colors. Several weeks later I was classified 1-A by the Selective Service System and was ordered to report for induction in the spring of 1969.

On the day of my induction I talked with some of the other young inductees traveling on the bus to Philadelphia with me. I could not get over how young they were. I was twenty-four. Many of the other draftees looked like they were just out of high school. At the processing center in Philadelphia, we stood in lines, filled out forms, and took written examinations. Much to my surprise, we had to undergo yet another physical exam before the induction process was complete. When I sat down for a brief interview with a doctor at the end of the exam, he looked at the same documents that had been in my file at the time of my previous physical, and asked me about a medication I had been taking for several years. I told him I was fine as long as I took my medication. He said he was classifying me as 1-Y, which meant that I was qualified for military service in the event of war but was being deferred for one year. His decision may have saved my life.

On 1 December 1969, the Selective Service System held its first draft lottery since 1942. All young men between the ages of eighteen and twenty-six were included. The procedure was simple. After a brief prayer, birthdates between 1 January and 31 December were selected at random. The first birthday chosen was 14 September, meaning that all registrants with that birthday were at the top of the list to be drafted. The last birthday drawn was 8 June, making military service for those born on that date highly unlikely. The first of April, the day before my birthday, was number 32, well within the draft-eligible range. The third of April was number 83, again a likely draft pick. My birthday, 2 April, was number 271. By a simple drawing of numbers, young men were selected for military duty, some of whose names now appear among the dead on the Vietnam War Memorial in Washington, D.C.

Not long after the draft lottery, I was informed that I had been accepted into the doctoral program in sociology at Penn State. Gina and I decided to spend the summer in California, where I spent several months making daily visits to the San José State University library, reading books that my academic advisor thought would be crucial for success in the doctoral program. I read and took copious notes on sociological classics such as Durkheim's *Division of Labor in Society*, Veblen's *Theory of the Leisure Class*, and Marx's *Kapital*. I struggled to make up for academic time lost while an undergraduate devoted to sports. I begged a San José State University professor to let me sit in on his statistics course for free. When I returned to Penn State, I felt as prepared for graduate school as I used to feel prepared for football practice at Notre Dame after working out all summer.

The Athletic Revolution

Although I was aware that athletes and former athletes were involved in radical politics in the sixties, I was slow to realize that sports itself reflected and reinforced many of the features of American life that political activists were challenging. Only after I returned to Penn State in 1970 to pursue my doctoral degree did I began to take a more critical look at sports as it relates to society and culture. My window into sports activism was a genre of books written during this period—often referred to as jock-raking literature—that examined sports through the critical lens of 1960s radical politics. Among the books in the popular literature that influenced my thinking were Jack Scott's *Athletic Revolution,* Dave Meggyesy's *Out of Their League,* and Harry Edwards's *Revolt of the Black Athlete.*

Jack Scott, a radical sportswriter who earned his Ph.D. at UC-Berkeley and remained there as director of the Institute for the Study of Sport and Society before accepting a position as athletic director at Oberlin College in 1972, was dubbed "the guru of jock liberation," most often scornfully, by leaders of the athletic establishment. Scott incorporated the politics of the New Left and the humanist values of the sixties counterculture into his vision of sports. The ultimate goal of the athletic movement, as he saw it, was to abolish the authoritarian, racist, sexist, and militarist nature of contemporary sports. The true joy of sports, he argued, was often stifled by a system that glorified violence, encouraged hatred of the opposition, and treated athletes like expendable parts in a machine obsessed with winning. Scott supported sports for everyone, regardless of level of ability or disability.

As athletic director at Oberlin, he supported the amateur notion that "athletics should be for athletes" rather than for the commercial entertainment of paying spectators, thus fusing elements of an older intellectual elitist view of college sports with the New Left's emphasis on participatory democracy. Scott argued that athletes should have a significant say in all policy decisions, such as the scheduling of games, the hiring of coaches, and the allocation of resources. He shocked the Oberlin administration by allowing the football team to interview the candidates for a new coaching position and submit their recommendations. He hired the Oberlin Athletic Department's first black coaches and instituted new coed classes in sports such as squash, handball, gymnastics, yoga, and karate—actions that were fairly revolutionary for the time. One of Scott's most controversial hires was Tommie Smith, one of the Olympic runners to give a black power salute while receiving a medal at the 1968 Mexico City Olympics.

David Meggyesy, a friend of Scott's, had been an outside linebacker for the St. Louis Cardinals for seven years when he quit at the height of his career, in part because his radical politics clashed with the values of the NFL. In 1971 he wrote *Out of Their League,* a book that exposed what he saw as the dehumanizing side of collegiate and professional sports. Meggyesy was appalled by the racism that pervaded sports and American society, and he viewed the war in Vietnam as having more to do with American and French imperialism than with the threat of communist expansion. Although he embraced the humanistic values of the New Left, his approach to politics embodied the pragmatism of an old-time labor union organizer. In his view, both professional and big-time college athletes were part of an exploited class whose most powerful weapon was the threat of withholding their labor.

Of the scores of sports activists who wrote exposés of sports in America in the 1960s and 1970s, none was more instrumental in launching an actual athletic revolt than Harry Edwards, then an instructor in sociology at San José State University. Unlike Jack Scott, Edwards was far less concerned with authoritarian coaches, participatory democracy, and finding a kinder and gentler approach to athletic competition than with purging sports of racial discrimination. The "revolt of black athletes" that Edwards helped to precipitate grew out of the civil rights and black power movements. Edwards was not advocating radical changes in the structure of sports and how they are played. Rather, he wanted equal opportunity for African Americans in sports and in society, and he viewed sports as a platform for raising the consciousness of Americans and people throughout the world about the plight of African Americans.

In 1967, not long after Ali was stripped of his heavyweight title, amateur black athletes, under the leadership of Harry Edwards, formed the Olympic Project for Human Rights (OPHR) to boycott the 1968 Olympics in Mexico City. The goal of the boycott was to show that although the success of black athletes gave the impression of racial progress, most African Americans were denied equal status with whites in American society. While a general boycott never materialized, black athletes Tommie Smith and John Carlos made history when they took the stand to accept their Olympic medals. When the two men took their positions on the awards platform, Smith and Carlos put on black gloves. They wore black socks and no shoes to protest poverty in America and a black scarf to represent black pride. When the U.S. national anthem was being played and the flag was going up the flagpole, both athletes bowed their heads and raised their fists in a black power salute.

The impact of this symbolic gesture was powerful. Smith and Carlos were stripped of their medals and expelled from the Olympic village within a couple of hours. Although they were attacked from all sides for using sports as a forum for political protest, Smith and Carlos, much like Muhammad Ali, became models for other black athletes who were beginning to challenge racism in sports and in society. According to one estimate, more than one hundred colleges and universities experienced athletic disturbances between 1967 and 1971.[3] The demands black athletes made included having black females represented on cheerleading squads, hiring more black coaches, putting an end to the practice of assigning black athletes to certain playing positions on the basis of racial stereotypes, and eliminating racial discrimination in campus housing. White college athletes also began raising questions about war, poverty, race, and gender inequality in America.

In 1970 National Guardsmen opened fire on students protesting the Vietnam War on the Kent State campus in Ohio, killing four of them. After this event, even students who had previously been politically inactive found themselves being swept up in radical campus politics. In the spring of 1970 seven football players from Notre Dame went to Ara Parseghian to ask if they could skip a day of spring football practice to participate in a moratorium march against Vietnam being held in South Bend. The group included both black and white ballplayers who had found it difficult to ignore such events as the assassinations of Martin Luther King and Bobby Kennedy and the escalating war.

Ara refused them, saying that they had every right to their political opinions but that missing practice was simply unacceptable. Half of the athletes defied Ara and went anyway. According to Bob Minnix, one of the African American athletes, the demonstration was peaceful. "We marched, we sang, we went home."[4] The next day Ara called the activist athletes into his office. He was upset that they had violated the rule of attending practice and said he could not ignore their actions. He could have withdrawn their scholarships—an action made legal by an NCAA rule change in 1967—but Ara simply had them spend an entire day picking up trash in the stadium.

When I talked to Ara about the campus disturbances of the 1960s, he told me that he was opposed to the Vietnam War and was fairly sure that the players knew it. He told the players, "I understand why you would want to demonstrate. But you can't go demonstrate while we are practicing. You cannot demonstrate rather than going to chemistry class. If you want to go any time other than that, it is your prerogative." He added that he was opposed to the Iraq War today. "I was in World War II; I was in the navy for three years. I do not think that people realize how devastating wars are. If I hadn't been in the war, would I still feel this way? I do not know, but I think I would." Ara's philosophy when dealing with team rules was to remain consistent, to treat each player, whether a star or a guy on the prep team, the same. This certainly squared with my experience of playing for him.

Although Ara had serious doubts about the nation's involvement in the Vietnam War, he had little sympathy for the sixties counterculture that espoused sex, drugs, and alternate lifestyles as a solution to society's ills. In an interview for *Sports Illustrated* in 1969 he said, "The fad started with the hippies. I saw them in Haight-Ashbury. Wearing a beard or a moustache or long hair doesn't necessarily make anyone look like the scum I saw there but it gives empathy for a movement that certainly is the direct opposite of what we strive for in football. Sports is goal-oriented. The hippie movement is geared to shiftlessness."[5] Much like Notre Dame's president, Father Theodore Hesburgh, Ara was liberal on many issues, but he would not tolerate the incivility and disruptive tactics that had become the hallmark of New Left politics.

Minnix, who is now an associate athletic director in charge of compliance at Florida State University, says that his political consciousness was primarily molded by the civil rights movement.[6] He has vivid memories of watching television while in high school and seeing race riots in places like Watts on hot summer nights, attack dogs and cattle prods used on civil rights workers, and Reverend King leading protest marches in Birmingham. At Notre Dame he majored in sociology with a minor in black studies. He was well aware of Tommie Smith and John Carlos's protest at the 1968 Mexico City Olympics. For him, taking part in a demonstration against the war in Vietnam was a matter of conscience. "At that point in my life," he said, "I didn't care if I lost my scholarship." He also said, however, that Notre Dame had awarded him a four-year scholarship, and that "Ara was unlikely to take it away for missing a single day of spring practice."

Comparing football players on our 1966 team with those who entered college a few years later, assistant coach Tom Pagna once commented, "We used to tell kids to do something and they would do it. Within a couple of years, we'd tell them to do something and they'd want to know why."[7] The ballplayers protesting the Vietnam War at Notre Dame in 1970 were part of the new generation Pagna was talking about. Minnix says he used to get into arguments with coaches. He would say, "You went out and found the best and the brightest. Now you want us to pretend we don't have any questions? Asking questions is how we became good students. Well, right now I have a lot of questions. And I am not hearing any good answers on why I should not be allowed to demonstrate."[8] Other players, such as 1969 team co-captain Mike Oriard, also had questions but kept politics and sports separate. "For me, ND was a place where I first discovered that my country fell short of its stated ideals and where I turned against the war along with most of my college generation, but the football field existed apart from that political world."[9]

The student unrest at Notre Dame in 1970 pales by comparison with the tumultuous events at Syracuse University at the same time. In response to the Kent State killings and President Nixon's decision to invade Cambodia, Syracuse students barricaded campus roads and called a student strike that emptied classrooms. In addition, nine African American football players accused Coach Ben Schwartzwalder of discriminatory practices and boycotted spring practice. Among the players' demands were that Syracuse hire an African American assistant coach, offer better medical support, and stop calling African American athletes "boy," a term used to humiliate African American men. The players were later kicked off the team for refusing to sign a statement refuting claims that the university had discriminated.

Four of the suspended players were reinstated for the season opener against Kansas, a game preceded by the worst riot in campus history. But the nine players refused to be divided and decided to boycott the entire season. The players paid a high price for their courageous stand for racial equality. Only two of them ever played for Syracuse again. Thirty-six years later, the university made a formal apology to the nine players during the weekend of the Syracuse-Louisville game. At the ceremony, the university's chancellor, Nancy Cantor, recognized the players for the courage they showed in standing up for their beliefs, and admitted that problems related to diversity remain a vexing problem in universities and society in 2006. During halftime of the Louisville game, the players finally received their letterman's jackets.[10]

Although a relatively small group of athletes and former athletes in the sixties generation stepped forward to support various left-wing causes, the vast majority of athletes were among the movement's most outspoken critics. The football players who offered to physically remove protestors from buildings they occupied during a Columbia University antiwar demonstration in 1968 are a good example. For me, leaders of the "athletic revolution" like Jack Scott, Dave Meggyesy, Muhammad Ali, Harry Edwards, Tommie Smith, and John Carlos were an inspiration at a time when athletes who supported radical causes were in short supply. They also raised the public's awareness that sports is a vital social institution that reflects and reinforces the values of society as a whole.

The Impact of the Sixties Uprising on Sports

For better or worse, the sixties generation left its stamp on sports. The late 1960s and early 1970s saw the growth of labor unions in all of the major professional sports leagues. By the mid-1970s the reserve clause, a rule created in 1880 to prevent professional baseball players from bargaining with teams other than the one on which they played, had been replaced by some form of free agency that allowed greater player movement. The organization of players into collective bargaining units had made these changes possible. The demand for equal rights spurred on by the civil rights and jock liberation movements, and the revolt of black athletes, had spilled over into professional sports and altered the relationship between players and owners forever. The average annual salaries of players in the four major professional leagues rose from about $20,000 in 1967—my teammate Alan Page worked as a used car salesman in the summer in his early years with the Minnesota Vikings—to about $2 million by 2000. And athletes now have a say regarding health care and other conditions of employment.

The impact of the women's movement on sports has been nothing less than spectacular. In the late 1960s Billie Jean King, a champion tennis player and an outspoken advocate for equality for girls and women in sports, challenged the pay differential between male and female professional tennis players. King was a central figure in the creation of the Virginia Slims Tour in 1971, which commanded enough loyalty from top women players to force the U.S. Lawn Tennis Association to change its sexist practices. In 1972, under considerable pressure from women's rights activists and supporters of the women's movement, Congress passed Title IX, a law that prevents gender discrimination in educational programs funded by the federal government, including sports. As a result of this law, millions of girls and women who might otherwise have been excluded are now playing sports.

The "revolt of black athletes" created opportunities for African American athletes that would have been unimaginable when I entered college in 1963. Today, African Americans dominate the rosters of football and basketball teams at both the professional and collegiate levels, and although African Americans are still underrepresented in many management positions in sports, their numbers are increasing. At the college level, African

American athletes in the 1960s and 1970s often boycotted or threatened to boycott athletic contests unless conditions for African Americans on campus were improved. That college athletes had no labor union protection when they confronted college administrators left them exposed to losing their scholarships and to other types of intimidation. But the activism of that period demonstrated the power that athletes, regardless of skin color, possess by virtue of being able to organize and withhold their services.

The athletic revolution of the sixties also challenged the conventional wisdom that sports is merely a game, an activity set apart from more practical concerns such as war, politics, and making a living. Among the writers—in addition to Jack Scott, Dave Meggyesy, and Harry Edwards—who wrote political exposés of sports during that period were Jim Bouton (*Ball Four*), Gary Shaw (*Meat on the Hoof*), Peter Gant (*North Dallas Forty*), Curt Flood (*The Way It Is*), and Paul Hoch (*Rip Off: The Big Game*). None of these books rose to the level of a scholarly treatise, but they all pointed to links between sports, politics, economics, and other social institutions that academics and serious journalists had previously ignored. The years that followed saw the birth of academic journals and even professional associations devoted to the scholarly study of sports. And the notion that sports is a business just like any other began to gain wide acceptance both inside and outside academe.

Laying the Groundwork for Professional College Sports

The Fighting Irish maintained their dominance in collegiate football in the years following my graduation. Notre Dame went 10–1–0 in 1970, beating Texas in the Cotton Bowl to finish number two in the country. In 1973 Ara Parseghian had his finest season ever, when the Irish defeated Alabama in the final minutes of the Sugar Bowl, finishing the season undefeated and winning the national championship. In 1969 Notre Dame had reversed its forty-five-year policy of not playing in bowl games, in part because the Associated Press began tabulating its rankings for the national champion after the bowl games. Notre Dame had little choice but to accept bowl bids if it wanted to compete for national titles. The lure of television money also played a role, as did a change in Notre Dame's academic calendar that allowed athletes to complete final exams in mid-December.

College football did not look much different to the average fan in 1973 than it did when Notre Dame battled Michigan State for the national championship in 1966. Players wore their hair a little longer in the seventies, and there were more African Americans on the playing field. Otherwise, the games themselves did not reflect the political turmoil often raging outside the stadiums. Behind the scenes, however, the NCAA was fomenting its own athletic revolution, one that radically altered the relationship between athletes and their universities. In a few short years the NCAA repealed the freshman ineligibility rule, allowed coaches to "fire" athletes for questioning authority, opened the floodgates to athletes with extremely low academic credentials, and transformed athletic scholarships from educational gifts into contracts for hire. And finally, in 1973, the NCAA formally separated the amateurs from the pros by restructuring into Divisions I, II, and III.

The Emergence of Counterfeit Amateurism

Most people are well aware that the founding fathers of the National Collegiate Athletic Association were deeply committed to the principles of amateurism. What they seldom realize, however, is that the NCAA took a strong stand against athletic scholarships at its first convention, viewing them as "pay for play." According to the organization's 1906 constitution, violations of amateurism included "the offering of inducements to players to enter colleges or universities because of their athletic abilities or supporting or maintaining players while students on account of their athletic abilities, either by athletic organizations, individual alumni, or otherwise directly or indirectly."[1] The NCAA had no problem whatever with awarding both athletes and nonathletes financial aid based on need, but its members were acutely aware that athletically related subsidies might attract athletes with little academic interest or ability and send the wrong message about the mission of higher education.

Given the unique role that sports was beginning to play in American universities in the early twentieth century, it is not surprising that the NCAA's principles were often ignored. Not only were winning teams an important source of revenue but they also created an emotional bond between the university and the external community that provided students and financial resources. No campus activity could attract more media coverage than athletics. And nothing had greater appeal for the practical-minded business leaders and alumni whose support was critical to institutional survival. Given the very high stakes involved, under-the-table payments to skilled athletes became commonplace, and many schools gave athletic scholarships in open defiance of the NCAA, which at that point had no enforcement power.

An article written by a graduate manager—coaches were often referred to as graduate managers in the 1920s and 1930s—provides an insight into how under-the-table scholarships were often funded in that era. According to this graduate manager, profits from football games were turned over to the college president under the condition that the university would return a similar amount for athletic scholarships. The president then appointed individuals sympathetic to athletics to the financial aid committee to make sure that the money was used to recruit talented athletes. One president allegedly said of the system, "At first it troubled me considerably, and then it got so it didn't worry me at all. My only alternative would have been to have taken a stand which would have brought down upon me the enmity, not only of coaches and undergraduates, but of the Board of Regents as well."[2]

Although many universities found innovative ways to subsidize athletes in the early to mid-twentieth century, the NCAA remained steadfast in its opposition to athletic scholarships and other payment schemes. The central theme running through Article III of the 1941 NCAA constitution was that just as athletic ability could not be considered when awarding financial aid, no athlete should lose financial aid because of failure to compete in intercollegiate athletics. In explaining its position, the NCAA noted that athletes in some institutions were losing financial aid if they gave up sports and that this practice had a "direct professionalizing effect."[3] Right up until World War II, the NCAA clung to its founding principle that athletic scholarships were a form of pay for play and that such financial subsidies blurred the distinction between college athletes and paid entertainers.

In 1957, following a decade of intense internal debate, the NCAA finally caved in to pressure from schools that favored subsidies for athletes by allowing athletic scholarships that paid the room, board, tuition, fees, and laundry expenses of athletes with no financial need or remarkable academic ability. Four decades later, Walter Byers, the executive director of the NCAA at the time, characterized the scholarship system he helped create as "a nation-wide money laundering scheme" whereby money formerly given to athletes under the table could now be funneled through a school's financial aid office.[4] Although the NCAA continued to present itself to the public as a defender of time-honored amateur principles, its adoption of athletic scholarships began its slide down the slippery slope to out-and-out professionalism.

The NCAA's abandonment of a central principle of amateurism did not go unnoticed. According to Walter Byers, "as the awarding of full athletic scholarships became commonplace, colleges began to fear that NCAA athletes might be identified as employees by state industrial commissions and the courts." In 1963, for instance, a California district court of appeals ruled that the family of Gary Van Horn, a football player who had been killed in a plane crash while returning from a game in Ohio, should receive death benefits under workers' compensation law. One strategy for meeting this threat—a strategy that was actually recommended by an NCAA senior staff member—was to return to true amateurism by reinstituting need-based financial aid. According to his argument, athletic scholarships, especially those that required athletic performance for yearly renewal, came perilously close to being employment contracts.[5]

For Walter Byers and the NCAA, there was no going back. Instead of returning to true amateurism, the organization decided to launch an aggressive public relations campaign to convince the courts and the general public that the NCAA remained as committed to amateurism as it was in 1905. The creation of the term "student-athlete" was the opening salvo in this campaign. According to Byers, "We crafted the term student-athlete and soon it was embedded in all NCAA rules and interpretations as a mandated substitute for such words as players and athletes. We told college publicists to speak of 'college teams,' not football or basketball 'clubs,' a word common to the pros."[6] Early rules preventing universities from withdrawing athletic scholarships from injured athletes or from athletes who decided not to play were as much an effort to protect universities from workers' compensation lawsuits as to ensure educational benefits for athletes.

At first, NCAA rules allowed athletic scholarships to be awarded for four years. The scholarship I received in 1963 was essentially a gift that allowed me to further my education. In the 1960s many athletic directors and coaches were concerned that athletes were accepting these gifts and then deciding not to participate. While doing research in the NCAA archives several years ago, I came across a letter to Walter Byers from an irate athletic director who complained that several players who had accepted scholarships had decided not to play. "I think this is morally wrong," he said. "This is a contract and this is a two-way street."[7] This administrator wanted athletic scholarships to be contractual agreements not unlike those that bind professional athletes to their teams. Yet he also wanted to retain the term "amateur."

In 1967 he got his wish when the NCAA passed a rule allowing athletic scholarships to be taken away from athletes who voluntarily withdrew from sports. This rule also gave coaches the authority to withdraw the scholarships of athletes who refused to follow the rules of conduct laid down by a coach.[8] It was probably no coincidence that this so-called fraudulent misrepresentation rule was passed, and subsequently extended, during the period when athletes on some college campuses were in revolt. For coaches faced with boycotts and protests, this legislation was a godsend. Ara could well have used this rule to discipline Bob Minnix and the other athletic activists who skipped practice to attend a protest rally, though he chose not to do so.

The fraudulent misrepresentation rule allowed coaches to "fire" athletes for insubordination and for not taking their athletic responsibilities seriously. It did not allow the withdrawal of aid from an athlete who suffered an injury or who was a recruiting mistake. Four-year scholarships represented an institutional commitment to athletes as students, regard-less of performance on the athletic field. In 1973 four-year scholarships were replaced by one-year renewable grants. With this relegation of four-year scholarships to the scrap heap of amateur traditions, the NCAA gave coaches almost total control over athletes' behavior both on and off the court and playing field. Athletes are now contractually obligated to make sports their top priority. Failure to meet the demands of a coach can lead to nonrenewal of financial aid.

I asked Ara Parseghian if he remembered the NCAA's adoption of the one-year renewable scholarship rule. He said, "Vaguely. But it didn't im-pact me. You are at Notre Dame and Notre Dame is a cut above all of that. If you get a scholarship you are going to keep the scholarship. There is no damn way that I am going to have a reputation by dismissing a kid from the squad; that kind of public relations would be disastrous." The one-year renewable scholarship rule was passed just as Ara's coaching career was coming to an end. Early in his career at Notre Dame he had worked with Father Edmund P. Joyce to have a letter of intent drawn up that would formally stipulate that Notre Dame offered a four-year scholarship and that aid could not be withdrawn because of injury or failure to make the team. In 1973 such agreements became a violation of NCAA rules.

Between 1957 and 1973, the NCAA instituted a payment system that would provide a predictable and steady supply of top athletes for the bur-geoning business of collegiate sports and give coaches the kind of control over them that employers generally have over employees. By continuing to apply the term "amateur" to athletic programs that generate millions of dollars from the labor of young athletes, the NCAA—not the players—engages in fraudulent misrepresentation. It is testimony to the NCAA's public relations machinery that many people continue to believe that schools give four-year scholarships that cannot be taken away if an ath-lete is injured or is not good enough to play. Even the courts and various legislative bodies blindly accept this myth, thereby shielding the NCAA and its member institutions from unrelated business income taxes and other costs related to running a business. The myth also obscures the dif-ficulty athletes often encounter trying to be students and paid entertain-ers simultaneously.

Another vestige from the age of amateur sports was scrapped by the NCAA in 1972 when the freshman ineligibility rule was repealed. The decision was justified as a necessary cost-cutting measure at a time when many universities were experiencing a severe budget crunch. Allowing freshman to play on varsity teams, it was argued, would save money by eliminating separate freshman athletic programs. It would also allow the schools that could not afford as many scholarships as their competitors to get talented freshmen into action as soon as possible. An alternative proposal was to reduce the total number of scholarships schools could offer. When coaches at big football schools threatened that their programs would secede from the NCAA if scholarships were cut, the NCAA voted to repeal the freshman ineligibility rule instead, thus ending a practice that had long symbolized the NCAA's commitment to athletes as students.

Reflecting on the repeal of the freshman ineligibility rule, Ara Parseghian says that he favored it. "I was in favor of freshmen being eligible," says Ara, "provided that athletes were academically capable of absorbing the first year, which was quite an adjustment to college. A pretty high percentage of athletes admitted to Notre Dame were good students with reasonably high board scores." Ara was also concerned that Notre Dame could not bring in the same number of players that state schools did. "If you bring in a hundred and 30 percent are blue chip, you end up with thirty really good players. If you start with only thirty, you end up with only ten." When I asked him what he thought of freshman athletes from disadvantaged educational backgrounds who now end up playing football on national television before they have attended their first class, he said that was wrong, adding, "I never had a guy that played as a freshman who did not graduate."

I once asked an NCAA representative who was participating on a panel on college sports reform if she could think of an academic justification for dumping the freshman ineligibility rule. To her credit, she admitted that the change had more to do with economics and competitive balance than with education. She did add, however, that many freshman athletes, especially women, seem quite capable of balancing the demands of sports and education. The fact remains, however, that most of the NCAA legislation passed since I left Notre Dame, including the elimination of four-year scholarships and freshman ineligibility, have had more to do with protecting revenue streams and the power of the NCAA cartel than with educational opportunity for athletes. The NCAA's current efforts at academic reform seem anemic when compared with policies that existed forty years ago.

The repeal of the freshman ineligibility rule was followed the next year by the NCAA's decision to rescind its 1.6 rule, a rule limiting athletic scholarships and freshman eligibility to play or practice to athletes likely to achieve a 1.6 (or C−) on a 4.0 scale. Because the rule relied in part on standardized test scores, it was alleged to discriminate against minority athletes. By dropping the 1.6 rule, the NCAA opened the floodgates to the recruitment of athletes with extremely limited academic skills, including minorities who had been segregated in poverty-stricken areas with very poor school systems.[9] There may be good reasons to admit athletes who are academically at risk to universities. But to throw them into the high-pressure world of big-time collegiate sports as freshmen is, in my opinion, unconscionable.

Separating the Amateurs from the Pros

The NCAA's adoption of athletic scholarships in 1957 represents a watershed in the history of collegiate sports and American higher education. In the years that followed, schools with major investments in big-time college sports became increasingly professionalized, binding athletes to one-year renewable contracts conditioned on athletic performance. Many others remained committed to the amateur principles upon which the NCAA was founded. Elite northeastern universities such as Yale, Harvard, and Princeton chose to pursue academic excellence rather than professional college sports in order to maintain their national prominence. In 1954 the Ivy League signed an agreement that reaffirmed its stand against athletic scholarships. Never again would Ivy League schools have the critical mass of quality football players that allowed the University of Pennsylvania to play Notre Dame to a 7–7 tie in 1952.

In the 1970s, leaders of many liberal arts colleges outside the Ivy League also came to the defense of the amateur model. John William Ward of Amherst College argued that athletic scholarships are at the core of all that is wrong with collegiate sports. "Contracted grants-in-aid at many schools," according to Ward, "force athletes to remain on a team in order to continue their education. Athletic programs that depend on media-oriented audiences compel college athletes to perform like professionals without anything near commensurate compensation. In the marketplace such practices run counter to standard labor ethics; in an educational context they affront common sense."[10] A major concern of the liberal arts colleges, one they shared with the early founders of the NCAA, was that athletic scholarships would create a class of athletic specialists who would be isolated from the student life.

Shulman and Bowen, in their landmark study *The Game of Life,* established that elite liberal arts colleges currently give hugely more weight in the admissions process to athletic excellence than to excellence in any other nonacademic pursuit. In this regard, schools that do not grant athletic scholarships are much like the superpowers in the NCAA's Division IA. What separates the amateurs from the pros, however, is that athletes in schools that grant no athletic scholarships can walk away from sports with no loss of financial aid. Coaches in nonscholarship institutions, such as those in the Ivy League, often vent their anger at the fairly large number of recruited athletes who at some point decide not to play. The coaches' frustration is understandable, but the freedom to give up sports to devote oneself to education full time is the essence of amateur college sports. If coaches are looking for hired hands, they should move to a Division I scholarship-granting school.

The passage of Title IX in 1972 not only created greater opportunities for women to participate in college sports but empowered women to pursue a model of sports not unlike the one espoused by liberal arts colleges. The Association of Intercollegiate Athletics for Women (AIAW), the organization that governed women's sports in the 1970s, took a principled stand against athletic scholarships, viewing them as payment for athletic performance. The AIAW was fundamentally committed to a form of governance that protected the rights of athletes to pursue college life in a manner similar to that enjoyed by other students, and argued that student welfare rather than revenue generation should guide ethical conduct and decision making.[11] The AIAW enthusiastically supported Title IX, but rejected the notion that women could attain gender equity only by adopting the exploitive practices so common in men's programs.

Although the AIAW fought a heroic battle to maintain sports as an integral part of the educational process, the NCAA used its power and resources to ensure its demise. The NCAA had originally opposed Title IX and attempted to have revenue-producing sports exempted from its provisions. When it became clear that collegiate sports would have to comply with Title IX with no exceptions, the NCAA strategy shifted to taking over women's sports altogether. This it did in 1980 by offering championships for women. Because the NCAA had far more financial resources than the AIAW, many women's programs left the AIAW for the NCAA. The AIAW challenged the NCAA takeover on antitrust grounds but lost. As a result, the AIAW folded, and its alternate vision of women's athletics solidly grounded in educational principles died with it.

Reverend Edmund P. Joyce, Notre Dame's vice president, led the charge for the more professional model of college sports that was emerging during the 1970s. When he rose to oppose the need-based aid proposals that came before the NCAA in the 1970s, he probably spoke for the majority of college administrators and coaches with big-time football programs. Father Joyce argued forcefully that athletes in revenue-producing sports deserve special treatment when it comes to financial aid. The football player, said Joyce, "is absorbed into a Spartan regime that places demands upon him both academically and athletically that few other students experience. . . . He also helps to bring in millions of dollars of revenue that generally redounds to the benefit of his fellow students in the non-revenue sports."[12] Joyce included women's athletics among the benefactors.

Father Joyce's position, in my opinion, came perilously close to an admission that big-time collegiate sports operates as a business whose preoccupation with revenue production makes it difficult to provide athletes with the same kind of educational experiences that other students get. Like many of the coaches of major football and basketball programs during this period, Joyce was claiming a special status for revenue-producing collegiate sports by virtue of its contribution to the bottom line. In a statement that must have shocked delegates from the elite liberal arts colleges, Joyce asserted that "football players cannot and should not be treated the same as the generality of students."[13] This statement was especially shocking in light of the NCAA's stated goal of maintaining athletes as an integral part of the student body.

There have always been philosophical differences among the members of the NCAA. In the 1970s, however, these differences became more open and divisive, perhaps because television had raised the financial stakes. In 1973 these philosophical differences were formalized by the creation of three separate divisions within the NCAA. Division I represented the large scholarship-granting institutions that received the lion's share of television revenue. Consistent with the basic principles of free enterprise, these schools saw no reason to share their profits with schools that had less media appeal. Division III comprised the schools that offered no athletic scholarships and generated little revenue from sports. Division II fell somewhere in between.

One of the things that people like Father Joyce found most frustrating about proposals for need-based financial aid was that they might be forced on them by schools whose conception of the role of collegiate sports in the modern university differed quite radically from their own. In his convention speech opposing need-based financial aid, Joyce argued for reorganization of the NCAA to give greater autonomy to the football powers. It was becoming clear that the schools that viewed collegiate sports as a business wanted to break away from the pack. Being associated with prestigious liberal arts colleges and their quaint amateur traditions was good for branding, but living by those traditions—by giving up athletic scholarships, for instance—would lower the quality of the sports entertainment product.

The major football powers were faced with a dilemma. On the one hand, they had to prevent schools that did not share their market-driven philosophy of collegiate sports from interfering with their policies and decisions. On the other hand, they could not leave the NCAA, as they often threatened to do, because they needed the academic legitimacy that comes from being associated with the Amherst Colleges and Yale Universities of the world. Pulling out of the NCAA would definitely raise a red flag for organizations like the Internal Revenue Service, which were already asking how multimillion-dollar television contracts, sponsorship deals, and licensing agreements are related to the tax-exempt purpose of higher education.

The big football schools ultimately dealt with this dilemma by using their financial clout to demand greater autonomy within the NCAA, thereby allowing them to call their own shots while at the same time remaining under the same umbrella as true amateur programs. The NCAA spends millions on public relations to perpetuate the myth that schools in its most competitive conferences are as committed to amateurism as members of the Ivy League. The NCAA's staff of attorneys and lobbyists ensures that this message gets out in the nation's courtrooms and in the halls of Congress.

In the 1970s, big-time college sports turned pro. It took another three decades for commercialism to go right through the roof, making college sports all but indistinguishable from professional leagues such as the NFL and NBA.

The End of Ara's Era

The Southern California Trojans defeated Notre Dame 55–24 on 30 November 1974 in what was arguably the most incredible turnaround victory in collegiate football history. By coincidence, it was also the day I received my doctoral degree from Penn State. Immediately following the graduation ceremony, I rushed with my family to the Rathskeller, one of my favorite college bars in State College, to watch the game. With my three-year-old son in one arm and my cap and gown in the other, I managed to grab a table with a good view of the television. The bar was packed with Penn State fans, many of whom resented the fact that Joe Paterno's teams of that era often ranked below the Irish in national polls, even when they had almost identical records. I had just become an alumnus of Penn State. But I remained in enemy territory when it came to college football.

The first half of the game was all Notre Dame. After each Notre Dame touchdown, our little group cheered, yelled, and engaged in behavior that bordered on obnoxious. Luckily, we had to leave at halftime, with Notre Dame ahead 24–6. In the second half, we watched elsewhere in disbelief as Southern California scored forty-nine points in seventeen minutes to humiliate the Irish totally. Had we stayed at the Rathskeller to watch Notre Dame's meltdown, I can only imagine the abuse we would have taken. The next day we walked around campus, stopping at one point to take a picture of my son sitting on the statue of the Nittany Lion. We were in good spirits, but the loss to USC dampened my celebratory mood.

Most longtime Notre Dame fans remember the 1974 USC game and, as with President Kennedy's assassination and the terrorist attack on the World Trade Center in 2001, they remember what they were doing when disaster struck. I remember commenting at the time that the rout appeared to be more than a simple momentum shift. The team simply stopped playing; USC was scoring at will against a defense that was ranked the best in the nation coming into the game. In a recent interview with Ara, I asked about that game. "I was stunned," he said, "I couldn't believe it." Ara says that the Irish had total control of the game at halftime and that he gave his normal motivational speech. "What occurred was a complete surprise to us. It was a momentum change that I never experienced in all of my coaching career, although I do remember being the beneficiary of such shifts, like when we beat USC 51–0 in 1966."

An explanation for Notre Dame's collapse that sparked considerable controversy appeared in an underground newspaper in Los Angeles several days after the game, and several weeks later made it into the pages of the *San Francisco Examiner and Chronicle*.[14] This account, based mostly on rumor, argued that Notre Dame's football team had been experiencing racial tension ever since several black players had been suspended for a year for a sexual incident involving a young woman in a campus dormitory. The young woman claimed that she had been raped. The players said the sex was consensual. It was alleged that black athletes on the squad felt that the whole matter should have been dropped and that Art Best, a white player, came to the black athletes' defense. Some months later, when Ara suspended Best before the USC game for some breach of discipline, several members of the team got angry, and, it was rumored, the racial tension that had been building for some time spilled over onto the playing field. The loss of momentum, so goes the argument, was actually a purposeful effort by several alienated players to throw the game and embarrass Ara.

When I asked Ara about these rumors, he responded unequivocally, "They are a joke, an absolute zero. Yes, I had disciplined Art Best. I spent more time counseling Art Best than I did my own son. He was a nightmare. How they could interpret this as a race problem is beyond me. He is white, not black." I accept Ara's explanation for what happened in the

Southern California game, but I am not surprised that Notre Dame may have experienced some racial growing pains during Ara's era. When I was playing for Notre Dame, there was only one black football player, Alan Page, on our team, and he has told me of the isolation he often felt being one of the few blacks on campus in a sea of white faces. It was during the final years of Ara's tenure that this began to change, and Ara and his staff had to manage this transition at a time when racial sensitivities were at an all-time high nationwide.

According to Ara, recruiting black athletes at Notre Dame was often difficult because the school had high admissions standards, and many black athletes came from economically and educationally disadvantaged backgrounds. Notre Dame's location and lack of diversity were also issues. One night, Ara (according to his own account) was having a booster party at his house and Fathers Hesburgh and Joyce were both there. Hesburgh came up to him at one point and asked why Notre Dame did not have more black football players. Ara said he told Hesburgh to go to the admissions office and see how many black players had been turned down. "We tried to recruit kids that we thought had a chance and we were turned down. Hesburgh obviously got the message, because the next year we brought in Ross Browner, Luther Bradley, and several other black athletes who helped the Irish win a national championship."

According to Ara, 1973 was the turning point for bringing many more black players into Notre Dame. He speaks proudly of the racial progress made during his tenure, although having to suspend some of the black players he brought in in 1973 was a painful episode in his life. "I am amazed," says Ara, "that during the 1980s there were nearly 50 percent blacks on the team. That is simply unbelievable. You go back to your years [1963–67], this was an all-male school. It was like a service academy with a religious affiliation. These were dramatic differences that I experienced in my eleven years at Notre Dame—women being admitted, blacks were being admitted in much larger numbers, and facilities being upgraded." Ara had performed brilliantly while meeting the almost impossible demands imposed on a Notre Dame football coach. By 1974 the stress was beginning to wear him down.

The actual cause of USC's stunning comeback victory against Notre Dame in 1974 will probably remain shrouded in the fog of history. The media's racial spin on the incident probably reflected the challenges many universities faced during that period in assimilating athletes from America's underclass into educational institutions that are bastions of elite cultural values. The tremendous influx of African American athletes into the revenue-producing sports of football and basketball also raised issues beyond the clash of cultures. Unlike the Poles, Irish, and other athletes from ethnic backgrounds that preceded them, African American athletes were being recruited at a time when the NCAA was abandoning the amateur principles intended to help maintain athletes as an integral part of the student body.

The influx of African American athletes into revenue-producing sports also differed from the experiences of previous ethnic groups in that it was in part a response to federal initiatives to liberalize admissions standards to attract larger numbers of minority students. Under the guise of furthering social justice and embracing diversity on college campuses, the college sports industry was able to subsidize its operations by awarding federal money to athletes who were often woefully unprepared for college level work. Large segments of the American public railed against affirmative action programs that give motivated minorities an edge in college admissions, but saw nothing wrong with admitting talented athletes, including minorities, with little academic interest or ability.

In December 1974, only a few weeks after the USC debacle, Ara Parseghian announced that he was resigning as Notre Dame's football coach. Notre Dame played an undefeated Alabama team in the Orange Bowl on 1 January 1975, winning 13–11. Ara's eleven-season coaching career at Notre Dame was over. The Orange Bowl victory allowed him to step down on a very positive note. Coincidentally, Ara had arrived at Notre Dame in 1964, the same year the Gulf of Tonkin Resolution gave broad congressional approval for the expansion of the war in Vietnam. In 1975, the year Ara coached his last game at Notre Dame, North Vietnamese troops seized Saigon. The war was over. Ara's era at Notre Dame paralleled a period of tremendous social upheaval. These had been challenging years for Ara. They were also among the most formative years of my life.

When the war ended, so too did the protests and the campus riots. After a tremendous outburst of energy that had spurred on the antiwar movement as well as movements for civil rights, women's rights, gay rights, athletes' rights, and the right to pursue open lifestyles, the nation seemed to be exhausted and ready to put the chaos of the sixties behind it. In 1974, just after receiving my doctoral degree, I accepted a position as an assistant professor at the University of New Haven, where I carried out research on intercollegiate athletics, taught a variety of sociology courses, and wrote extensively on the role of sports in society. Although I often incurred the wrath of the administration with my radical politics, my critical position regarding college sports, and my efforts to unionize faculty at my university, I was granted tenure in 1980.

During this period I began to take a very close look at the concept of amateurism and its transformation into an exploitive ideology. The more I read about and studied the topic, the more convinced I became that

big-time college athletes—much like the "million-dollar slaves" in the
NBA and NFL—are employees under law and deserve the same rights and
benefits that go along with that status, including the right to organize to
gain greater control over their working conditions. Being a product of the
sixties, I believed that faculty who build their careers writing about social
injustice have a moral responsibility to do something about it. This led
me to take a leave of absence from the University of New Haven in 1980
to join with several community organizers and sports activists from New
York City to build an organization to defend athletes' rights. A community
center in the South Bronx, not far from the police precinct often referred
to as Fort Apache, served as our organization's headquarters.

6

Taking a Stand at Fort Apache

Sports for the People

In 1976 a group of politically progressive athletes, some of whom met while playing on an interracial touch football team at Riverside Park on Manhattan's Upper West Side, began meeting regularly to discuss the state of sports and recreation in New York City, especially in its minority communities. One of their major concerns was that during periods of fiscal crisis, sports and recreation were often the first public services to be cut. Out of these meetings evolved an organization called Sports for the People, the founding principle of which was that public recreation, like healthcare, should be a right.[1] At that time I had no idea that Sports for the People existed, or that it would one day play an important role in my life.

The group's first big projects were a senior citizens' sports festival in Riverside Park and a "People's Opening Day" at Yankee Stadium in the Bronx. In the latter initiative, Sports for the People joined with other activist groups in protesting the city's willingness to subsidize the renovation of Yankee Stadium while failing to invest in the neighborhoods and public parks surrounding it. Sports for the People broadened its focus in 1977 by supporting a boycott of the Davis Cup tennis matches being held in Forest Hills because a team representing South Africa was being allowed to participate. At that time South Africa was banned from the Olympics for excluding blacks from its teams. Sports for the People, from its inception, was an aggressive advocate for athletes' rights in the United States and around the world.

Among the founding members of the group were activists who had been intimately involved in the radical politics of the sixties. Mark Naison, who had just finished his doctoral dissertation at Columbia on the Communist Party in Harlem in the 1930s, was a professor of African American Studies at Fordham University. While a student at Columbia, Naison participated in the 1968 student strike that led to the takeover of several campus buildings. He later became a member of SDS, and did a brief stint with the Weathermen before deciding that the violent tactics advocated by that group were unlikely to lead him anywhere but to jail. For Naison, a multiracial activist organization like Sports for the People provided an opportunity for grassroots organizing that could bring much-needed resources into the city's desperately impoverished communities. Naison also viewed Sports for the People as an affinity group for athletes like himself who seldom ran into other athletes who supported left-wing causes.

Another founding member was Phil Shinnick, an Olympian whose world record in the long jump at the 1963 California relays was not recognized because an official failed to set a wind gage needed to monitor the achievement. In 1974 Shinnick and his sports activist friend Jack Scott allegedly provided newspaper heiress Patty Hearst with a safe haven after several members of the Symbionese Liberation Army, which had kidnapped her, were killed in a shootout with police. Shinnick spent fifty days in federal prison for refusing to cooperate with the FBI investigation. Shinnick, the athletic director at Livingston College at Rutgers when Sports for the People was founded, often angered the athletic establishment by supporting closer athletic ties with communist nations.

The men and women who created Sports for the People ranged across the political spectrum from left-liberal to radical and were racially and ethnically diverse. A belief they shared in common, however, was that important issues related to sports were seldom addressed by radicals and intellectuals on the left, many of whom viewed sports as trivial. Stephanie Twin, a founding member who was writing a book on women and sports for the Feminist Press, was a strong advocate for women's rights in sports. Sports for the People worked to develop a Women's Sports Network composed of female athletes, community organizers, sports educators, and coaches to increase opportunities for women in sports. Another concern was that young athletes, especially minorities, were being exploited by the nation's universities. Almost from its inception, some members of Sports for the People began formulating ideas on how to defend the educational, legal, and medical rights of high school and college athletes.

The quarterback of the Riverside Park football team that spawned Sports for the People was Cary Goodman, a young radical whose charisma and ability to inspire spilled over from the playing field into his life as a political activist and community organizer. Goodman, who had played football at Colgate, was a passionate advocate of racial equality.

For Goodman, Sports for the People was more than an advocacy group for community recreation. He saw it as a mechanism for raising political awareness in minority communities and providing a focal point for community organizing. Sports for the People, as he saw it, could use an activity that grabbed people's attention—sports—to raise much broader issues concerning the quality of life in their communities ranging from healthcare and substance abuse to protecting the rights of senior citizens. Over the next couple of years, Goodman played a significant role in transforming Sports for the People into a multimillion-dollar community agency.

It was during the Yankee Stadium protest demonstrations that Goodman forged a relationship between Sports for the People and Gerena Valentin, a South Bronx politician who was running for a seat on the New York City Council. Valentin, a Puerto Rican nationalist with ties to the Old Left, was impressed by Goodman as a political strategist and community organizer and hired him as his campaign manager. With Goodman's help, Valentin managed to unseat Ramon Velez, a South Bronx political boss described by one of his opponents (hopefully with a bit of hyperbole) as a "ruthless if not a murderous human being." Valentin's victory said a great deal about Goodman's skills as a political infighter, as well as his fierce determination to win even when at a competitive disadvantage. These qualities would serve him well when taking on organizations with far more power and resources than Sports for the People.

After Valentin's election, Sports for the People began its meteoric rise. With Valentin's help, the organization was able to acquire an abandoned building in the South Bronx and convert the six-story structure into a multiservice community center offering recreation as well as health and entitlement programs to community residents. The center was named after Roberto Clemente, a former Pittsburgh Pirate All-Star and Hall of Famer much revered in the South Bronx for his contributions as an athlete and humanitarian, and Paul Robeson, an exceptional athlete, actor, singer, scholar, and political activist whose black nationalist views and support for oppressed people throughout the world led to his persecution at the anticommunist McCarthy hearings in the 1950s. Not only was Valentin instrumental in helping Sports for the People acquire the Clemente-Robeson Center, but he also used his political connections to help procure grants necessary to fund its programs.

Within a relatively short time, Sports for the People was attracting hundreds of thousands of dollars from the New York City Youth Board, Division of Substance Abuse Services, Department of Aging, the Community Development Agency of New York, and a variety of other foundations. Although shabby by comparison with "state-of-the-art" recreation centers in more affluent communities, the Clemente-Robeson Center became a hub of community activity, providing exercise classes for seniors and fit-ness programs and aerobics for women. The center also provided weight training, gymnastics, and martial arts for local youth. Bronx residents used the center to become more involved in the political process. Valen-tin was able to point to Sports for the People as one of his success stories, thereby strengthening his political base. Sports for the People began to build its reputation within the city as a whole.

The early successes of Sports for the People are all the more impres-sive when one considers the impoverished community it served. By 1980, New York City's South Bronx had become an international symbol of urban decay and desolation. What had once been a multiethnic working-class community was rapidly being transformed into an urban wasteland overwhelmed by crime, unemployment, substance abuse, and abandoned housing. Both Ronald Reagan and Jimmy Carter used the crumbling hulks of burned-out buildings in the South Bronx as a backdrop for policy statements on poverty and its eradication in their 1980 presidential cam-paigns. In 1981 Paul Newman played a police officer in a film called *Fort Apache, the Bronx*. Fort Apache was the nickname used by police officers in the 41st Precinct in the South Bronx because they often felt surrounded by a population that viewed them as an occupying army.

In this area of urban devastation, located only several miles from the Fort Apache police station, Sports for the People was launching its experi-ment of using sports not as an opiate to distract people from their social problems but as a way of engaging in political action to confront problems directly. In 1979 a board of directors composed of a diverse assortment of former athletes, lawyers, feminists, professors, and other politically pro-gressive New Yorkers was created to address the fiscal, administrative, and personnel challenges that accompanied the organization's rapid growth. Mark Naison was named chairman of the board, and Cary Goodman became executive director. Although the leaders of Sports for the People were effective agitators and political organizers, they often lacked the attention to detail needed for effective management. In time this lack of administrative expertise would leave Sports for the People struggling for survival.

Creating a Center for Athletes' Rights and Education

I first became aware of Sports for the People, an organization that would have an impact on my life comparable to that of playing football for Notre Dame, in 1980. In the spring of that year I organized a conference at the University of New Haven that focused on issues that emerge when sports is transformed from a recreational activity into a form of professional entertainment. In the morning session of this one-day conference, I brought together a panel of experts to discuss labor relations in the National Football League. The afternoon session was devoted to college sports and the question of whether recent changes in NCAA rules had created an employer-employee relationship between scholarship athletes and their universities. The conference, which examined the relationship between work, sports, and alienation, was very well attended, largely because of the quality of the speakers.

The first person I invited to the conference was Alan Page, my friend and former teammate at Notre Dame. At that time Page was an All-Pro defensive lineman for the Minnesota Vikings as well as the Vikings' player representative to the National Football League Players Association (NFLPA). Page believed back then, and still does today, that the issues raised by the Players Association were very similar to those raised by the civil rights movement. The issue as he saw it was freedom—"freedom for athletes to sell their services, and to have the same rights as other workers and citizens."[2] In 1980 the NFLPA was gearing up for a tough round of negotiations with the league over the players' demand for a percentage of the gross income they generated, a demand that if not met was likely to lead to a players' strike. Page, who had worked as a used car salesman in the summers to supplement his salary when he began playing for the Vikings, was an articulate spokesman for the NFLPA.

Once Page agreed to speak at my conference, I had little trouble getting other key people on board. Other panelists included Vince Lombardi Jr., a member of the National Football League Management Counsel and son of former Green Bay Packer coach Vince Lombardi. John Toner, the president of the NCAA, also spoke at the conference. To round out the morning panel, which included Page and Lombardi, I looked for someone from the far left who could address the issue of worker alienation from a socialist perspective. After a little research, I found the name of a community activist from New York City who seemed perfect for what I had in mind. As fate would have it, I had stumbled upon Cary Goodman, the executive director of Sports for the People, a group I had never heard of. What I remember most about Goodman is that no sooner had he entered the room where the conference was being held than he began passing out literature on Sports for the People and otherwise working the crowd. Before he even reached the podium he was shaking hands, exchanging business cards, and extolling the virtues of his organization. After his talk I had a chance to meet with him briefly and was struck by how much we agreed on a variety of issues, especially the need for an organization to defend the rights of collegiate athletes. For a year or so I had been working to create an advocacy group on my own campus composed of athletes, former athletes, faculty, and others who could assist athletes in disputes with coaches and other athletic personnel. I had considered establishing similar advocacy centers on other campuses but had no idea how that could be accomplished.

Goodman and his colleagues at Sports for the People had come up with a very similar idea and had already drafted a concept paper on how an "athletes' advisory center" could be created and funded. According to their proposal, Sports for the People, in conjunction with the National Conference of Black Lawyers, would provide young athletes with services and information to defend their rights during the recruiting process, throughout their careers as big-time college athletes, and beyond. What really excited me about their proposal was that their advisory center would mobilize crisis intervention teams to provide immediate and concrete negotiating or litigation services to athletes facing serious difficulty. The center would ultimately provide professional services to professional athletes in contract negotiations, endorsement arrangements, and career development.

In the months following the conference at UNH, Goodman and I stayed in touch. I made a number of visits to the Bronx to visit the Clemente-Robeson Center and met with other members of Sports for the People. The ideas in the early concept paper were refined and expanded into a proposal for the creation of an organization called the Center for Athletes' Rights and Education (CARE). CARE would incorporate many of the ideas contained in the concept paper but would focus primarily on the rights of high school and college athletes. In addition to providing services to young athletes in the New York City area, CARE would establish advocacy centers on college campuses throughout the country. Crisis intervention on behalf of athletes remained a central focus, as did the provision of legal expertise. With the help of a grant writer, we submitted a proposal to the Fund for the Improvement of Postsecondary Education (FIPSE), an agency within the U.S. Department of Education.

A major breakthrough for CARE came in the fall of 1980, when Goodman, Milton Brown, another founder of Sports for the People, and I traveled to Washington, D.C., to meet with Ed Garvey, the executive director of the NFLPA. We realized that an attempt to unionize collegiate athletes was premature, but our national network of advocacy groups on college campuses could certainly serve as the foundation for such a union effort further down the line. More important, the message we took to the NFLPA was that CARE could help raise the consciousness of college athletes about to enter the NFL regarding the issue of athletes' rights and labor unions. Most college athletes are unlikely to have given such issues much thought.

As we had hoped, the NFLPA leadership gave us a very warm reception, as if they had been waiting for an organization such as ours to come knocking on their door. Not only did they support our efforts to educate college athletes about their legal, financial, and medical rights, but they were solidly committed as well to our effort to defend college athletes' right to an education comparable to that of other college students. They had absolutely no problem with our argument that NCAA rules had transformed collegiate athletes into semiprofessional entertainers who often struggled to reconcile their roles as students and college athletes. Before our meeting ended, the NFLPA leadership offered to be a primary sponsor of CARE and to help in any way they could to get us funding. Goodman, Brown, and I left Washington feeling that our meeting could not have gone any better.

Several months after our meeting with the NFLPA, Sports for the People was informed that it had been awarded a three-year $250,000 grant by the U.S. Department of Education through FIPSE. We also learned that further funding for CARE would be coming from the Hazen Foundation and New York Community Trust. Although this money was small change compared to the resources at the disposal of the NCAA and its member institutions, CARE's partnerships with the NFLPA and the National Conference of Black Lawyers, plus its grassroots network of activists, would allow it to launch the most aggressive movement ever undertaken in the history of collegiate sports to defend the educational and legal rights of college athletes.

The first order of business for our new organization was to staff key leadership positions and to create an organizational structure consistent with the goals laid out in our grant proposal. I agreed to serve as CARE's director. The next position we had to fill was that of field representative. For this position we chose Kermit Alexander, a former All-Pro defensive back for the San Francisco 49ers. Alexander was employed by the NFLPA to meet regularly with player representatives and teams throughout the country to keep them informed of the status of talks with management. We paid half of Alexander's salary to combine his trips on behalf of the NFL with efforts to build local affiliates of CARE on college campuses. The money from CARE helped with the NFLPA's budgetary situation. We benefited by having a well-known professional athlete on our staff whose travel expenses were paid by the NFLPA.

We also needed a writer/researcher who understood NCAA rules and could produce educational materials to help athletes and their families better understand their rights. This person would also write press releases and provide data to be used in grant proposals or when preparing for congressional hearings. Jack Scott, the person most often associated with the "athletic revolution" of the 1960s, possessed skills that would make him an ideal candidate for this job. In July I received a letter from Dave Meggyesy, who was now working in the western office of the NFLPA, recommending Scott for the position in glowing terms. Support from the people within the NFLPA, plus Scott's tenure as athletic director at Oberlin College, made him a strong candidate.

Scott's prior involvement with the Symbionese Liberation Army (SLA) created a stumbling block. Scott's efforts to provide a safe haven for Patty Hearst were probably well intentioned, but his association with the SLA, an organization that had robbed banks and claimed responsibility for the murder of a school superintendent in Oakland, was part of his background. We knew that the athletic establishment would try to discredit CARE as soon as it went public. Scott would provide them with ammunition to go on the attack. Scott had been an inspiration for me and many others. He had given Tommie Smith a job at Oberlin after Smith had been blacklisted for his gesture of protest at the 1968 Olympics. This was a painful decision. In the end we hired Carl Johnson, an African American intellectual with a good feel for the problems faced by college athletes.

CARE moved into its offices on 149th Street and Third Avenue in August 1981 and went to work trying to fulfill its obligations under the FIPSE contract. I commuted to New York City by train and stayed overnight in the South Bronx several nights a week in the Clemente-Robeson Center or in our new 149th Street office. Much of the time I slept on a cot in a sleeping bag I brought from home. At times the modest accommodations, lack of basic office equipment such as fax and copy machines, and the grinding poverty of the South Bronx gave me a hint of what it must be like to work in a Third World nation. The difference was that I could jump on a train and be in Connecticut in half an hour. The contrasts between the South Bronx and the wealthy bedroom communities I passed on the train to New Haven were jarring, and constantly reinforced my conviction that the game of life was seldom played on a level playing field.

CARE Goes Public

In the fall of 1981 Sports for the People had reached its high-water mark. CARE was up and running with its FIPSE grant. At about the same time, the Human Resource Administration awarded Sports for the People a several-million-dollar grant for a home attendant services program, which was administered out of the Clemente-Robeson Center. The Sports for the People headquarters on 149th Street acquired new desks and furniture, and even a water cooler, giving the organization an almost corporate look. When staff from the Clemente-Robeson Center visited the offices, there was some grumbling about the disparity in working conditions at the two locations, but things were going well and morale was high. Goodman, who was thriving in his position as executive director, was named one of the top ten New Yorkers by the *Village Voice* for his work with Sports for the People.

Buoyed by this string of successes, we decided that the time had come for a major press conference to announce the creation of the Center for Athletes' Rights and Education and make the public aware of our mission. To ensure a good media turnout, we held the press conference in Washington, D.C., at the NFLPA headquarters. Ed Garvey, the executive director, was present, as were representatives of the other groups sponsoring and funding CARE. When we arrived at the room where the press conference was to be held, reporters were already milling around. When the press conference actually began, the room was packed, with standing room only in the back. Among those present were writers from the *Washington Post, New York Times,* Associated Press, and United Press International. The headline of our press release, "Athletes Rights' Group to Organize Nationally: Blames NCAA for Athletic Corruption," had generated substantial interest.

Cary Goodman gave some introductory remarks. He then turned things over to me to present our "athletes' bill of rights," which we displayed on a large poster in the front of the room. Our preamble went right for the jugular. "College athletes," it began, "are students and workers. Their time and sweat bring in millions of dollars to their universities. . . . As students, they are entitled to an education similar in quality to other students. As workers, they are entitled to safe working conditions and fair compensation for the money they generate." I then went through the list of ten specific rights, among them legal assistance and due process in disputes with athletic departments and coaches; the right to sports free from discrimination by race and gender; and the right to a multiyear grant-in-aid to help an athlete graduate even if injured. Although important, these rights were not particularly radical.

The reporters began scribbling feverishly in their notebooks, however, when we proposed that athletes have the right to a fair share of the revenue they generate and the right to form unions and bargain collectively on all issues affecting financial aid and working conditions. We stated clearly that CARE had no intention of trying to unionize college athletes. Our goal was to establish advocacy centers on campuses throughout the nation to give athletes legal support and to provide them with the information they needed to make informed choices about sports, education, and their future careers. Ed Garvey noted that 65 percent of the players in the NFL failed to receive college degrees. The NFLPA was not interested in launching an effort to unionize college athletes; it supported a grassroots effort to make college athletes more aware of their educational and legal rights.

The media response to our press conference was overwhelming, at least from my perspective. The story went out via the wire services immediately. Don Cronin, a UPI sportswriter, wrote, "A group headed by a former Notre Dame defensive end Monday announced plans to organize high school and college athletes to fight for their rights to a share of revenues generated by their sports."[3] Within a few hours, I found myself in a small office at the NFLPA doing phone interviews with reporters and radio stations around the country. I blasted the NCAA and the big football powers (especially those associated with the College Football Association) for engaging in a shameless legal battle over the sale of broadcast rights to the networks while athletes were leaving college without an education or financial security. Later in the day I appeared on CNN discussing similar themes and laying out CARE's plan of action.

My connection with Notre Dame football provided a hook for the media. Dave Anderson, the veteran *New York Times* sportswriter who had been assigned to ride the train with our team on the way to the Michigan State game back in 1966, used my Notre Dame background to frame his article on CARE and its "bill of rights."[4] Anderson included our entire list of rights in his column and accurately presented the message CARE had delivered at its press conference. Tom Hansen, the assistant executive director of the NCAA, was quoted in the column as saying that our bill of rights was "totally contrary to the spirit of college athletics." For the most part, however, Anderson gave CARE a very sympathetic treatment, perhaps because he too was disturbed by the big television deals and the increasing tendency of the NCAA and the powerbrokers in collegiate sports to put property rights and profits ahead of the educational needs of athletes.

The *Washington Post* gave our press conference front-page coverage in its sports section. Sportswriter Bart Barnes put a spin on the press conference that undoubtedly caught the eye of powerful groups in the nation's capital but unfortunately misrepresented what we had actually said at the press conference. The headline on Barnes's article was "Group Plans Union of College Players." Barnes went on to say that "during the coming weeks, CARE staff members will be visiting college campuses across country to organize union locals."[5] Unionization was on our minds as a long-term goal, but we emphasized at the press conference that although we supported the right of athletes to form unions, neither we nor the NFLPA were prepared to launch such an effort. In fact, we were fully aware that engaging in union organizing with Department of Education grant money was a clear violation of our FIPSE contract.

Garvey demanded that the *Washington Post* print a retraction, and after reviewing a video of the conference, the *Post* agreed to do so.[6] We had been damaged nonetheless. Once conservative members of Congress and officials from the newly elected Reagan administration read in the *Washington Post* that the Department of Education—a federal agency already under attack by the Reagan administration—had funded a group from the South Bronx to unionize college athletes, we knew we were in for a battle. The article also evoked an angry response from a number of NFL players' representatives who were convinced that Garvey must have lost his mind. How, they asked, could the leadership of a union about to go on strike against the NFL be diverting its resources to organize college athletes?[7] It took Garvey several days to set the record straight.

The NCAA's response to the CARE proposals left no doubt that we had struck the central nerve that runs to the very core of the collegiate sports industry. In his book *Unsportsmanlike Conduct,* Walter Byers, the former executive director of the NCAA, says that upon hearing about the creation of CARE, "there was an immediate red alert. The NCAA staff was told to get on this one right away. We asked legal counsel for a briefing about the labor rights of college students."[8] In Byers's view, we were creating a players' union. The *NCAA News* ran an article several weeks after our press conference laying out in some detail the NCAA legal counsel's preliminary examination of the question of unions for collegiate athletes. The conclusion was that both state and private institutions "normally will be held to have no obligation to bargain collectively with organizations claiming to represent college athletes."[9]

According to Byers, the legal opinions were reassuring to the NCAA leadership. Mike Scott of the Washington, D.C., Squire, Sanders and Dempsey firm, however, warned against being too complacent. "It is unlawful in virtually every state for firemen and policemen to strike," he said, "but it happens. Similarly, most labor contracts prohibit strikes during the life of the contract, but they happen. The simple fact is that whenever a group of people band together and insist upon acting in concert, they usually have to be dealt with in some fashion or another."[10] CARE was certainly an organization to be "dealt with." In 1981 the NCAA signed a football television contract with ABC and CBS for $263.5 million. The schools making up the College Football Association (CFA) signed with NBC for another $180 million. The rush for television money was on. The last thing the big-time programs wanted was for players to demand a piece of the action.

The controversy swirling around our project focused almost entirely on the union issue and on our argument that college athletes are employees who deserve a share of the revenue they generate. These are the issues that attracted media attention and helped us get our fifteen minutes of fame. What most sportswriters failed to grasp was our argument that the employment issue went to the very core of the education issue. One of the reasons why athletes do not receive the education they deserve, we argued, is that they are contractually obligated to give sports top priority. Athletes who fail to meet the performance expectations of coaches can lose their room, board, and financial assistance. In other words, an athlete on a one-year renewable scholarship can be "fired" like any other employee. By insisting that athletes are merely amateurs engaged in sports as an extra-curricular diversion, we argued, the NCAA trivializes the conflicts athletes often face when trying to reconcile their student and athlete roles.

From our perspective, any attempt at educational reform that failed to recognize the employment issue and the NCAA's abandonment of amateurism had little chance of succeeding. Unfortunately, FIPSE, our primary funding source, was unable to acknowledge the destructive impact of NCAA policies without alienating powerful interests in Washington and elsewhere that viewed CARE as a threat. About one week after our press conference, we received a letter from Leslie Hornig, our FIPSE program director, saying that she was "taken aback to find the project operating under . . . a philosophy of supporting athletes' rights as workers as well as students."[11] Hornig warned that if we got involved in a "two-front war" that gave too much attention to athletes' rights as workers, FIPSE would have problems renewing our grant. The signatures on our contract letter had barely dried and already FIPSE was threatening to cut our funding.

In spite of this warning from FIPSE, we refused to give in to what we perceived as a gag order. When I appeared on *Good Morning America*, David Hartman, who was then the show's host, asked if I thought college athletes should be paid. I responded that college athletes were already receiving pay for play in the form of one-year renewable athletic scholarships. The relevant question, I argued, was not whether they should be paid, but whether they should be paid more than the NCAA currently allowed. CARE's position was that once the NCAA abandoned amateur ideals by making athletic participation a contractual obligation, it lost the moral authority to dictate what constitutes adequate compensation for services rendered. We opposed socialism for athletes and free enterprise for everyone else.

On my subway ride uptown to my office after the show, I thought about how out of touch NCAA policymakers were with the daily realities of life in communities like the South Bronx, where teenage unemployment was close to 50 percent and poverty was the norm. In the 1980s America's ghettos became a major recruiting ground for coaches in search of athletes whose exceptional talents could generate millions of dollars of revenue for the burgeoning collegiate sports industry. Yet the myth of amateurism was denying these athletes an opportunity, while in college, to create financial security for themselves and their families. Why shouldn't an athlete be allowed to endorse products and engage in the same kinds of business deals as their coaches? What moral or educational justification could there possibly be for arguing that making money is bad for college athletes but fine for everyone else? These were just a few of the questions CARE was asking.

Fighting for Survival

In January 1981 Ronald Reagan was sworn in as the fortieth president of the United States. There is no way to know whether Reagan ever heard of the Center for Athletes' Rights and Education, but there is good reason to believe that if he had, he would have done everything in his power to cut our grant from FIPSE. During the 1980 presidential campaign, one of Reagan's campaign promises was to abolish the fledgling Department of Education, an agency he dubbed "President Carter's new bureaucratic boondoggle." Once in the White House, Reagan made it clear that even if he could not abolish the Department of Education, he was going to cut its budget. And it is hard to think of a DOE-funded program more likely to end up on Reagan's chopping block than one that supported labor unions for college athletes.

Just months after taking office Reagan made his position on unions very clear when he fired fifteen thousand air traffic controllers who had gone on strike. PATCO, the Professional Air Traffic Controllers Union, was demanding safer working conditions, including a thirty-two-hour workweek, updated computer equipment, and retirement after twenty years of service, as well as higher wages. Reagan's antiunion stance did not bode well for CARE. That Reagan, a former Hollywood actor, was well known for his portrayal of Notre Dame's legendary football star George Gipp in the 1940 film *Knute Rockne, All American* may also have worked against us.

It is unlikely that a union-busting president whose campaign slogan was "Win One for the Gipper" was going to tolerate an organization support-ing collective bargaining rights for collegiate athletes.

I first realized that the CARE project was in serious trouble when Cary Goodman and I were called to Washington in January 1982 to meet with Leslie Hornig, our FIPSE program officer. In her letter announcing the meeting, Hornig said that "this turns out to be a hotter topic with far more political complications and ramifications, than we suspected when we funded CARE."[12] Hornig said she was concerned that CARE was "stray-ing from its mission" and that its aggressive advocacy of athletes' rights as students and workers was diluting its focus. Hornig invited Bob Atwell, the vice president of the American Council on Education, and Roscoe Brown, the president of Bronx Community College, to help us get back on the road to what she viewed as positive educational reform. Hornig was sending a signal that continued funding depended on CARE's willingness to tone down its rhetoric and avoid controversial issues.

In the months that followed, we tried to respond to FIPSE's concerns, but we found it impossible to abandon CARE's stated mission. We were activists, and our goal was to defend the legal and educational rights of high school and college athletes. We continued our efforts to develop advocacy centers on college campuses and discussed our athletes' bill of rights whenever we had the opportunity. We also continued to argue that athletes deserve a share of the revenue they generate. For instance, we tried to introduce a resolution at the NCAA convention in support of what we called an "academic trust fund" for college athletes. Our proposal was to put a certain percentage of the revenue from the NCAA's multimillion-dollar television deal into a trust fund to be used by athletes to finish their degrees after their athletic eligibility had run out. The money could also be used to get them started on a graduate or professional degree. Although the resolution was not passed, CARE was able to generate public dialogue around such issues.

Media coverage of CARE continued unabated. Even if we had tried to pass ourselves off as an educational counseling service for educationally disadvantaged athletes, the media was unlikely to buy it. Years after our initial press conference, columnists continued to write articles—most of them very supportive—about CARE and the stand it was taking on behalf of college athletes. No other organization had ever brought such passion and resources to bear on the issue of athletes' rights, and no other organi-zation had ever posed a greater threat to those who profit from the educa-tional and financial exploitation of college athletes in revenue-producing sports. In less than a year, CARE was putting processes in place that could help restore the integrity of sports in higher education. It had also created enemies among those with a vested interest in growing college sports into a multibillion-dollar industry.

I was not totally surprised when Goodman and I received a letter in May 1982 informing us that FIPSE would not be renewing its grant to Sports for the People. What did surprise me was FIPSE's candid admission that the decision was largely political. In his response to Congressmen Garcia, Biaggi, Simon, Peyser, Rangel, and Weiss—U.S. congressmen who had befriended CARE and who were concerned about the decision to cut CARE's funding—Sven Groennings, the director of FIPSE, stated that "it was our feeling, after careful monitoring, that the activities CARE was undertaking with public educational dollars were primarily advocacy and not educational. Although we recognized CARE's excellent ability to raise public awareness of abuses in college athletics, we felt that their treatment of the issues was often one-sided and confrontational."[13]

At about the same time that I heard that CARE's primary source of funding had been cut, I realized that Sports for the People, CARE's parent organization, faced an even greater crisis. One afternoon while I was in the middle of an important phone call, Ivette Borras, our secretary, informed me that a moving company had just arrived to repossess our furniture. The movers had been sent, she said, by the Human Resources Administration, the agency that had provided a couple of million dollars to fund Sports for the People's home attendants program. As I continued my phone conversation, movers came into my office and carried away my desk and my chair. I remember asking myself if things like this ever happened at NCAA headquarters in Mission, Kansas. I finished the workday sitting on the floor. I was grateful they had not removed the new carpets. This tragicomic episode was the first inkling I had that the finances of Sports for the People were being monumentally mismanaged.

The reason our furniture had been seized, I later learned, was that it had been bought with funds that were supposed to be used at the Clemente-Robeson Center, the site of the Home Attendants Services Corporation project. I also discovered that Sports for the People had accumulated large debts to utilities and contractors and had transferred funds between programs without keeping accurate records, and that tax payments had been so erratic that the organization's bank accounts were regularly seized by the IRS and the state of New York. As more and more of these irregularities began to surface, Cary Goodman, the executive director of Sports for the People, became increasingly estranged from the board of directors and its chairman, Mark Naison. The only positive thing I could see in all of this was that in my position as CARE's director, I was not directly responsible for grant money and its administration. The major downside was that I was caught in the battleground between my two friends and colleagues, Naison and Goodman.

Goodman was ultimately removed as executive director. One could argue that all of us in leadership positions shared some responsibility for not keeping closer watch over accounting procedures and financial management. When the smoke cleared, I decided to remain with Sports for the People and the friends I had made at the Clemente-Robeson Center. I spent my final months in the South Bronx working at the community center on 165th Street, sleeping over several nights a week on my cot. Once the FIPSE grant was gone, the NFLPA backed off from the CARE project, as did the National Conference of Black Lawyers. Without a solid financial base or a major sponsor like the NFLPA, CARE lost whatever potential it had for influencing educational policy at the national level. After an incredible burst of energy and creativity, CARE was about to take its place in the graveyard of failed attempts at collegiate athletic reform.

I returned to my teaching job at the University of New Haven in the fall of 1982. What I left behind was an organization fighting for survival. Sports for the People was able to keep a scaled-down version of CARE up and running for a while, and it struggled to raise enough money to pay off its debts and to retain its remaining grants. The organization managed to limp along for several more years. In the end, crippling tax liens, lawsuits filed by creditors and former employees, and the inability to liquidate its debts led to the demise of Sports for the People. The Clemente-Robeson Center closed in 1984. The building is now occupied by United Bronx Parents, an organization that has been able to procure the financial resources needed to maintain it.[14] Mark Naison told me recently that a professor at Columbia University once used Sports for the People as a case study of how not to run a community agency.

Epilogue

In recent years there has been a slight economic upswing in the South Bronx. The arson has subsided and new housing has been built. Poverty persists, however. Classrooms in public schools are overcrowded, and qualified teachers are in short supply. Bathrooms in some schools have no toilet paper or hand towels, and parents and teachers often buy their own supplies. By some estimates, nearly a fifth of the city's schools lack gymnasiums. Ninety-four percent have no athletic fields. More than half have no playgrounds.[15] Yet in 2004 the city signed on to a project to build a new $1.4 billion stadium to house the New York Jets on the posh West

Side of Manhattan. There was no money for playgrounds for kids, but the city and state actually considered giving $600 million to help billionaire Woody Johnson build his stadium. If Sports for the People had still been around, its supporters would have been marching in the streets. The project ultimately died in the state legislature, but other stadium deals are on the horizon.

Colleges and universities now sell their athletic programs to networks and corporate sponsors for billions of dollars, and everyone who can write a business plan is cashing in on these collegiate athletic spectacles. Yet the athletes whose exceptional talents attract the capacity crowds continue to work under the same salary cap of room, board, tuition, and fees that was imposed in 1957. Some coaches' salaries have soared over the $3 million mark as universities engage in bidding wars for their services. Athletes, many of whom are recruited out of economically disadvantaged communities, are treated like criminals for accepting modest financial benefits that exceed NCAA limits. CARE was a bit ahead of its time, but the corporate takeover of college sports in the twenty-first century has spawned a modern version of CARE called the Collegiate Athletes Coalition, which recently changed its name to the National College Players Association (NCPA). I discuss NCPA initiatives in the final chapter of this book.

A handful of Notre Dame students protest as segregationist George Wallace, governor of Alabama, gives a speech on campus in 1964. Two of Notre Dame's African American football players, Jim Snowden and Richard Arrington, joined the protest outside the field house. Notre Dame Archives.

Ara Parseghian's coaching tenure at Notre Dame paralleled a period of tremendous social change and political turmoil on America's college campuses. Here Ara (*right*) and back coach Tom Pagna (*left*) talk strategy with players before a home game. Notre Dame Archives.

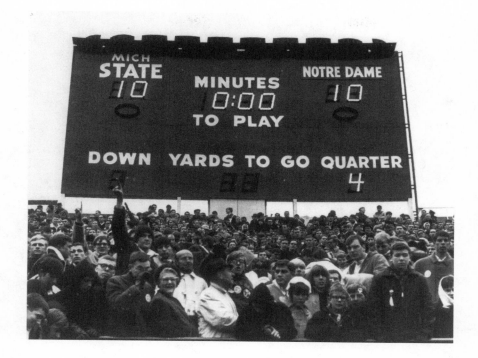

(*opposite*) Allen Sack (88) and Alan Page put pressure on Purdue's Bob Griese in the 1966 season opener. Notre Dame Archives.

(*above*) Fans appear to be stunned as time runs out in the 1966 Michigan State–Notre Dame game, which ended in a tie. This game, which had the highest television rating of any regular season college football game up until that time, foreshadowed the rampant commercialism to come. Michigan State University Sports Information.

(*left*) Jack Scott, Oberlin College athletic director and leader of the "athletic revolution" of the 1960s, was an outspoken critic of racism, sexism, and authoritarian coaching practices in sports. Oberlin College Archives, Oberlin, Ohio.

(*right*) Tommie Smith—shown here in 2005 and in the background poster—and his teammate John Carlos were expelled from the 1968 Olympics for giving the black power salute while receiving their Olympic medals. This courageous act inspired other athletes to fight discrimination on their campuses. AP Images.

(*left*) Billie Jean King, a champion tennis player and an advocate for equality for girls and women in sports, became a national symbol for gender equity in the 1970s, while women's rights advocates worked to pass Title IX. AP Images.

(*right*) With Walter Byers at the helm, the NCAA passed rules between 1967 and 1973 that transformed athletic scholarships from educational gifts into contracts for hire. In his later years, Byers characterized athletic scholarships as a "nationwide money-laundering scheme" whereby money formerly given to athletes under the table could be funneled through the financial aid office. Rich Clarkson/Rich Clarkson and Associates.

(*above*) In the 1980's poverty-stricken areas such as this devastated section of the South Bronx became recruiting grounds for college athletic recruiters. Athletes from these areas generated millions for universities but were treated like criminals for accepting benefits in excess of the NCAA's arbitrary salary cap. AP Images.

(*opposite, above*) Notre Dame's executive vice president Father Edmund Joyce (*right*), shown here with President Theodore Hesburgh and Ara Parseghian, worked closely with the College Football Association to challenge the NCAA's monopoly control of football television broadcasts. Notre Dame Archives.

(*opposite, below*) Kent Waldrep, a running back at Texas Christian University, sued TCU for workers' compensation benefits in 1992, decades after being rendered a quadriplegic during a football game against Alabama. The testimony of Walter Byers, Waldrep's star witness, was barred from the proceedings, even though Byers had served as the NCAA's executive director from 1951 to 1987. Courtesy of Patrick J. Bricker.

(*left*) Linda Bensel-Meyers, a founding member of the Drake Group, reported plagiarism and altered grades among University of Tennessee football players but was told by university administrators to let the matter drop. AP Images.

(*right*) NCAA president Myles Brand argues that commercialism is "not a four-letter word" in college sports as long as it is consistent with the academic mission of higher education. Courtesy of the NCAA.

USC sold thousands of Reggie Bush's number 5 jerseys while he played, but Bush could not share in the revenue. Notre Dame Archives.

Ramogi Huma, founder of the Collegiate Athletics Coalition, now called the National College Players Association, believes that college athletes must organize to make sure they get adequate health coverage and enough money for basic necessities. AP Images.

PART III

Shouting from the Ivory Tower

7

Building an Industry on Athletes' Backs

Workers' Compensation

I often tell people, only partly in jest, that the short time I worked in New York City for Sports for the People may have taken five years off my life. I worked long hours, traveled a lot, and spent a great deal of time away from my family. Even at home I often found myself on the phone with reporters, or distracted by the crises that invariably beset a fledgling organization dedicated to political activism. The youthful idealism that drove this project also made it emotionally draining because we took what we were doing so seriously. The positive side was that I was forced out of my comfort zone on a daily basis, taking on new challenges and learning new skills. On any given day my schedule might include going to Washington to meet with a member of the Congressional Black Caucus, appearing on the *McNeil-Lehrer NewsHour,* or attending a fund-raiser in an upscale loft in Greenwich Village. For someone as sociophobic as I am, these things were as stressful as they were exciting.

When I returned to the University of New Haven, I was emotionally drained, but I had learned organizational, political, and interpersonal skills that have served me well ever since. And I gained an understanding of college sports that I never could have acquired without actually being involved in a movement to challenge the powerful interests that benefit from the current system. Although CARE had lost its major funding, it had built up enough momentum during its short existence to influence public debate on issues related to college sports for years to come. Even after my return to academic life, I continued to be called upon as CARE's former director to present an alternate opinion on major issues in collegiate sports. CARE's network of contacts in the media and in the college sports industry, in addition to my own research and consulting related to college sports, kept me constantly in touch with new developments and controversies that emerged in the 1980s.

In the summer of 1982, Charley McKenna, a writer for the *Minneapolis Star and Tribune,* sent me a note to thank me for spending so much time talking with him about an article he had written on CARE and its athletes' bill of rights. He also gave me a heads-up on a court ruling that he thought would significantly reinforce CARE's argument that one-year renewable scholarships had transformed college athletes into employees. On 16 June, said McKenna, an Indiana court of appeals judge ruled that a student attending college on a sports scholarship is entitled to workers' compensation for injuries received on the playing field. I immediately grasped the significance of the ruling. If such a ruling were to be upheld on appeal, it would lend overwhelming support to the argument that athletic scholarships are contracts for hire.

I read the actual court ruling as soon as possible to better understand the facts of the case. In the spring of 1976, Fred Rensing, a scholarship football player at Indiana State University, was injured when he tackled a teammate during a punting drill in spring practice. Rensing, who was covering a punt, made what his coach described as "a very hard tackle," his head hitting the shoulder pad of the receiver. "It was the kind of hit that can be heard all over the stadium," the coach said.[1] When I read the description, I thought of the times I had made similar hits and how amazing it was that more football players do not suffer similar injuries. Rensing suffered a fractured dislocation of the cervical spine, rendering him a quadriplegic. Even after treatment, which consisted of traction and spinal fusion, Rensing was left 95 to 100 percent disabled.

Although this was a personal tragedy of immense proportions, I was well aware that the determination of whether Rensing was an employee of Indiana State University when injured would be based on complex legal arguments rather than emotion. According to the ruling of Judge Stanley Miller, "The benefits received by Rensing were conditioned upon his ability and team participation. Consequently, the scholarship constituted a contract for hire and created an employee-employer relationship." If I had received a catastrophic injury in 1966, I would not have been able to make a similar claim on my own behalf. When I was at Notre Dame, I had a four-year scholarship, which was a gift for the purpose of furthering my education. Even if I had abandoned sports to devote all of my time to educational pursuits, my scholarship was guaranteed as long as I performed well in the classroom.

Not long after this landmark ruling, I presented my views on workers' compensation for college athletes in a number of public forums. The first was the *Notre Dame Magazine,* which had accepted an article I wrote for an issue on intercollegiate athletics. This issue included articles by John Underwood, a senior writer with *Sports Illustrated,* and a piece by Notre Dame's president, Father Theodore Hesburgh. Neither Underwood nor Hesburgh mentioned the issue of workers' compensation in their articles, even though the case was receiving national attention and Notre Dame's location in the state of Indiana placed it near the epicenter of the workers' compensation controversy. My article made employment issues its centerpiece.

In language not much different from Judge Miller's in the Indiana court of appeals ruling, I argued that because athletic performance and participation are conditions of continued financial aid, coaches in big-time college sports programs, like any other employer, "can control the time, manner and discharge of their players' duties." I pointed out that few occupations have a higher injury rate than professional football. In order to cushion the blow of the more debilitating injuries, professional athletes have a right to state workers' compensation. Such athletes are also covered by the Fair Labor Standards Act, the Occupational Safety and Health Act, and the National Labor Relations Act. Scholarship athletes—whose responsibilities are indistinguishable from those of the pros—are denied these protections because they are supposedly amateurs.[2]

The *Notre Dame Magazine* article was scheduled to appear in February 1983. By coincidence, I was also asked to join a panel of experts to discuss the legal impact of the Rensing case in February at a conference sponsored by the Indiana University School of Law in Bloomington. Included on my panel was John N. Shanks II, chairman of the Industrial Board of Indiana, the board that first denied Rensing's request for workers' compensation benefits and whose decision had been reversed by the appellate court. Other conference attendees had written amicus curiae briefs in the Rensing case. I was excited and honored to have an opportunity to test my ideas against people directly involved in one of the most important cases in the history of collegiate sports. As I was writing my *Notre Dame Magazine* article and doing research for my Indiana University School of Law presentation, Fred Rensing's case was on its way to the Indiana Supreme Court.

On February 9, the day before I was to give my panel presentation at the conference, the Indiana Supreme Court ruled against the plaintiff, Fred Rensing. I was stunned and dismayed. My anger over the court's decision has never fully gone away. I had little time to study the court's ruling carefully before my presentation the next day, but even a quick read revealed that the court had misrepresented the true nature of athletic scholarships. What I found most misleading was the court's contention that "under the applicable rules of the NCAA, Rensing's benefits could not be reduced or withdrawn because of his athletic ability or his contribution to the team's success. Thus, the ordinary employer's right to discharge on the basis of performance was missing."[3]

The actual NCAA rule was, and still is, that "an athlete's financial bene-fits cannot be reduced or withdrawn *during the period of their award* because of his athletic ability or his contribution to team success" (emphasis added). Because the period of the award was changed in 1973 to one year, an athlete in Rensing's era could indeed lose financial aid for failing to live up to a coach's performance expectations. The coach could simply decide not to renew the grant of an athlete who was perceived to be a recruiting mistake. Just as universities that fire nontenured faculty often give them until the end of the year or longer to pack their bags, athletes who did not make the grade could finish out the school year. The court also chose to ignore the 1967 "fraudulent misrepresentation" rule, which allows immediate withdrawal of aid for defying the directions of depart-ment staff members or voluntarily withdrawing from sports.

The next day, in my presentation at the conference, I aggressively attacked the court's ruling, especially its misleading language regarding the supposed irrevocability of financial aid for athletic ability or contribu-tion to team success. If such language—which implied that NCAA rules do not allow an athlete to be discharged on the basis of performance— were used by a college coach during the recruiting process, I said, it would constitute a breach of professional ethics. According to a record of my comments that appeared in the *Chronicle of Higher Education,* I "admon-ished" the audience of university officials—I was pretty full of myself back then—to return to amateurism. "Return to sanity," I said. "Return to really caring about education in our universities. If you don't do that, you've got to recognize the rights of the employees that you are putting through this system. You can't have it both ways anymore."[4]

In the question-and-answer period that followed, Chuck Neinas, the commissioner of the Big Eight (now the Big Twelve) and the first execu-tive director of the powerful College Football Association, agreed with my contention that the one-year scholarship rule gave coaches an oppor-tunity to "eliminate deadwood." He disagreed, though, that the rule was motivated by a desire by coaches to gain the kind of control over athletes one finds in an employment situation. Neinas argued that the rule was actually a humanitarian gesture, passed primarily to prevent the common practice of "running off" players who were not very good athletes in order to make room for better ones. Not renewing a scholarship made the cruel practice of running off athletes unnecessary. I responded that that might well have been one of the motivating factors, but that what he seemed to be saying was that it is more humanitarian to "fire" players than to beat them up to get them to quit. And when you can fire people, I asked, aren't you talking about employment?

Reflecting on that meeting, I recall how disturbed I was by the celebratory mood I sensed among many of the attorneys present, especially those who represented major football schools. I am not suggesting that they did not empathize with Rensing in the personal tragedy that had befallen him. But they were applauding the clever way the court had spun the facts to defend the interests of big-time college sports. The court, as they saw it, had saved college sports from financial ruin. Recognizing college athletes as employees would have opened a Pandora's box of labor unions, unrelated business income taxes, and athletes demanding a share of the revenue they generate. Fred Rensing himself was quoted in the *St. Louis Post-Dispatch* as saying that when his case was on appeal, people came up to him and said that if he won, he might destroy college sports as we know it.[5] I could not comprehend how anyone could say this to a young man who would spend the rest of his life in a wheelchair.

The Indiana Supreme Court decision applied only to the state of Indiana, a state with a reputation for having some of the least progressive workers' compensation laws in the country. Nothing would prevent other cases like this one from popping up in other places and under slightly different circumstances, which might give an injured athlete a little more of an edge. Nonetheless, the Rensing decision was a tremendous victory for an emerging industry that derived a huge chunk of its profits from the relatively cheap labor of athletes. The clear message was that college athletes are amateurs whose compensation can be capped at room, board, tuition, and fees, regardless of the revenues they generate. The Indiana Supreme Court had helped smooth the way for universities to build a sports industry with few of the labor costs of other business enterprises.

A week after I returned from Indiana, I received a letter from Ernie Chambers, a Nebraska state senator who had just read my article in *Notre Dame Magazine*. He told me that it was heartening to see that there were people willing to speak out openly on the matters I had addressed in my article. Enclosed was a copy of a bill he had introduced in the Nebraska state legislature to provide that football players at the University of Nebraska at Lincoln be treated as university employees. Senator Chambers ended his letter by saying, "Keep doing what you are doing. I won't release my hold on this issue until the players receive equitable treatment and a piece of the financial pie which their efforts produce."[6] Twenty-one years later his bill, which included a provision to pay football players a stipend in addition to their scholarship, was passed by the Nebraska legislature and signed into law by the governor.

Socialism for the Athletes, Free Enterprise for Everyone Else

In the early 1980s, at the same time that major football powers were extolling the virtues of amateurism to justify denying workers' comp benefits to an athlete paralyzed from the neck down by a football injury, they were also gearing up for a major court battle over how the megabucks generated by athletes like Fred Rensing should be distributed. Now singing the praises of free enterprise, major football powers like Notre Dame, Penn State, Oklahoma, and Georgia argued that they had a property right to sell football television broadcasts to the highest bidder, and that the NCAA was behaving like a cartel, in illegal constraint of trade, by insisting that it should negotiate television deals for its entire membership. To understand this dispute more fully, let's take a step backward.

The hallmark of big-time college football, almost from its inception, has been its commitment to commercialism. Walter Camp, the father of the American game, argued that "demand should determine ticket prices, and Yale should profit from the attraction."[7] As early as 1885 Camp was trying to run Yale's football program on gate receipts alone. Paying athletes may have offended Camp's amateur sensibilities, but making as much money as possible from their games was the American way. By the late 1940s a new invention called television was already making it possible for college football to enter new markets and exploit revenue streams that would have warmed Camp's entrepreneurial heart. The NCAA feared, however, that television might have a negative effect on game attendance.

In 1951 the majority of NCAA membership, convinced that televising college football should be limited, passed a rule that gave the NCAA monopoly control over negotiations with the networks and permitted only one national and several regional telecasts a week. The NCAA eased up on these controls over the years, but powerhouse schools like Notre Dame fought the television agreement from day one because it limited their television exposure and distributed some of the revenue they generated to schools whose teams had far less spectator appeal. Notre Dame's president, Father Hesburgh, viewed the NCAA's monopoly control over television rights as "socialist in nature." Howard Stassen, the president of the University of Pennsylvania at a time when Penn fielded terrific football teams, called the NCAA policy to restrict a college's right to broadcast its own games a violation of the Sherman Antitrust Act.[8]

In 1976, sixty-one of the major football powers formed the College Football Association—Notre Dame was a powerful behind-the-scenes player—to lobby within the NCAA to get a television contract that would give them a bigger share of television football revenue. This group, led by Chuck Neinas, was convinced that TV controls were keeping millions of dollars out of their reach. In 1981 the CFA began negotiating a separate deal with NBC-TV, thus declaring war on the NCAA. The CFA backed out of the NBC deal when the NCAA made a number of concessions. In 1982, however, the Universities of Georgia and Oklahoma, with financial support from the CFA, decided to sue the NCAA on antitrust grounds. The case, which was heard in a federal district court in New Mexico, ruled in favor of Georgia and Oklahoma, declaring the NCAA a classic cartel that was limiting these schools' right to sell their football rights in an open market.

In 1981, while I was working in New York, I was well aware of the impending battle between the NCAA and the CFA. In a guest column I wrote for the *New York Times,* I said that this battle "should dispel any romantic illusions the public may still harbor about amateurism and big-time college sports. Property rights and profits are the prominent concerns, not the education of amateur athletes." "Who is going to defend the financial and educational interests of athletes?" I asked. "The NCAA and the CFA are negotiating television contracts worth nearly one-half billion dollars. Yet, the athletes whose sweat and sacrifice make these revenues possible in the first place, have been excluded from the negotiations altogether."[9] I closed by arguing that professional athletes had joined together in players' associations and that it was time for college athletes to do the same.

Several months later I received a call from a producer of *Good Morning America* who asked me to come on the show to discuss the ongoing lawsuit from an athletes' rights perspective. The NCAA had just lost round one and the case was making its way to the U.S. Supreme Court. The other guests joining David Hartman for this segment were the attorneys for the NCAA and the University of Oklahoma. The producer told me that I would be last in the batting order. Leading off would be the attorney from Oklahoma, followed by the attorney from the NCAA. I would be given the final word. I could not have been happier with the arrangement. I knew that they would focus on law, money, and antitrust law and totally ignore the needs of athletes, so I prepared my sound bite with that in mind.

The NCAA attorney argued, among other things, that a victory for the Universities of Georgia and Oklahoma would be a terrible setback for college sports because it would allow a handful of big-time programs to get richer while the others would languish. The Oklahoma attorney took the position that allowing schools to negotiate their own deals would increase the number of games on television, give consumers a wider variety of choices, and reward excellence. I responded, "I cannot believe these gentlemen and the universities they represent are fighting over millions of dollars of TV revenue, yet there has not been one mention of the educational consequences of these big-money deals for the athletes themselves." "I cannot think of a better example," I argued, "of how distorted the values of big-time college sports have become." At this point there was a commercial break, and the two attorneys never had a chance to respond.

In July 1984 the U.S. Supreme Court ruled in favor of the plaintiffs, Georgia and Oklahoma, in a 7–2 verdict. Justice John Paul Stevens, writing for the majority, said that "there can be no doubt that the challenged practices of the NCAA constitute a 'restraint of trade' in the sense that they limit members' freedom to negotiate and enter into their own television contracts."[10] College sports programs in America were now free to negotiate their own TV contracts; they could now sell their broadcast rights to the highest bidder. In the years that followed, there was a dramatic increase in the number of football games on TV. When I was in high school, I used to watch what was called the "NCAA Game of the Week." There was little choice. Now games flood the networks. Schools fight over weekend timeslots and even weeknight slots.

Although football revenues fell somewhat in the years immediately following the ruling, there was a rapid rise in revenue in the 1990s.[11] Free enterprise appeared to be working for the moguls who run college sports. And even schools that no one had ever heard of before began to enter the college sports arms race, figuring that they too could use television to catapult themselves to millionaire status. The increased competition for television money also put coaches under greater pressure to win, which in turn forced them to put more pressure on their players. In this highly competitive market, the salaries of celebrity coaches began to rise into the million-dollar range. Compensation for players, by contrast, remained capped at room, board, tuition, and fees. The major football powers that control the business of college sports had created the best business plan imaginable, one that combined socialism for the players with free enterprise for everyone else.

The most poignant statement I have ever read regarding the 1984 Supreme Court ruling was written by Justice Byron "Whizzer" White, the author of the dissenting opinion. White, an All-American football player at the University of Colorado in 1930, wrote that his fellow justices "err in treating intercollegiate athletics under the NCAA's control as a purely commercial venture in which colleges and universities participate solely, or even primarily, in the pursuit of profits."[12] Although I think White was wrong in saying that the justices had erred, his characterization of what they were saying was right on target. Contrary to the rhetoric of the NCAA, the Court had ruled that big-time college sports had become a business much like any other and that the NCAA was a classic cartel. The question I asked myself at that time was how long it would take for athletes to challenge on antitrust grounds NCAA rules that restrict how much schools can offer athletes for their services.

Prop 48: A Masterpiece of Public Relations

As I mentioned in an earlier chapter, the NCAA dropped its long-standing ban on freshman ineligibility in 1972. Few students needed the breathing space provided by freshman ineligibility more than minority athletes who were now flooding into revenue sports like never before. I supported affirmative action programs in undergraduate education back then and I still do now. But letting athletes from educationally disadvantaged backgrounds compete as freshmen was in my opinion morally unconscionable. One-year renewable scholarships compounded this problem by allowing coaches to demand that athletes give sports top priority as a condition for continued financial aid. Given these NCAA rule changes, combined with the transformation of collegiate sports into a highly competitive industry, the widespread failure of college athletes to obtain a meaningful education became a national embarrassment in the 1980s.

Media accounts of the most egregious instances of academic abuse were common. One of the most cited examples was the case of Kevin Ross, a basketball star at Creighton University who completed four years of college literally not knowing how to read and write. Similar cases of athletes being admitted and pushed through school, even though functionally illiterate, attracted media attention. Other studies during that period found that athletes who were academically qualified were also having a hard time reconciling the often contradictory demands of being both a student and a big-time college athlete. In other words, recruiting athletes with limited academic ability or interest was only a part of the problem. The unreasonable demands of commercial sports also played a role.

Between 1983 and 1985 I carried out my own survey of 644 male and female basketball players representing forty-seven universities in thirty-five conferences nationwide to determine whether athletes in the most competitive programs experience greater role conflict than others, and I presented my findings at the annual meeting of the American Sociologi-cal Association.[13] As expected, I found striking differences among NCAA divisions. When asked if they often felt pressure to be athletes first and students second, 41 percent of Division I athletes said yes. This was true of only 12 percent of athletes who played at the Division III level. Division II athletes fell somewhere in between. Division I athletes were also far more likely to report that being an athlete had forced them to take fewer courses a semester, cut classes, take a less demanding major, miss impor-tant exams, and take a variety of academic shortcuts, including cheating.

Between media exposure of extreme cases of academic corruption and a growing body of research that documented other abuses, the NCAA was faced with an erosion of public confidence in higher education's commit-ment to educating athletes. To salvage its image as a defender of academic integrity, the NCAA passed legislation in 1983 called Proposition 48. This rule, which was to go into effect in 1986, stated that entering freshmen would be eligible for athletic grants and game competition only if their high school grade point average was at least a C in eleven core courses and they achieved a minimum 700 of the combined 1,600 points on the SAT or 15 of 36 points on the ACT exam. Because students received a com-bined SAT score of 400 for merely signing their names and answering one question, a student needed only 300 more points to meet the minimum.

Proposition 48 can be viewed as an effort to reinstitute freshman ineli-gibility, but only for athletes at considerable academic risk. In retrospect, I think this was probably a good idea. One problem was that the mini-mum standard was so low that most athletes at risk academically would be denied the educational benefits of freshman ineligibility. Another problem was that many black leaders thought that Proposition 48 was flawed by the racial bias inherent in standardized tests. In the years that followed, Proposition 48 went through a number of versions, each one generally watering down the test score component. Athletes can now have a combined SAT score of 400—the lowest score possible—and compete as freshmen, provided they have a very high GPA in the core high school courses. In the 1990s the College Board, the sponsor of the SAT, recen-tered the test downward so that a score of 400 today would literally be off the bottom of the chart under the old system.

The "recentering" of the average SAT score has gone largely unnoticed by the American public. In 1995 the College Board concluded that an average score of 1,000—the average score in 1941—was an unrealistic standard for the diverse body of students taking the test in the 1990s and beyond. The board thus decreed that the average score be adjusted downward by basing results on the performance of students taking the test in 1990. For instance, a student who received a 505 on the verbal test today would have received a score of 428 on the original scale.[14] By this stroke of statistical legerdemain, a combined verbal and math SAT score of 700—the minimum standard for freshman athletic eligibility set by the NCAA in 1984—was raised to 820 without any tightening whatever of the test score requirement. Many unknowing sportswriters and others praised this seeming increase in the test score minimum as another sign that the NCAA was "getting tough" on academics.

Over the years sportswriters have generally characterized Proposition 48 and the watered-down versions that followed as examples of "tough new standards" imposed by the NCAA. In actuality, the standards have done little to raise academic standards or graduation rates. Even with these supposedly rigorous new standards in place, graduation rates in many athletic programs have remained embarrassingly low. In 2006, for instance, only 44 percent of Division I men's basketball players finished their degrees within six years. The rate for black players was 38 percent.[15] Students do not graduate for a variety of reasons, the biggest being lack of financial resources. Given that most big-time athletes have full athletic scholarships and access to academic support services, one would expect them to graduate at much higher rates than other students. This has not been the case.

Responding to the dismal graduation rates reported for the teams competing in the NCAA's Men's Basketball Tournament in 2004—by this point Prop 48 had had more than enough time to have worked its magic—NCAA president Myles Brand reportedly said, "It's reprehensible and disappointing. I think the current system permits student-athletes in basketball to move through school without getting a degree."[16] There is probably no greater indictment of Proposition 48 and its failure to raise the academic bar for athletes than the fact that Brand and the NCAA have had to launch a whole new initiative, a so-called Academic Performance Rating (APR), to raise graduation rates. Sportswriters, without skipping a beat, have embraced the APR rule with the same enthusiasm they showered on Prop 48, as the latter continues its slide into the dustbin of failed reform efforts. In the meantime, freshmen continue to be thrown into the pressure cooker of big-time college sports.

The Scope and Morality of Under-the-Table Payments

In 1986 I received a call from Stanton Wheeler, a professor of law and social science at Yale University, asking me to be a consultant on a multi-million-dollar project being done on behalf of the NCAA by the American

Institutes for Research (AIR). The project included a survey comparing a sample of 4,083 Division I athletes with students in other extracurricular activities in terms of their academic experiences. My job was to provide input into the research design and the kinds of questions to be included. Although I contributed to the final product, I wanted to include questions that the AIR people would not consider. The whole issue of compensation for college athletes was definitely taboo, even though most colleges and universities were facing NCAA probation at that time because of what the NCAA calls "improper benefits" given to athletes.

I knew it would be futile to come right out and ask college athletes if they were violating NCAA rules. I suggested more indirect questions such as: Do you think it is wrong for athletes to accept benefits that exceed NCAA limits? Do you think athletes should receive a stipend, in addition to their scholarships, that would cover a variety of living expenses? I argued that this survey would offer a once-in-a-lifetime opportunity to explore athletes' attitudes on a problem that had plagued college sports almost from its inception. I quickly recognized that regardless of how important the topic might be to the well-being of big-time college athletes, it was too politically charged to make the AIR's study. I let the issue drop.

On my flight back to New Haven, I decided that although I did not have a million dollars to spend, I would do the study of college athletes' attitudes concerning amateurism and under-the-table payments on my own. I worked out a research design that, while not perfect, might be doable. Instead of surveying current college athletes who would be neither accessible nor likely to admit violating NCAA rules, I decided to survey all current and former players in the National Football League. These players had little to lose by telling the truth, and their many years of experience could yield insights unattainable from a sample of current college players. Before the plane landed in New Haven, I knew that the key to this project would be getting the NFLPA to support it and to provide the names and addresses of more than thirty-five hundred active and former players.

I had good contacts in the NFLPA from my years of working with CARE. Intruding into the private lives of players to get them to fill out a survey, however, was no small matter. I got a lucky break when the issue of agents becoming involved with college football players before they graduated became a national scandal. The NFLPA wanted to know more about this and saw my survey as a way to retrieve vital information they needed from their membership. It took me one year to prepare the survey and work out the details. In 1989 I crammed boxes filled with thirty-five hundred envelopes into a Volkswagen Rabbit and delivered them to the NFLPA offices in Washington, D.C., where they were mailed out to the athletes. I then went to Wyoming for spring break and waited to see what would happen.

When I returned, I went to my mailbox at the University of New Haven to find it totally filled with returned surveys. I was euphoric. Then the guys in the mailroom informed me that there were four more boxes full of surveys on the floor in the back room. I was overwhelmed. The surveys kept on coming in over the next couple of weeks. About twelve hundred players had responded. I knew that I was raising very important issues in the survey and that a return rate of this magnitude would make the findings difficult to ignore. I immediately began to enter the data with the aid of graduate assistants, and then moved on to the analysis stage. The preliminary analysis revealed that many of the players in my sample had accepted payments in college that violated NCAA rules and that large numbers of them saw nothing particularly wrong with doing so. I worked for several months analyzing the data and preparing a paper to present at a meeting of the North American Society of Sport Sociology in Washington, D.C., in the fall of 1989.

To ensure that my study would reach an audience beyond my colleagues in sports sociology, I hand-delivered a copy to the sports editor of *USA Today* at his office across the Potomac in Arlington, Virginia, immediately following my presentation. Then, on my drive back to New Haven, I made further deliveries to the *Philadelphia Inquirer* and the *New York Times*. I also had the University of New Haven send out a press release to the Associated Press. The media response far exceeded my expectations, and many papers, including the *New York Times* and *USA Today*, included charts or graphs of my findings along with interviews I did with reporters over the phone. Most of the articles also included interviews with NCAA officials and other leaders in the collegiate sports industry to gauge their response.

What I found in my study was that a large percentage of former NFL players had accepted illicit payments while in college. The cheating was most pervasive in major conferences, particularly the Southeast Conference, where 57 percent of the players whose classes graduated after 1970 admitted taking payments. In an Associated Press article, I commented that "for me, the results said that there are far more violations than they say at the NCAA—that it is not just a renegade institution or the deviant player. There's a substantial underground economy that's likely to be unstoppable."[17] I added that it was humiliating for the athletes to be treated like criminals for accepting benefits that they deserve to be getting above the table, and that it was degrading for universities as well.

My findings revealed that the vast majority of illicit benefits were made by alumni, although some players said that coaches were involved. Payments came in the form of cash slid under dormitory doors or palmed in congratulatory handshakes after games. One player said that he typically found cash in his helmet every Monday morning. An important source of illicit cash was the sale of complimentary tickets each player received back then. One player admitted getting as much as $1,000 per ticket. In addition to cash, players received free meals and clothing. A new suit was a common benefit among older players. Most of the payments were very small. One player, however, said he received $80,000 over the course of his college career. Another said he was offered an interest in an oil well but turned it down.

The response to my study by college sports officials was fairly predictable. David Berst, the NCAA enforcement director, said in *USA Today* that in his opinion payments were "less of a problem now than in the past."[18] Southwest Conference commissioner Fred Jacoby, also quoted in *USA Today,* said my study did not reflect new rules to clean up programs: "We've gone through an agonizing period, and we've gotten everything in order. We're in a new era—it's called live by the rules." Mark Womac, acting commissioner of the Southeast Conference, was quoted in the *New York Times* as saying that "he doubted it [my study] reflected an accurate picture of illicit payments in his conference because it surveyed only players who made it to the N.F.L."[19] Womac's point was well taken, but I found it significant that of all of the players in the NFL, those from the Southeast Conference topped the list in terms of accepting illicit benefits.

At about the same time that I was doing my study, a football player at Auburn—a member of Womac's Southeast Conference—was doing his own study of under-the-table payments, although his approach was much more surreptitious than mine. While I was mailing out my questionnaires, Eric Ramsey was secretly tape-recording conversations—twenty-two microcassettes' worth in all—with boosters and coaches detailing the exchange of money and other extra benefits for his athletic services. Ramsey's tapes showed, among other things, that Coach Pat Dye had used his connections as a bank director to arrange a car loan for him, thus leading to Dye's dismissal. Ramsey had also received assistance with auto insurance payments, $100 bonuses for making interceptions, and cash subsidies funneled by alumni through coaches. There was also mention of players mingling with alumni on Friday nights before home games to receive cash while doing "the Auburn handshake."[20] Ramsey's tapes gave some life to my dry statistics.

Probably the most significant finding of my study, from my perspective, concerned the athletes' perceptions of the propriety of accepting under-the-table benefits and the adequacy of their financial aid packages. Overall, 53 percent of those responding said they saw nothing wrong with accepting under-the-table payments for living expenses, with the number rising to 72 percent among black players. And 78 percent of all respondents said that athletes deserve greater compensation than NCAA rules allow. When a *New York Times* reporter asked why black players were less likely than others to view under-the-table payments as wrong, I responded that "blacks in general may be more cynical about rules imposed by the white power structure because of their race's historic experience as victims of exploitative legal codes." The plantation system was still a part of their collective memory.

At the end of my survey I had left a space for respondents to include their names and phone numbers if they were willing to be interviewed. More than a hundred players were. One of the athletes I interviewed was Roman Gabriel, my childhood role model and one of the finest quarterbacks in NFL history. I mention him here because his views are typical of many Americans who support NCAA policies. "I played football because it is a game," he said. "The kids should learn it that way instead of listening to some of our professional players who say it is a business."[21] Gabriel argued that it was wrong to take money under the table. In his view, professional athletes who wait a couple of years after leaving college to admit they accepted illegal benefits "should have to pay the money back and also pay the school the cost of the scholarship they received." (He may have had Eric Ramsey in mind.) He added, "You play because it's fun and it's enjoyable to be part of it. Amateurism is worth preserving."

I appreciated Gabriel's passionate defense of amateurism. But when I hung up the phone, the same old questions started going through my mind. If, as Gabriel asserted, college football is merely a game, like club rugby, and not a highly competitive business, why did the Universities of Georgia and Oklahoma go to the U.S. Supreme Court to claim they had a property right to the sale of football broadcasts to television networks? And why did the Court rule in their favor, concluding that the NCAA's cartel behavior constituted a violation of the Sherman Antitrust Act? Do rugby clubs generally find themselves in the Supreme Court arguing these kinds of cases? Of course not, because club rugby is merely a game played by amateurs, not a multimillion-dollar business built on the backs of underpaid professionals.

A question that no one has ever been able to answer for me is this: If the Supreme Court says college football is a business and that universities have a property right to the sale of football games in an open market, why don't the players who are recruited and subsidized to put fans in the seats and in front of their television sets have a similar property right to sell their labor to the industry that makes millions of dollars off their backs? When the economic interests of college sports are threatened, everyone concedes that college sports is a business. But when athletes ask for a fair share of the revenue, or for protection under workers' compensation laws, the NCAA insists that college sports is merely an amateur recreational outlet for college students. The miracle of college sports in the 1980s was that universities were able to build a massive entertainment industry with virtually no one questioning this charade.

Brian Boulac, an assistant football coach at Notre Dame from 1970 to 1982, and I recently had a long phone conversation about how college recruiting has changed since the sixties. In his opinion, NCAA rules that have barred alumni from recruiting athletes have most probably reduced the numbers of players accepting "under-the-table" payments in college sports compared with my era. He may be right, but my NFL study in 1989 presented convincing data to the contrary. In addition, instances of colleges and universities being sanctioned by the NCAA for "improper benefits" appear on the sports pages on a regular basis. If these accounts are to be believed, the size of these payments far exceeds the living expenses I received from Leonard Tose while I was at Notre Dame. Reggie Bush, for instance, allegedly received nearly $280,000 in cash from agents while playing for Southern Cal. Chris Webber, a Michigan basketball player, has admitted receiving $40,000 from a booster who testified before his death that he had given $616,000 to Webber and three other Michigan players.[22] Does anyone actually believe that under-the-table payments are a thing of the past?

8

Fighting for Market Share in the 1990s

The 1984 Supreme Court ruling that busted the NCAA's monopoly control over television broadcasts of college football games was a victory for free enterprise. Every school willing to make the investment could now compete for national television exposure and a piece of commercial college football's pot of gold. In this hypercompetitive environment, teams like Notre Dame could no longer live off the glory of impressive squads of the past. They too had to invest in new stadiums, state-of-the-art training facilities, high-priced coaches, and all of the other amenities necessary to recruit and train the nation's best athletes. This heightened level of competitiveness raised a crucial question for the future of college sports: Could the nation's top academic institutions remain major players in sports without sacrificing academic and moral integrity? A look at Notre Dame in the 1990s sheds light on this crucial issue.

Notre Dame Football: A Cut Above the Rest

The only conversation I ever had with Father Hesburgh, before the lengthy interview I did with him for this book, took place more than forty years ago when I was a student at Notre Dame. My roommate, Joel Maturi—now the athletic director at the University of Minnesota—Roy Perry, another close friend, and I were on our way back from a night in South Bend and saw that the light was on in the president's office in the administration building. Joel insisted that we stop in to say hello. Because Hesburgh spent a great deal of time off campus raising funds and traveling the world, Joel figured that this might be one of our few opportunities to meet him. I suggested that an unannounced visit, especially after a night of bar hopping, might not be a great idea. Joel reassured me that other students had done this in the past and that dropping in on the president when he was working late was a campus tradition.

We knocked on his door and, as Joel had predicted, Father Hesburgh invited us into his office, a fairly spacious room with a beautiful view of the campus through the window behind his desk. His desk was scattered with papers in the lamplight. Classical music played softly in the background. We introduced ourselves. Joel told him proudly that two of his older brothers had gone to Notre Dame and that he was following in the family tradition. Joel also mentioned that I was a football player. After we spent a few minutes discussing topics ranging from sports to disciplinary policies on campus, we apologized for disturbing him and let him get back to work. This late-night talk with our distinguished college president remains one of the fondest memories of my four years at Notre Dame.

Father Hesburgh, who was president of Notre Dame for thirty-five years, retired in 1987 and now holds the title of president emeritus. During his career he counseled seven U.S. presidents and several popes. His stature in the academic community is perhaps best reflected in the 150 honorary degrees he has been awarded by other universities. After Hesburgh became president in 1952, he began to transform Notre Dame into a modern university, one that ranks today among the finest in the country. Under his leadership, Notre Dame also continued its tradition of excellence in college football. During Hesburgh's presidency Notre Dame finely tuned its image as a school that could win national championships without lowering its academic standards or breaking the rules. Notre Dame's ability to excel in both sports and the classroom is what led me to choose it over several Ivy League schools when I was being recruited in high school.

In 1989 Hesburgh became the co-chair of the Knight Foundation Commission, an organization charged with proposing a reform agenda for college sports. Because the Knight Foundation Commission reports of 1991 and 2001 focused on issues I had been debating for decades, I decided to begin my interview with Hesburgh by addressing some of those issues as they relate to Notre Dame. The Knight Foundation placed rampant commercialism in college sports at the top of its reform agenda, fearing that it was compromising the academic mission of many universities. "Sports as big business for colleges and universities is in conflict with nearly every value that should matter for higher education," says the 2001 report. "The big business of big-time sports all but swamps those values, making a mockery of those professing to uphold them."[1]

My question for Hesburgh was how he could reconcile the position on commercialism he took in the Knight Foundation Commission report with the "free-enterprise" approach Notre Dame had taken over the years. I specifically mentioned Notre Dame's support for the 1984 Supreme Court decision that recognized each university's right to sell football television broadcasts to the highest bidder. "First of all," Hesburgh replied, "athletes should be educated. That's the number-one thing. If you are educating athletes and you can also get on television, you should be free to use that money any way you want. I welcome the money we made on athletics and can point to the results in a positive academic way. We have buildings we were able to build—academic buildings—thanks to extra income, and we have a scholarship program for minorities."[2]

I asked him if he thought that lifting NCAA restraints on the number of television appearances football teams can make might have actually heated up the arms race, leading many schools to place their desire for television money above the academic needs of athletes. Didn't the Supreme Court ruling encourage universities to treat football as just another business? Hesburgh's response was that he never gave the 1984 antitrust case serious thought but that he supported the views of Ned Joyce, his executive vice president. Notre Dame should "control its own internal show," Hesburgh said. In his view, though, making money does not require compromising academic standards. For instance, he said, "we would not play on Friday night and we don't play during the week." According to Hesburgh, "some universities are going to do everything in the world to maximize their income and use the kids just as moneymakers. That is wrong."

Hesburgh has little tolerance for schools with low graduation rates for athletes. "If schools do not graduate 50 percent of athletes, they should not be eligible for the conference championship or a bowl game. That would straighten it out in a hurry if you hit them in the pocketbook," he said. The Knight Foundation Commission actually included this among its proposals for reform, and it was the source of the NCAA's recent APR legislation geared toward increasing graduation rates. Hesburgh speaks with pride of Notre Dame's very high graduation rates for football players, estimating that the figure is around 90 percent over the years. The method used by the NCAA to calculate graduation rates in 2005 puts the figure for Notre Dame closer to 80 percent, but Notre Dame continues to rank with top schools like Duke, Boston College, and Northwestern in NCAA rankings.

The key to maintaining high graduation rates for athletes, according to Hesburgh, is to admit only those who fit the profile of the rest of the student body. "Our coach has absolutely no say about who gets accepted.

The director of admission's word is final." Hesburgh admits that Notre Dame takes students who would not have been admitted if not for their athletic skills, but not very many, and even those athletes, in his opinion, are capable of handling college-level work. "I once made an exception," he told me, "for a football player from a rough area in East St. Louis whose disadvantaged educational background placed him at the extreme low end of the applicant pool." His supportive family and determination to succeed, however, convinced Hesburgh to give him a chance. Says Hesburgh, "The young man graduated, played professional football, and is a wonderful citizen."

Toward the end of our talk, I mentioned to Hesburgh that the Knight Commission Foundation report had included a reference to my 1989 survey of NFL players, which found that many respondents had accepted what the NCAA refers to as "improper benefits." I asked if he thought it was wrong for athletes to accept payments beyond what the NCAA allows, especially when college coaches, the universities, and just about anyone else who can write a business plan can exploit these games for commercial gain. I obviously touched a nerve. "It is wrong for an athlete to take five cents beyond what they are offered," Hesburgh replied. "A $40,000 scholarship to Notre Dame is more than enough. You know what you are getting into when you decide to attend, and you agree to certain terms. It is wrong for an athlete to accept any more than that."

Throughout his tenure as Notre Dame's president, Father Hesburgh had skillfully leveraged college football for university advancement. As executive vice president in 1949 he negotiated Notre Dame's first television contract with Dumont television, selling five games for $55,000. Today, the Irish sell six games to NBC for $9 million. Hesburgh was an aggressive academic entrepreneur, and college football became a crucial part of his overall business plan. He took great pains, however, never to let football appear to overshadow his primary mission, which was to create a great university. For instance, he held back on building a new stadium to avoid the perception of overemphasizing football. He insisted that the amount of money spent on the new athletic and convocation center not exceed what was spent on the library. Under his watch Notre Dame developed a national reputation for being a cut above the rest when it came to combining excellence in sports and education.

Losing Some of the High Ground

When Father Hesburgh turned over the leadership of Notre Dame to Father Edward ("Monk") Malloy in 1987, the football strategy he and his executive vice president, Father Edmund Joyce, had carefully crafted over thirty-five years was paying substantial dividends. The pivotal role they had played in the College Football Association and its successful challenge to the NCAA's monopoly control of football television revenues boded well for Notre Dame's future negotiations with major networks. Even Father Joyce's ill-conceived decision to hire former Moeller High School football coach Gerry Faust, after Dan Devine stepped down, had an upside for preserving the Notre Dame mystique. Faust, who recruited the kind of athletes admissions officers dream about, had a lackluster record (30–26–1). Notre Dame patiently honored his five-year contract and sent him on his way with a touch of class. One of Joyce's last decisions as executive vice president was to hire Lou Holtz, a tremendous motivator with a knack for winning, as Faust's successor. In just three years Holtz took his team to a national championship. As the 1980s came to a close, Domers had good reason to brag that when it came to playing football with integrity, the Irish were in a league of their own.

By 1990, however, Notre Dame's new leadership seemed more willing than their predecessors to sacrifice a little moral high ground if the right business deal came along. For instance, Notre Dame's 1990 decision to break with the CFA to sign its own five-year, $38 million deal with NBC led critics to quip that tarnish was beginning to accumulate on the Golden Dome. That Notre Dame was trying to make some money on this deal was not the major issue. As Father Hesburgh made clear in my interview with him, Notre Dame makes no apologies for running its football program with an eye toward profit. In this case, however, Notre Dame appears to have worked behind the scenes to undercut an organization with which it had established a relationship of good will and mutual trust over the years. People have come to expect behavior like this on Wall Street, but not at Notre Dame.

Notre Dame had been a strong supporter of the College Football Association since its founding in 1977. Father Joyce, one of the CFA co-founders, worked very closely with Chuck Neinas, the CFA's executive director, often being asked by Neinas to be a national spokesperson for the organization. When the CFA won its antitrust case against the NCAA, Notre Dame was a primary benefactor. In 1984 and 1987, Joyce privately turned down two opportunities for Notre Dame to negotiate separate agreements with the television networks out of loyalty to the CFA and its television package.[3] After Joyce retired in 1987, Father Bill Beauchamp, the new executive vice president under Monk Malloy, maintained Notre Dame's strong ties with the CFA, serving on the CFA board of directors and later becoming its secretary-treasurer. Notre Dame and the CFA spoke with one voice.

In 1990, when the CFA was negotiating with ABC and ESPN, Beau-champ was on the negotiating team and Notre Dame was represented at every major meeting. After months of difficult negotiations, the CFA announced a deal with ESPN and ABC that would bring in $350 million to the sixty-four members of the CFA over five years. Notre Dame football was an important part of the package. Unbeknownst to Chuck Neinas and the other members of the negotiating team, Notre Dame had been meeting secretly with NBC while the CFA negotiations were going on.[4] Several weeks after the CFA deal was announced, Notre Dame sent shock waves through the world of sports by announcing that it was out of the CFA package and had closed its own separate deal with NBC for $38 million. Without Notre Dame in the CFA package, the CFA lost $35 million. Many CFA members were in a state of disbelief. Vince Dooley, Georgia's athletic director, exclaimed, "I wasn't surprised by this, I was shocked. Surprise, shock, greed, and ultimate greed—that is the reaction I am getting from people."[5]

In a recent phone conversation with Roger Valdiserri, Notre Dame's former sports information director, I had a chance to discuss the public relations impact of Notre Dame's bolting from the CFA. I first asked Valdiserri if Father Bill Beauchamp and Dick Rosenthal, the new athletic director, had any concerns about how the public might respond to the decision. Valdiserri said that at a meeting with the Athletic Department called by Beauchamp and Rosenthal to announce the NBC deal, several of those present asked if they expected a lot of criticism. Rosenthal said there might be a little and inquired why they had asked. These people expressed a concern that Notre Dame had a long history with the CFA and that now the school was abandoning it. There was a concern that the response was going to be nationwide and that it would not be favorable.[6]

At this meeting people raised the possibility that other schools might decide to boycott Notre Dame. According to an Athletic Department source who preferred not to be identified, Beauchamp and Rosenthal "sort of laughed at that suggestion and could not imagine schools refusing to play Notre Dame in sports." The next day, according to this source, "the athletic director at the University of Kansas called and wanted out of our basketball game with them and then the AD at the University of Houston comes out in the paper and says Houston will never play Notre Dame in anything." As predicted, the criticism was hostile. Sportswriters, including those with no history of bashing Notre Dame, used terms like selfish, greedy, and arrogant to describe Notre Dame's decision. Most disturbing was the implication that Notre Dame had fallen to the level of any other football factory by putting money ahead of other considerations.

Michael DeCicco, legendary fencing coach and former director of academic advising at Notre Dame, had worked with Father Joyce for many years. When I talked with him about the transition from the Hesburgh-Joyce administration to the Malloy-Beauchamp administration, he said, "In my opinion, the new guys were not in the same league."[7] He thought this was especially evident in the way the new administration handled the CFA television decision. According to DeCicco, although CFA executive director Chuck Neinas was very close to Joyce and Hesburgh, the latter were not even consulted on the decision. "You certainly would have thought they would have talked to Joyce, knowing that he was close to the CFA and the CFA was going to be toppled by this decision," says DeCicco. DeCicco, who was very close to Father Joyce, said that he is certain that Joyce had no idea this was coming and was really upset.

Notre Dame's abandonment of the CFA was significant for the larger world of collegiate sports. Once Notre Dame jumped ship, other schools and athletic conferences began to see the attractiveness of doing their own negotiating. In the 1990s conferences began to realign to extend their markets. The Big Eight became the Big Twelve. Penn State joined the Big Ten. The Atlantic Coast Conference added Florida State. One by one the major conferences broke off from the CFA and cut their own deals with major networks.[8] Notre Dame's decision to go it alone spelled the beginning of the end for the CFA, which ceased to exist in 1996. Of course, Notre Dame alone did not cause the CFA's downfall. The same drive toward free enterprise that had motivated the CFA to break the NCAA cartel had predictably led others to seek independence from the CFA. There was money to be made from college sports, and no one was interested in sharing it.

Trying to Steal the Halo from the Golden Dome

Not long ago, while browsing through the sports section of a used bookstore, I came upon a book entitled *Under the Tarnished Dome: How Notre Dame Betrayed Its Ideals for Football Glory*. This book, written by author Don Yaeger and *Sports Illustrated* writer Douglas Looney, was published in 1993, the same year that a stunning upset by Boston College cost the Irish a second national championship under Lou Holtz. I vaguely remember the controversy the book created at the time of its publication, but I had never gotten around to reading it. Because I was just beginning to write this book, and because *Under the Tarnished Dome* was selling for $4.95 in 2003, I decided to take it home and give it some close attention. The authors had interviewed eighty-four former Notre Dame football players who had played for Lou Holtz, and I found some of the issues they raised difficult to ignore.

The authors' major thesis was that by hiring Lou Holtz, Notre Dame had struck a bargain with the devil. In order to get a coach who could win national championships, said the authors, Notre Dame had sold its soul. Among other allegations, the authors accused Holtz of turning a blind eye to rampant steroid abuse, recruiting athletes who had little commitment to Notre Dame's traditions and academic values, pressuring seriously injured players to return to action before medically advisable, and using abusive behavior with players and coaches. The book was a national best seller. Ted Koppel devoted an episode of *Nightline* to the authors' accusations, interviewing several Notre Dame athletes. The authors had breached the defenses of fortress Notre Dame, and to this day Notre Dame loyalists grimace when the book is even mentioned.

One of my first reactions to the book as a former Notre Dame football player was that some of the things the authors took Holtz to task for, such as grabbing players' face masks, slapping their helmets, and screaming at them, were common practices even when I played. Joe Yonto, a coach whom I continue to hold in high regard, did all of those things to me, often making me so mad I wanted to slug him. But this was football, not croquet, and the mind games coaches played to prepare athletes for conditions in some ways analogous to combat were part of the culture. Maybe this culture does not belong in a university, but that is a different question. My point is that Holtz, while a bit over the edge at times, was not much different from other coaches I have known when it came to using drill instructor tactics on the practice field.

Although I cannot imagine Ara's coaching staff risking the long-term health of an athlete, their attitude toward injury and pain could have been taken from Lou Holtz's playbook. I recently had a long talk with my former coach, Johnny Ray, regarding this issue. Ray, Ara's defensive coordinator in the sixties, became head coach at Kentucky after leaving Notre Dame and later coached for the Buffalo Bills. Lou Holtz asked him on two occasions to join his staff at Notre Dame, but Ray declined. Ray, a paratrooper in World War II, has survived a heart attack and has had operations for lung and colon cancer. He continues to fight on. As a coach, he was as demanding as they get. One of his favorite sayings was, "Anybody can play when they're healthy." Regarding injuries he often said wryly, "It's only pain."

When I mentioned the authors' allegations in *Under the Tarnished Dome* that Lou Holtz regularly shunned players, or humiliated them in some other way in order to get them back into action when injured, Ray said that "if there was any question about a boy's health, Ara's and my policy was that we were not going to screw around and embarrass him."[9] He added, however, that "you have to get to know your athletes to really determine if they are babying themselves, or if they are really injured." He admits that he sometimes used embarrassment to motivate players. He would sometimes call a player gutless, or a disgrace to the uniform. "We would do this to drive you to your utmost ability. I sometimes appeared to be madder than hell, but it was just an act. I could motivate some guys that way, but I would never use that kind of psychology with an athlete who was seriously injured."

Pain defines a violent game like football. I once played an entire game after breaking my jaw on the opening kickoff. Ron Jeziorski, a friend and teammate at Notre Dame, has memories of football practice that are much like mine. Ron, a platoon leader in Vietnam, where he was wounded in a mortar attack, says in all seriousness that football practice at Notre Dame was often more physically demanding than the physical training he experienced in Marine Corps boot camp. For one whole season he played with a sprained ankle that never healed. To this day we often marvel at how players would literally sacrifice their bodies for the team. George Goeddeke, our starting center, had an appendectomy and came back to play in two weeks. Mike McGill, a linebacker, dragged himself off the field after a very serious knee injury to avoid wasting a timeout. The list could go on.

Holtz, in my opinion, was not much different from a lot of other football coaches in his use of ridicule to motivate players to ignore minor injuries. James Baugus, one of Holtz's players quoted in *Under the Tarnished Dome*, is now in his late thirties. When I asked him about Lou Holtz in a recent interview, he said, "Holtz is a great coach and a great motivator. I think that because of what I learned from him, I am a better person than I would have been."[10] Despite the passing years, Baugus stands firm on what he said to Yaeger and Looney about Holtz's treatment of injured players. "The coaching staff would shun and ignore injured athletes as if they did not exist. It was a motivational technique to make you feel you were not part of the team. The idea was that if you felt left out, you would try to play, even when you were experiencing pain and discomfort."

An obvious question is where does one draw the line between a minor injury and one that could cripple an athlete for life if not adequately treated? Baugus says he made that judgment on his own. Baugus had a serious back injury and pushed himself to play through the pain, often questioning whether he was babying himself or really risking long-term injury. Just before his senior year, he went to Holtz and told him that because of his back he simply could not play anymore. According to

Baugus, Holtz said he understood perfectly and wished him well. Baugus kept his scholarship and graduated in 1989. Baugus says that he regrets not being on the 1988 national championship team but knows he made the right decision. "I ultimately had successful back surgery. I can still roughhouse with my kids, and I have my health."

Another image one would not associate with Notre Dame is football players bulked up on steroids. Yet, according to Yaeger and Looney, the Notre Dame football team became awash with anabolic steroids starting in about 1986, the year that Holtz arrived. Their argument is that Holtz was well aware that athletes he was recruiting were using steroids. He simply ignored it. In addition, by insisting that linemen be strong—which he defined as being able to bench press at least four hundred pounds—he was actually encouraging players to use steroids. Because few players were able to bench press that much naturally, Holtz was sending out an indirect message that if you want to play, you had better "juice up." Yaeger and Looney interviewed enough former players who had played for Holtz at Notre Dame to give some credibility to that claim.

Even many of Holtz's strongest defenders admit that some Notre Dame ballplayers were using steroids in the Holtz era. According to Chris Kvochak, an athlete who played for both Faust and Holtz, "there were steroids going on. But there were steroids going on everywhere. It was a sign of the times. Holtz came to Notre Dame at a time when steroid use was on the rise nationally. Sure, there were guys much bigger and faster than seemed natural. But it wasn't rampant, as Yaeger and Looney argued. It was five or ten guys, and there were about five or ten guys under Faust as well." According to Kvochak, "it was Holtz's knowledge of the game of football, attention to detail, and ability to motivate that turned Notre Dame around, not steroids."[11]

Jim Baugus stated in *Under the Tarnished Dome* that Holtz recruited a different kind of character than Faust did, and that he had never seen a steroid until Holtz's first class came in. When I talked with him, I asked if he would still stand behind that statement. His answer was yes, but he wanted to qualify it. "It wasn't the entire class that was made up of steroid users and discipline problems. It was a few kids that stood out. Some were from Chicago and did not finish Notre Dame. They were the ones that introduced me to steroids." Baugus says that what led him to try steroids was a fear that he would not be able to compete with some of the guys Holtz was bringing in. "I came into Notre Dame as a 215-pound lineman. The biggest I ever got was 260. These guys were coming in as freshmen at 260 and 270, and hard as rocks. I figured that if I didn't do something,

I was going to be left behind. I got caught after a random drug test and was warned that I would be dismissed from the team if it happened again. They sent a letter to my parents. That was the end of it."

According to Baugus, everyone could see that Holtz was going to turn the program around and wanted to be a part of it. This, he says, put pressure on some of the players, especially those who had played for Faust, when there was a more laid-back attitude about strength training, to do whatever was necessary to excel. "It's not like Holtz was telling players to take steroids. It's just that he set the bar so high and put such an emphasis on size, strength, and speed in his players that steroids seemed like the only way for some of the older guys to hang in there." Both Kvochak and Baugus say that although there was some steroid use, the team was not overrun by steroids, as one might conclude from reading *Under the Tarnished Dome*. In fact, only eight of the eighty-four athletes interviewed for the book admitted using or briefly experimenting with steroids. There is no hard evidence in the book that Notre Dame was "awash with anabolic steroids," as the authors claim.

Yaeger and Looney went right for the jugular with their allegation that Notre Dame, a school long viewed as the model to emulate when it came to combining athletic and academic excellence, had seriously compromised its academic standards during the Holtz era. It is undeniable that Lou Holtz recruited some players with very questionable academic credentials. Tony Rice and John Foley, two players who helped turn Notre Dame into a national championship football team in 1988, failed to earn a combined verbal and math score of 700 on their SATs and thus had to sit out their freshman year. Other players recruited by Holtz ended up leaving Notre Dame for academic reasons. Dan Saracino, however, who became Notre Dame's director of admissions after Holtz's departure in 1996, says that although SAT scores for ballplayers were on the average below those of other Notre Dame students in the Holtz years, a similar gap existed during previous coaching regimes.[12]

Mike DeCicco, the director of academic advising at Notre Dame under Holtz and during previous regimes, provided a slightly different perspective on the kinds of athletes Holtz recruited. DeCicco said that Notre Dame has an academic board that would decide whether to take a risk with a student who might not fit the Notre Dame profile. DeCicco said that "Gerry Faust was the best recruiter Notre Dame ever had for bringing in Notre Dame–type people—choir boys." DeCicco cannot remember Faust's having to take an athlete before the admissions board. With Holtz, by contrast, "you had to take a closer look to make sure they [the athletes] belonged here," said DeCicco. "I sensed that there were some rough kids that came in. I found that I had to push kids to get to class a little bit more. Actually more than a little bit."

According to DeCicco, the issue with Holtz was not so much that he was recruiting athletes who did not meet Notre Dame's minimum academic requirements, but that some of his recruits were just not very interested in Notre Dame for what it offered educationally. Roger Valdiserri echoed these sentiments when he told me, "I do not think they were checking the character of players as well as they could have during the Holtz years." Not everyone agrees with this assessment. "I don't think that the Holtz athletes were that different from the Faust group," says Chris Kvochak. "In both groups, there were a certain number of guys who didn't do so well academically, and who had some discipline problems. Tony Rice struggled, but guys that weren't Prop 48 struggled too. These were the exceptions, and you could find them under both Faust and Holtz." Kvochak thinks Yaeger and Looney distorted reality in order to bash Notre Dame.

Some observations by Mike Wadsworth, a former teammate of mine at Notre Dame and Notre Dame's athletic director at the end of Holtz's tenure, support the position taken by DeCicco and Valdiserri. When Wadsworth met with Holtz to talk about his contract in 1996, one of the things they discussed was the low graduation rates. According to Wadsworth, who is quoted in Steve Delsohn's book *Talking Irish,* "Some players, like Jerome Bettis, left because they had an outstanding pro opportunity. But other players left for disciplinary reasons, or academic reasons, or because they transferred. Well, that does become a concern because somewhere along the line in our recruiting, we did not get the proper fit for Notre Dame."[13] This bad fit may have had more to do with lack of motivation than with lack of minimal academic ability to get by. As one former athlete, referring to academic support services, put it, "You almost have to want to flunk out; they make sure you pass."[14]

A close look at NCAA graduation rates for Notre Dame in the Faust and Holtz years suggests that Wadsworth's concerns about "fit" were justified.[15] The graduation rate for freshman football players recruited by Faust between 1983 and 1985 was 86 percent, giving Notre Dame the highest graduation rate of any Division IA football program in the country. Classes recruited by Faust never ranked lower than third in the country on graduation rates, with only Boston College and Duke ranking higher. By contrast, the first Notre Dame classes recruited entirely by Holtz— 1986 through 1989—had a 76 percent graduation rate. Over the next ten years, the rates fluctuated a bit before hitting a low point of about 74 percent for players recruited by Holtz between 1992 and 1996. These figures, plus my interviews with DeCicco and Valdiserri, lead me to conclude that Notre Dame did compromise its admissions policies during the Holtz years, allowing some tarnish to accumulate on the Golden Dome.

Can Notre Dame Have It Both Ways?

Even if one accepts the argument that Yaeger and Looney were out to get Holtz and therefore distorted facts and selectively manipulated interviews with players to present the worst possible image of Notre Dame, I find it hard to dismiss their book as pure fiction, as some of the Notre Dame faithful have. Holtz was a gifted coach. He was funny, charismatic, and, like Parseghian, he was a tremendous motivator and football strategist. But I do not think that Holtz was a good match for Notre Dame, and I am not alone in this assessment. Johnny Ray, my former coach, says that "Holtz was a good match when he got there. He brought the alumni back, because they of course love winning." According to Ray, "Holtz had a tendency to wear out his welcome after about four years, wherever he was. He is the kind of guy that would win at all costs."

I asked an athletic administrator who knows both Parseghian and Holtz to comment on how they compared as coaches. One of his insights was that "Holtz started to think he was bigger than Notre Dame; Ara never made that mistake." He also said that "Holtz, unlike Ara, often lives on the edge, if not over the edge. I think that it is a fact that at every place Lou has left there have been NCAA violations, some more serious than others." Not long after leaving Notre Dame, the Irish received their first NCAA probation ever for violations that occurred on his watch. More recently, NCAA violations marred Holtz's tenure as South Carolina's football coach. I cannot imagine Ara leaving a similar trail of devastation in his wake. I also cannot imagine Parseghian literally jumping on a player's back and knocking him to the ground, as Holtz allegedly did to Tony Rice during practice, even if this was merely a motivational technique. Stylistically, Holtz and Parseghian were in different worlds.

Lou Holtz left Notre Dame in 1996—some would argue he was given a push—after compiling a remarkable record of one hundred wins, thirty losses, and two ties, leaving him only five games shy of Knute Rockne's record in total wins. Over the next five years, with Bob Davie at the helm, the Irish went 35–25, a mediocre record almost identical to that of Gerry Faust's. When Tyrone Willingham replaced Davie in 2002, it looked like Notre Dame was about to turn things around. After beginning his Notre Dame career winning eight games in a row, however, Willingham's teams went 13–15 over the next couple of years, leaving him with an overall record of 21–15 that included some of the most lopsided losses in Notre Dame history. Fearing that Notre Dame was losing its relevance as a major football power, alumni and fans demanded that Willingham be replaced, although he had completed only three years of his five-year contract. Notre Dame hired the blunt and hard-nosed Charlie Weis, former offensive coordinator for the New England Patriots, as their next coach.

Throughout the Bob Davie and Tyrone Willingham years, there was unending debate in the Notre Dame community and the media over whether the Irish could compete for national championships without significantly lowering academic standards for their football players. Paul Hornung, a 1956 Heisman Trophy winner at Notre Dame and a star for the Green Bay Packers, shocked many Americans when he said in a radio interview that "we can't stay as strict as we are as far as the academic structure is concerned, because we've got to get the black athlete, and we must get the black athlete if we are going to compete."[16] Hornung later recanted, saying that Notre Dame had to ease up for all players, not just blacks. Bob Davie has chosen his words more carefully, but he too has complained that Notre Dame's admissions office has made it difficult to find enough talented recruits who qualify academically.[17]

Davie's position is consistent with the argument that Holtz's success at Notre Dame was in part a result of looser admissions standards for athletes after the changing of the guard from Hesburgh to Malloy in 1986. According to proponents of this thesis, Notre Dame alumni, smarting from the humiliation of the Faust years, demanded a turnaround. In addition, Notre Dame's exclusive television deal with NBC in 1991 and its privileged position in the bowl coalition—a precursor to the Bowl Championship Series—made winning absolutely imperative. In other words, Notre Dame hired Lou Holtz and charged him with restoring Notre Dame football to its former glory, even if this required some academic compromises. A corollary to this argument is that Notre Dame football's slide into mediocrity under Davie and Willingham resulted from a return to tougher standards toward the end of what Douglas Looney refers to hyperbolically as "Holtz's reign of terror."

Dan Saracino knows that Notre Dame's admission standards pose a challenge for its football coaches. Nonetheless, he insists that the standards are not so high—football players average about 1,048 on the SAT— that Notre Dame cannot continue to be a major player. In response to Bob Davie's complaint that admissions was responsible for the decline in Notre Dame's football fortunes after Holtz stepped down, he says, "There are and were good athletes who are also good students; we just haven't been getting our share." The problem, as he sees it, is coaching and recruiting.

"All coaches at Notre Dame," says Saracino, "are working under the same constraints. Some get the job done better than others." Saracino holds Charlie Weis up as a coach who "gets it." Even before Weis's first season at Notre Dame, Saracino told me that Weis had gotten verbal commitments from ten students whose academic credentials were higher than the profile of any group of players he had seen for years. They were also very good athletes.

That Charlie Weis compiled a 19–6 record during his first two seasons as the Irish coach, including trips to major bowl games, speaks to the importance of coaching. Weis's impressive start reinforces the claim that Notre Dame can be a very good Division IA football team without tarnishing its academic reputation. Of the top twenty schools in the *U.S. News & World Report*'s academic rankings of national universities in 2006 and 2007, only Notre Dame was also ranked in the top twenty of the Bowl Championship Series final standings. Notre Dame football also had the highest graduation rate of any school in the top twenty Bowl Championship Series schools in those years.[18]

Despite the success that Weis has brought to Notre Dame's football program, the jury is still out on whether Notre Dame can win against perennial powers like Ohio State, Michigan, USC, and Florida without easing up on its admissions standards. Notre Dame's crushing loss to LSU in the 2007 Sugar Bowl set an NCAA record for consecutive bowl games lost. Notre Dame's nine-game losing streak in bowls extends back to Lou Holtz's victory in the 1994 Cotton Bowl. In the 2006 season USC, Michigan, and LSU, the only really strong opponents the Irish played, unloaded on Notre Dame unmercifully. Notre Dame's football performance since the departure of Lou Holtz does not inspire confidence that the Irish can regain the stature of the impressive squads of the past. I agree with Joel Maturi, my old roommate and the current athletic director at the University of Minnesota, when he says, "I think they [Notre Dame] can be good, and very good occasionally, but I don't think they can have the glory days of the past consistently."[19]

Notre Dame possesses most of the ingredients necessary to produce national championship contenders on a fairly regular basis. Notre Dame's upgraded athletic facilities, unequaled television exposure, history of football excellence, and ability to attract coaches who can prepare athletes for careers in the pros give the Irish a decided recruiting advantage. The problem, as I see it, is that elite academic institutions such as Notre Dame, Duke, Stanford, and Northwestern are fishing in a smaller pond for marquee players than are many of the schools listed in the top twenty in BCS rankings. To quote Notre Dame admissions director Saracino,

"Notre Dame could not do what Stanford does and field a competitive football team. But at least I review a full application before the football coach can offer a grant in aid. At many top-twenty schools," Saracino says, "if a kid is NCAA eligible, then boom, you do not have to run it by admissions. Are you kidding? It's automatic."

Notre Dame's 77 percent graduation rate for football players—measured by the federal graduation rate in 2005—indicates that the school accepts players likely to graduate from Notre Dame in six years. Graduation rates for some of Notre Dame's major competitors during this same period paint a very different picture. The University of Southern California is a fine university with an acceptance rate of only 27 percent and an overall graduation rate of 83 percent. Yet the Trojans graduated only 58 percent of their football players. Among the three schools that pummeled Notre Dame in football in the 2006 season—Michigan, Southern California, and Louisiana State University—the graduation rate for black players was 47, 52, and 35 percent, respectively, suggesting that many athletes were selected with something other than education in mind. Notre Dame's 76 percent graduation rate for black players jumps out in sharp contrast.

The harsh reality that emerges from these data is that pressure for Notre Dame to make some academic compromises will increase the longer it goes without a national championship or a major bowl victory. The stakes are very high. In 1993, when Notre Dame last seriously contended for a national championship, 6.2 million households watched Notre Dame football games. That number dropped to 2.6 million in 2003.[20] Ratings have undoubtedly improved in the Weis years, but if Notre Dame wants to maintain its market share in the face of threats from new entrants such as Rutgers, Boise State, Louisville, and other schools that could not care less about Notre Dame's storied past, the Irish may have little choice but to put education on the back burner for a while and go after some athletes whose major goal is to "play football on Sundays."

Notre Dame in the 1980s and 1990s played a central role in transforming the landscape of college sports. A major player in the College Football Association, Notre Dame led the charge against the NCAA's monopoly control of college football television broadcasts. The Irish took the laissez-faire model of college sports to another level in 1990 by breaking with the CFA, its former ally, to negotiate its own television deal with NBC, thus solidifying Notre Dame's privileged status at the pinnacle of big-time college football. NBC continues to pay millions of dollars to nationally televise all of Notre Dame's home games. The road games are shown by ABC, CBS, and ESPN. Notre Dame remains a major independent and has spurned overtures to join major BCS conferences because it prefers not having to share its television revenue. Notre Dame remains in a league of its own.

Ironically, the same free-market philosophy that turned Notre Dame into a money-making machine is threatening its football program's competitive advantage. Now that networks televise hundreds of games, Notre Dame's competitors have been able to extend their reach beyond their states and regions to build their brands at the national level. Not only does this allow schools like Nebraska, Southern California, and Tennessee to recruit more effectively at the national level, but teams like Boise State, Rutgers, and Louisville—teams not even on the major college football radar screen a decade ago—now dip into the blue-chip recruiting pool. Because many of these schools have few qualms about admitting great athletes with limited academic promise, Notre Dame is slowly being squeezed out of the national spotlight.

Notre Dame football is at a crossroads. Even though the football team's average SAT score of about 1,048 falls well below that of the rest of the student body, and the demands of football make it difficult for players to receive the same quality of education available to other students, Notre Dame delivers on its promise of an opportunity to earn a college degree. High graduation rates, a refusal to accept junior college transfers, a stadium that contains no skyboxes, no luxury seating, and no corporate signage—these are just a few of the outward symbols that Notre Dame's business model retains a focus on education. Whether the Irish can retain their educational focus and still compete in college football's upper echelon remains an open question, and one that is relevant for all universities engaged in corporate college sports.

9

Inside the Billion-Dollar Beast

Fighting Against the Odds

Over the past three decades I have focused primarily on athletes' rights when thinking about reform issues in college sports. My tenure as director of the Center for Athletes' Rights and Education in the 1980s provided a unique opportunity to build an activist organization based on that model. After the demise of CARE, I continued my involvement with athletes' rights issues through writing, speaking engagements, and appearances in the media. In 1996 I began writing a book that gave considerable attention to legal issues in college sports, including workers' compensation law as it applies to scholarship athletes. In the course of doing research for that book, I discovered the case of Kent Waldrep, a former college athlete who was seriously injured playing college football many years ago. The Waldrep case, which went to court in the 1990s, highlights why I cannot make peace with big-time college sports and its fraudulent amateur myth.

In the fall of 1974 I attended graduation ceremonies at Penn State and received my doctoral degree. Several weeks before I donned my cap and gown and walked across the stage to accept my diploma, Waldrep, who was then a twenty-year-old running back from Texas Christian University, began a very different rite of passage, one that was devoid of handshakes and pomp and circumstance. As I celebrated the start of my career as a college professor, Waldrep lay near death at the University of Alabama Medical Center, steel rods embedded in his skull to support the broken neck he had sustained several weeks earlier in a game against Alabama. Waldrep, who was paralyzed from the shoulders down, drifted in and out of consciousness. As he struggled to breathe, the thought kept running through his mind that this couldn't possibly be happening to him.

Being knocked out for a few seconds in a violent game like football occurs so often that players refer to it euphemistically as "having your bell rung." When Waldrep crashed headfirst into the artificial turf at Alabama's Legion Field, his instincts told him that the dizziness would soon pass and he would be able to return to action. He quickly realized, however, that the crushing blow to the top of his helmet was not the typical bell ringer. As he returned to consciousness, excruciating pain ripped through his shoulders and neck and exploded into his head. He then panicked for several moments, thinking he would not be able to breathe. He was taken from the field on a stretcher and transported immediately to the Alabama Medical Center. After several weeks, during which it was not clear that he would survive, his condition stabilized. Doctors regretfully informed him that his paralysis was permanent, but he never accepted the common belief that spinal injuries are incurable.

At age twenty-five Waldrep founded the National Paralysis Foundation and raised millions of dollars for spinal cord research. Ronald Reagan appointed him to the National Council on Disability. As vice chair, he helped to draft the Americans with Disabilities Act. He later married and had two children through artificial insemination. He regained the use of his arms and recovered feeling in his toes through physical therapy. He defied the medical community early in his career as an advocate for spinal research by traveling to the Soviet Union, where intensive research was already starting.[1] Waldrep has spent his life fighting for a cure for spinal injuries against overwhelming odds, and defending the rights of persons with disabilities. It comes as no surprise that he also challenged the overwhelming power of the college sports establishment by filing a claim with the Texas Workers' Compensation Commission in 1991, arguing that he was an employee of TCU when he was rendered a quadriplegic.

Kent Waldrep and I met for the first time in 1997, brought together by a shared passionate belief that college athletes are employees and deserve the same benefits as other workers, including coverage by workers' compensation laws. In March 1993 the Texas Workers' Compensation Commission found that Waldrep was an employee when playing for TCU and awarded him $70 a week for life plus medical expenses dating to the accident. TCU's insurance carrier—Texas Employers Insurance Association—appealed the decision, and after an agonizing delay, a trial date was set for fall of 1997. Early in 1997 I invited Waldrep to San Antonio to present his views on workers' compensation in a forum I was co-chairing on sports, ethics, and the law. We met at that conference. I have been in touch with him on and off ever since. In 1998 he wrote the foreword to the book I wrote with Ellen Staurowsky entitled *College Athletes for Hire.*

The Kent Waldrep case represented the greatest challenge to the NCAA's amateur myth since the case of Fred Rensing in the early 1980s. The Indiana Supreme Court ruling against Rensing in 1983 had been a defining moment in my thirty-year personal struggle against NCAA hypocrisy. Like Waldrep, Rensing had been rendered a quadriplegic while playing football for a major university. After a favorable lower court ruling that upheld his right to workers' compensation benefits, the Indiana Supreme Court stripped him of those rights in part because it accepted uncritically the NCAA's claim that college athletes are amateurs whose scholarships are educational gifts rather than payment for athletic services rendered. The court simply ignored the reality of what Rensing was contractually required to do to retain his scholarship and used the NCAA's "friend of the court" brief as a template for writing its decision.

I was aware that Waldrep's case had implications that went well beyond his personal struggle with disability and beyond the limited area of workers' compensation law. The myth that scholarship athletes are amateurs engaging in sports as a healthy diversion from their schoolwork is the lynchpin of corporate college sports. Without it, billions of dollars generated by athletic labor would be vulnerable to what the Internal Revenue Service calls unrelated business income taxes. A court ruling recognizing scholarship athletes as employees would not only raise a red flag with the IRS but could also give players the right to demand a larger share of the revenue, to form players' associations, and to bargain collectively for other employee benefits. From the perspective of the movers and shakers of big-time college sports, a favorable ruling for Waldrep could expose college sports to added costs that would threaten the industry's very survival. A decision in Waldrep's favor could force schools to abandon the sports business for bona fide amateurism.

Realizing how high the stakes were, I followed the progress of the Waldrep case very closely. I talked with Waldrep fairly often in the months leading up to his trial, and I sent him articles I had written on workers' compensation, as well as information I had retrieved from the NCAA archives while doing research for my book. Some of this research focused on strategies the NCAA and its attorneys had developed to protect universities from workers' compensation lawsuits filed by athletes. Waldrep asked if I would be interested in serving as an expert witness. I appreciated the offer but suggested that there was someone else whose testimony would cut right through the NCAA rhetoric that I knew would be the foundation of TCU's case. I recommended that Waldrep hire Walter

Byers, the former executive director of the NCAA, as an expert witness. I had recently interviewed Byers, and I had read his book, *Unsportsmanlike Conduct: Exploiting College Athletes*. "Byers," I told Waldrep, "would rip the defense's arguments to shreds."

Byers, who served as the executive director of the NCAA from 1951 to 1988, shepherded the growth of the NCAA from an organization with limited resources and little enforcement power into a massive college sports cartel. Not only did his forty-year tenure inside the NCAA make him uniquely qualified to discuss issues central to the Waldrep case, but his book—written after he stepped down as executive director—is also the most devastating critique of NCAA hypocrisy ever written. Six years after he retired, Byers used his book to release frustrations that had apparently been building within him for some time. He argues in the book that athletic scholarships are contracts for hire and that they constitute pay for services rendered. Amateurism, he argues, "is not a moral issue; it is economic camouflage for monopoly practice." The people most exploited by this system, according to Byers, are the athletes.[2]

Waldrep and his attorney, John Collins, immediately grasped the significance for their case of what Byers had written. They flew to Mission, Kansas, for a videotaped deposition with Byers, who said he had no informed opinion regarding the incident involving Waldrep but was pleased to answer any questions related to his book. Byers testified that scholarship athletes are under contract on a pay scheme that is set in place by the NCAA. He also testified that the term "student-athlete" was invented by the NCAA to counter the perception that scholarships had transformed athletes into professional entertainers, and to avoid workers' compensation lawsuits such as those that rocked the college sports establishment in the 1960s. Instead of supporting athletes' rights to workers' compensation for catastrophic injuries, the NCAA launched a public relations campaign to convince the public and the courts that the new scholarship system, which had all of the earmarks of pay for play, was no different from the amateurism supported by the NCAA's founding fathers.

When the trial finally began in Austin, Texas, the attorneys for TCU's insurance carrier pursued a strategy that came right out of the NCAA playbook. The defense's major argument was that "NCAA rules made the principle of amateurism foremost, and that these rules prohibited student-athletes from taking pay for participation in sports."[3] According to this argument, the NCAA is the final arbiter of what constitutes pay, and the courts should blindly accept its definition. An obvious counterargument is that the courts should not blindly accept the NCAA's definition because the NCAA represents the interests of schools like TCU, one of the contesting parties. Waldrep and his attorney had sought out and deposed Walter Byers precisely because they intended him to use his extensive knowledge of NCAA rules to debunk the amateur mythology upon which the defense's argument was premised.

Unfortunately for Waldrep, the district court excluded the deposition of Walter Byers on the grounds that his "rhetoric" and "apparent knowledge" would somehow result in unfair prejudice. The court had no problem with the testimony of Steve Morgan, an employee of the NCAA, who stayed close to the party line, spinning facts and revising history to fit the NCAA's amateur mythology. To this day, Waldrep is outraged that the court allowed TCU and the NCAA to advise the jury on what amateurism is and is not, while the testimony of his star witness, Walter Byers, was barred from the proceedings altogether. Byers had blown the whistle on the NCAA. Doing so made him an outcast among NCAA loyalists and apologists for corporate college sports. Barring his testimony protected those interests but denied Waldrep an opportunity to have a fair hearing based on all of the facts.

The jury of eight women and four men deliberated seventy-two minutes before returning a 10–2 verdict against Kent Waldrep. Waldrep believes that the outcome would have been quite different had a person of Byers's stature and knowledge of NCAA policy been allowed to present an alternate point of view. I agree that the exclusion of Byers was significant, but I also think that the fact that Waldrep was injured before the introduction of one-year renewable scholarships worked against him. As Steve Morgan, the NCAA's expert witness, emphasized at the trial, Waldrep's scholarship, which was awarded in 1972, was guaranteed for four years and could not be removed during that period because of injury or poor athletic performance. TCU could have removed his scholarship if he had voluntarily withdrawn from sports or openly defied the directions of athletic staff. But this latter point does not appear to have been pursued aggressively by Waldrep's attorney.

Waldrep appealed the decision to the Texas Court of Appeals, where his petition for review was denied in 2000. Although the panel of judges denied Waldrep's petition, they concluded their opinion by noting that college athletics has changed dramatically over the years since Waldrep's injury, and that their opinion in the Waldrep case was based on facts and circumstances that existed twenty-six years earlier.[4] They added that they could not say what their ruling would be if an analogous case were to arise today. Thus they cautioned that their opinion should not be read too broadly. Although the judges did not come right out and say it, it does appear that their concluding remarks were meant to be a warning that runaway commercialism and the change in scholarship rules over the years could lead to a court decision in support of a player seeking workers' compensation.

I recently asked Waldrep if he thinks anything positive came out of his protracted battle with the college sports establishment. "Yes," he said. "We opened the eyes of the educated observer to the hypocrisy of big-time college sports, and I think that if an athlete took a case like mine to court today, he or she would win. The commercialism, the outrageous salaries paid to college coaches, the control that comes with a one-year renewable scholarship—the ingredients are all there today for anybody who wants to take it to court." He also thinks the lessons learned from his case will inform the strategies of attorneys representing clients like him in the future. Finding a cure for spinal injuries will take time. Fixing college sports is also unlikely to happen overnight.

Taking Back Our Classrooms

The Kent Waldrep case highlighted once again the David and Goliath relationship that exists between the NCAA and those who challenge it, and that unlike David, who used a slingshot, reformers have yet to find a weapon to bring the monster to its knees. In the aftermath of the Waldrep court case, I began to doubt whether I had the stamina to continue throwing myself under the big-college sports juggernaut. The odds against making a difference seemed overwhelming. Just when I began to think that my days as a sports activist were over, however, I received a call from Jon Ericson, a former provost and professor of rhetoric and communication studies at Drake University, inviting me to participate in a conference on corruption in college sports. Out of this conference, held in Des Moines, Iowa, in 1999, there emerged a reform-minded organization called the Drake Group.

When Ericson sent out his meeting announcement, his intention was not to create another NCAA, replete with bylaws, executive boards, and a ponderous bureaucracy. His idea was much simpler, yet far more ambitious. His plan was to assemble a distinguished group of scholars, authors, and activists who had been outspoken critics of big-time college sports, and to have them engage in an intensive twenty-four-hour think tank on how to end athletic corruption once and for all. Ericson, a passionate believer that big-time college sports is seriously undermining academic integrity, assumed that the problems are so obvious that those attending would have little problem reaching consensus on what had to be done. The goal was to produce a ringing manifesto for change and to send it out to every faculty senate in the country for action. With this accomplished, the Drake conference would have fulfilled its charge.

The group that descended on Drake University for what many hoped would be a history-making conference included an impressive array of college professors, representatives of faculty senates, journalists, athletic directors, and members of organizations such as the NCAA and the Knight Foundation. Although most of those present—about forty in number—shared a passionate commitment to change, I could see from the outset that the group was deeply divided over what was wrong with college sports and how to fix it. There was no shared vision of what college sports should be at its very best. Because the conference organizers decided to launch into a discussion of specific proposals for change without first building consensus on the nature of the problem, a barroom brawl was virtually guaranteed. With each new proposal, and the seemingly endless debate that followed, I could see that any hope of creating a unified action plan was slipping away.

Over the past couple of years I have given a great deal of thought to the factional strife that turned the Drake University conference into a modern-day Tower of Babel. At the core of the breakdown, in my opinion, were three very different mindsets, or models, that people use to organize their thinking about college sports reform. The names I have attached to these models are intellectual elitist, athletes' rights, and academic capitalist. I realize that these are crude caricatures rather than rigorous academic models. Nonetheless, they have helped me to make sense of the debates that continue to rage over sports in higher education. Some of the issues on which supporters of these models are likely to slug it out are the relationship of commercialism to academic values, the educational impact and legal status of athletic scholarships, and the mission of higher education.

William Dowling, a professor of English at Rutgers University, took an intellectual elitist stand at the Drake conference. From his perspective, commercialized athletics undermines American higher education. When universities sell their athletic programs to television networks or corporate sponsors, he argued, they are prostituting academic values. To win games and keep the revenue flowing, universities recruit athletes with embarrassingly low academic credentials and keep them eligible by turning a blind eye to cheating or by steering them into courses with little academic substance. Intellectual elitists often ask, with a note of derision in their voices, "What is the magic that allows athletes with SAT scores 300 points below the schoolwide average to maintain athletic eligibility, especially when coaches demand that they give most of their waking hours to sports?" Intellectual elitists suspect that the answer lies in widespread academic corruption.

At the time of the Drake Group meeting, Dowling was organizing a student-alumni-faculty group called Rutgers 1000 to withdraw Rutgers from the Big East and enter a Division IAA nonathletic scholarship conference. Dowling argued that athletic scholarships attract athletes who have little respect for traditional academic values. In a moment of exasperation at my unrelenting defense of athletes' rights, he said to me quite candidly, "Screw the [big-time] college athletes. What I care about are the thousands of regular students whose educations are degraded by the presence of athletes on campus who are merely masquerading as students." The mission of higher education, as intellectual elitists see it, is to encourage intellectual and personal growth, and this entails much more then being dragged to class half-asleep by an army of academic counselors, or putting in time in a mandatory study hall.

I spent a great deal of time talking to Dowling and others like him at the Drake conference, and I shared their concern that commercialism undermines academic integrity. Dowling, however, had little sympathy for my view—grounded in the athletes' rights model—that because athletic scholarships are contracts for hire, college athletes deserve the rights and protections that other employees take for granted, such as workers' compensation insurance and a fair share of the revenue they generate. In an article written not long after the Drake University conference, Dowling argued that my support for open professionalism in college sports was comparable to support for legalized prostitution.[5] I see nothing sordid or debased about athletes playing sports to work their way through college, as long as they are fairly compensated both educationally and financially.

The Drake conference attracted a number of people whose views on college sports reform fit neither the intellectual elitist nor the athletes' rights model. These people, many of whom identify with the NCAA, embrace what I call academic capitalism. Unlike intellectual elitists, academic capitalists view commercialism as a good thing as long as it is consistent with what they perceive to be the core educational mission of the university. In their view, negotiating a billion-dollar contact with CBS for rights to March Madness and building a stadium replete with corporate skyboxes are both perfectly consistent with educational values. While academic capitalists are firm believers in free enterprise for those who control college sports, they insist that paying athletes in excess of what the NCAA allows would violate the amateur spirit they say sets college athletes apart from the pros.

According to the academic capitalist model, athletic scholarships are awards that help college athletes further their education. Far from reducing college athletes to indentured servitude, these scholarships have had a democratizing effect on higher education, adding to campus diversity and increasing opportunities for minorities and women. Although many of the athletes who are recruited to play revenue-producing sports are admitted by lower admissions standards than other students, the provision of academic support services and efforts to recruit athletes who meet minimum academic standards can improve graduation rates. A central focus of the academic capitalist model is public relations and protecting the image of the college sports brand. Most athletic corruption, academic capitalists would argue, is caused by a few "bad apples" and is not endemic to the system.

Given the conflicting models that conference participants used to make sense of college sports, the failure to produce a unified plan of action after countless hours of debate was to be expected. To quote Jay Weiner, who covered the Drake conference for the *Minneapolis Star Tribune*, "the more the critics and faculty debated and sought solutions, the more the details became devilish and their directions became fuzzy."[6] Although the conference had fallen short of the goal set by its organizer, Jon Ericson, I was fairly optimistic. From the confusion and frustration emerged the rough contours of an organization that could help faculty defend their academic turf from inroads being made by athletic commercialism run amok. Agreement on details was elusive, but the anger of many faculty over the corporate takeover of college sports was palpable. Faculty, especially those in the intellectual elitist camp, viewed reform as a battle to take back their classrooms.

I left the Drake conference convinced that although corporate college sports wields awesome power, the industry would come to a grinding halt without the college faculty, who act as a release valve for the academic pressure it invariably creates. Faculty not only stand by quietly as commercialism erodes academic values but they also often aid and abet corruption by tolerating gut courses, inflating grades, and making a wide variety of other academic compromises to keep commercial college sports afloat. Faculty can do little to control the NCAA and its excesses. But they can control what goes on in their classrooms, and by so doing they can have a powerful effect on college sports. Through my discussions with faculty at the Drake conference, especially Ericson, I began to realize that college athletic reform might best be viewed as a "family feud"—an effort to get the faculty's house in order.

When I returned to my room after the first day of meetings, I began thinking seriously about making a proposal the next day to create an organization composed of a national network of faculty and others committed to defending academic integrity in college sports. I knew that if the opportunity to make such a proposal presented itself, I would have to be ready with a name. Before going to bed, I decided on the National Alliance of Faculty for Collegiate Athletic Reform (NAFCAR). The next day, when I made the proposal, Bill Dowling, the intellectual elitist with whom I had sparred throughout the conference, seconded the motion. Although several people expressed displeasure with my acronym NAFCAR because it conjured up images of stock cars and anti-intellectualism, the motion was carried unanimously.

When the conference ended at noon, the ringing manifesto Ericson had hoped to forward to faculty senates of all Division I universities and colleges had not materialized. Instead of a plan for ending the hypocrisy of professional college sports, the group produced a working document containing a wide assortment of proposals that would be a starting point for a future meeting to be held at Drake University in March. At the second meeting, attended by faculty and others with a strong commitment to intellectual values, a more coherent set of proposals began to emerge. The most daunting challenge at this point was to identify proposals most likely to be implemented. At this second meeting, Ericson finally embraced the idea of building a national organization. The name of the organization was changed from NAFCAR to the Drake Group.

Taking to the Streets

The Drake Group became a formal organization in November 2000 in Colorado Springs, where it adopted bylaws and elected officers. Jon Ericson, the man who had spoken out vociferously against the creation of yet another reform organization, became the Drake Group's first director. I was among the founding members. Throwing in my lot with the Drake Group required that I tone down some of my athletes' rights rhetoric. I continued to hammer away at how athletic scholarships have made athletes contractually obligated to give sports top priority, but I conceded that other compensation issues, such as medical benefits, monetary stipends, and workers' compensation, fell outside the Drake Group's mission. The Drake Group was the only organization in the country looking at sports from a faculty perspective rather than from the perspective of the NCAA. I was proud to be in on the ground floor of this unique experiment.

From its inception, the Drake Group has been strongly influenced by intellectual elitism—supporting proposals such as freshman ineligibility, making scholarship renewal dependent on academic rather than athletic performance, and insisting on measurable outcome assessments (disclosure) of athletes' performance in the classroom. Although proposals such as these represent educational best practices, they have been viewed as radical by those who view the NCAA as the final arbiter of educational policy in the realm of college sports. In reality, Drake Group proposals are extremely conservative; several of them are modeled on practices that worked well before the frenzy for television money and exposure in the 1970s led the NCAA to abandon them. Not only has the Drake Group supported educational best practices for athletes, it has been an advocate for faculty who have been attacked and vilified for merely doing their jobs.

For instance, one of the Drake Group's first activist interventions was undertaken on behalf of Linda Bensel-Meyers, a rhetoric professor at the University of Tennessee who blew the whistle on academic fraud in the Volunteers' football program. When she reported plagiarism and altered grades for players to the administration, she was told to let the matter drop. She refused. When ESPN did an investigative report on the episode, Bensel-Meyers became a pariah on campus, even among faculty, whom one would have expected to come to her defense. To support Bensel-Meyers, members of the Drake Group—labeled by *New York Times* columnist Robert Lipsyte "academic integrity's SWAT team"—spent several days in Knoxville, meeting with faculty and attending a faculty senate meeting at which Bensel-Meyers turned to her colleagues for support.[7]

The tepid response from the Tennessee faculty to the issues raised by Bensel-Meyers, one of their tenured colleagues, was an embarrassment to the teaching profession. But, in my view, the deafening silence was as much a matter of fear as of indifference. Towering in the midst of the University of Tennessee campus is a massive football stadium that literally casts a shadow on nearby classrooms. Faculty who spend their daily lives in that shadow tend to lose their voices when confronted by the awesome power of the college sports juggernaut. The Drake Group did the right thing by coming to Bensel-Meyers's defense, but we could not stop the harassment that ultimately led her to leave Tennessee for a campus where faculty view their charge as defending academic integrity, not the business of college sports.

Over the next couple of years I became increasingly involved in the Drake Group, serving on its executive board and sharing in the excitement of creating an organization from scratch. At the annual Drake

Group meeting held in Chicago in 2003, a statement of the group's mission and objectives I had written was formally adopted. The mission that grew out of what the Drake Group was already doing was "to help faculty and staff defend academic integrity in the face of the burgeoning college sport industry." The goals were to lobby for proposals that ensure quality education for college athletes, support faculty whose job security is threatened when they defend academic standards, and disseminate information on current issues and controversies in sports and higher education. We would also seek to form coalitions with other groups that shared our mission and goals.

The year of the Drake Group's Chicago meeting, 2003, was a tempestuous one for college sports. At California State University at Fresno a team statistician admitted that he was paid to write papers for members of the men's basketball team. The chairman of St. Bonaventure's board of trustees committed suicide, leaving a note explaining that he was despondent over an academic scandal in the school's basketball program. The University of Georgia fired an assistant basketball coach, Jim Harrick Jr., for giving players As in a bogus course called "Principles of Basketball Coaching." A Baylor basketball player was arrested for murdering Patrick Dennehy, whose decapitated body was found in a field near Baylor. While these and scores of other collegiate sports scandals rocked the nation, major athletic conferences such as the Atlantic Coast Conference were realigning to get a bigger slice of college football's "pot of gold."

At the Chicago conference, Linda Bensel-Meyers agreed to serve as director of the Drake Group when Ericson stepped aside to devote his energy full time to the disclosure issue. Under new leadership, and with the addition of some younger members, the Drake Group was prepared to take bold measures to get its message out. Bensel-Meyers suggested that we hold a protest demonstration in San Antonio, the site of the NCAA's 2004 Final Four. At first I thought the idea was crazy. But I agreed that we needed to do something edgy to get people to at least look at our proposals. Organizations such as the NCAA spent millions to pound their message into the public consciousness. Our fledging organization had no paid staff and a budget of about $2,000 derived from our $10 annual membership fee. Taking to the streets seemed like our only option.

March Madness, fueled by a $6 billion deal with CBS, is academic capitalism on growth hormones. When the Drake Group rolled into San Antonio, the streets around the Alamo Dome were full of scalpers hawking $800 tickets and merchants selling every kind of licensed product imaginable. The logos of big-spending corporate sponsors like Coca-Cola, General Motors, and Cingular were prominently displayed. The Drake Group figured that if the corporations could use the NCAA's Final Four to hawk everything from Buffalo wings to cell phones, we could exploit the tournament to sell education. Even if we had chained ourselves to the Alamo Dome, it is unlikely that anyone would have noticed, given the clutter of advertising that defines this event. But we were not deterred. We had no intention of engaging in civil disobedience or alienating the fans, but we believed that an informational protest at a strategic location near the Alamo Dome could be effective.

The Drakes used their three days in San Antonio to maximum advantage. On Friday night we awarded the first Robert Maynard Hutchins award, named after the former University of Chicago president who had not only fought for academic integrity in college sports but also had vigorously defended academic freedom. Jan Kemp, a whistleblower on academic corruption in the 1980s, was the recipient. Kemp, who was fired and suffered sexual harassment, eventually won reinstatement and a $1.1 million settlement in court. Not only had Kemp been vindicated, but her suit also detailed Georgia's practices of enrolling, and keeping eligible, athletes who could barely read and write. Kemp lamented in her acceptance speech that there was no organization like the Drake Group around when she went through her dark days in 1986.

The next day we held a press conference in a hotel not far from the Alamo Dome to announce four major proposals the Drake Group was trying to implement. Although the press conference was sparsely attended, we managed to attract the *Washington Post*, the *Chronicle of Higher Education*, and the *Indianapolis Star*—papers that served the nation's capital and the NCAA's hometown. We proposed (1) to require that students have a cumulative C average (2.0 GPA) to play college sports, (2) to make freshmen ineligible for varsity teams, (3) to replace one-year athletic scholarships with five-year scholarships that can't be revoked because of injury or athletic performance, and (4) to publicize information about the academic courses athletes take, as well as their choice of professors, academic majors, and aggregate grade point averages, to ensure that they are getting a legitimate education. These proposals, we argued, would be a big step in the right direction.

Later in the afternoon we took our message right into the belly of the beast, carrying signs listing each of our proposals as we walked back and forth in front of the Hyatt, the hotel where the Division I basketball coaches were staying. Our informational protest was simultaneously humorous, pathetic, and inspiring. Drake member David Ridpath was not far wrong when he predicted that we would be received like animal rights activists at a circus. *Washington Post* writer Liz Clarke described us as "graying university professors trying to sell something radical amid the basketball crazed marketplace that has sprouted up around the NCAA Final Four. The product they're pushing? Education."[8] To add a bit of humor, I asked a young police officer nearby if he would attack me with his nightstick while a *Washington Post* photographer snapped pictures. He laughed.

Drake Group member Bruce Svare likened our protest demonstration to a scene from a Michael Moore documentary. At one point I saw him, picket sign in hand, chasing University of Syracuse coach Jim Boeheim to get his views on five-year no-cut scholarships. Some of the coaches—such as Jerry Tarkanian, whom I asked about freshman ineligibility—responded like deer stunned by a car's headlights. Others were incredibly candid. Among the coaches' responses that Svare jotted down at the time were:

- "We need to win. I need to put food on the table. This [these proposals] won't allow me to do it."
- "If it's a five-year guarantee, how will I get them to perform? You're taking away my hammer."
- "Make freshmen ineligible and they won't come to school at all. They want to play right away. The better ones will go to Europe."
- "The kids want to play the game. There is only so much I can do to get them to perform in the classroom; they want to play in the NBA."
- "Freshmen ineligibility is great in theory, but sometimes I need a kid to play right out of high school if I am going to win, and winning is how I keep my job."

After our exposure to the commercialism of March Madness and interviews with the coaches, both Svare and I were in culture shock, like anthropologists who had just spent time in another civilization.

While the Drake Group's activities went virtually unnoticed by most people in San Antonio, the NCAA's overreaction to our activism attracted more attention to our proposals than we would ever have gotten had they merely ignored us. A few weeks after the tournament, Myles Brand, the new NCAA president, attacked the Drake Group in a column he wrote for the *New York Times,* labeling us "self-anointed radical reformers and incorrigible cynics" for criticizing the NCAA's reform efforts. "The Drake Group," he said, "wants to end university support of intercollegiate athletics. They want to turn college sports into professional teams."[9] The only thing that I can imagine would have provoked such a libelous attack is that the Drake Group had had the audacity and courage to bring its educational message to the doorstep of the NCAA's premiere sporting event, the Final Four.

Young Drake Group members refer to those of us who carried picket signs at the Final Four as the "San Antonio Seven" because there were only seven of us and we looked like remnants of the sixties generation. Although I can appreciate the humor in what we did, I often reflect on the kind of reaction we would have gotten had there been five hundred of us marching that day. We managed to intimidate the NCAA with a team of seven mostly graying college professors. If five hundred or a thousand faculty members and others began to show up in front of the coaches' hotel during the Final Four every year, the NCAA would have no choice but to give our proposals, all of which are consistent with educational best practices, serious consideration.

Several weeks after Brand's attack on the Drake Group, I wrote a guest editorial for the *NCAA News* in which I commended Myles Brand and the NCAA for passing legislation that would punish colleges and universities that fail to meet minimum graduation requirements by using disincentives such as barring them from postseason tournaments. I then pointed out that one of the most provocative features of this legislation was that it leaves it up to universities to decide how they will meet these requirements, thus issuing a "clarion call to faculty to step up with concrete proposals not only for increasing graduation rates but also for ensuring that athletes leave college as educated citizens." I then laid out the proposals that the Drake Group had presented in San Antonio as clearly and reasonably as I could.

Not long afterward, Brand dropped me a note telling me he had enjoyed my article and appreciated my positive comments about the NCAA's new legislation. Even though the specific proposals advanced by the Drake Group were unlikely to be supported by the NCAA, said Brand, the NCAA encourages cooperative relationships with faculty organizations. I appreciated Brand's letter, and I think it is possible that his misrepresentation of the Drakes' mission and reform agenda in the *New York Times* was in part a consequence of his not knowing enough about our organization's stated mission. He may also have viewed our strategy of working outside the NCAA framework as a threat. And I must admit to having a history of going for the NCAA's jugular vein.

Terry Holland, athletic director at East Carolina State University, Drake Group member, and the winningest basketball coach in University of Virginia history, suggested to fellow Drakes recently that "what we must acknowledge is that these people [the NCAA] are well intentioned and are actually honorable, intelligent human beings simply doing their jobs to the best of their abilities. When we attack the job they are doing, they simply become defensive. As we yell louder, they stop listening all together."[10] Over the past couple of years, NCAA representatives have accepted invitations to Drake Group conferences and members of the two groups have engaged in constructive dialogue, while agreeing to disagree on a number of major issues. The gulf between Brand's academic capitalism and my combination of intellectual elitism and athletes' rights advocacy is very probably unbridgeable.

Several years have now passed since the Texas Supreme Court refused to review Kent Waldrep's workers' compensation case. Since then, my involvement in the Drake Group has forced me to back off a bit from athletes' rights issues such as Kent's. Nonetheless, I have followed closely and supported in any way I can the efforts by young college athletes to challenge the NCAA and its absurd claim that big-time college athletes are amateurs. If the court cases emerging in the first decade of the twenty-first century are any indication of what is going on in the minds of college athletes, the NCAA has far more to fear from the younger generation than from the intellectual types that make up the Drake Group. In this new age of "academic capitalism," athletes are more likely than ever to demand that their schools "show them the money."

College Sports in the Age of Academic Capitalism

Brand Management

Over the past forty years, college sports has become increasingly commercialized, but so has higher education in general. When I began teaching in the 1970s, most faculty would have been appalled by the use of the term "customer" when referring to students. I saw my role as shaping minds and encouraging critical discourse, not as selling a product to consumers who, in the business model, "are always right." Today the language of business pervades the academy. I often sit in faculty meetings where the discussion focuses on niche marketing, building the university's brand, and developing business strategies for differentiating our "educational products" from those of our competitors. The wide use of business vocabulary indicates that universities have embraced a way of thinking that is a marked departure from the past. Scholars have referred to this business way of thinking as "academic capitalism."[1]

The emergence of the entrepreneurial university may help to explain the apparent lack of concern among most faculty and college administrators that college sports has taken on the look and feel of professional sports. In an era when academic departments are viewed as revenue centers and students as customers, and when the priorities of higher education are determined less by the institution and its faculty than by donors, corporations, and politicians, the NCAA's emphasis on marketing college sports and aggressively pursuing new revenue streams seems perfectly normal. Over the past couple of years, Myles Brand has emerged as an articulate spokesman for the academic capitalist model of college sports, waging a one-man public relations assault on what he calls the cynics and radical reformers who insist that selling college sports to the highest bidder invariably leads to academic compromises and outright corruption.

Brand's views on commercialism in college sports come right out of the academic capitalist's handbook. "When it comes to generating revenue for intercollegiate athletics," he says, "commercialism is not a four-letter word. Quite frankly, the collegiate model depends on commercial activities to succeed, as does higher education itself."[2] Commercialism is a good thing, he told me in a recent interview, "as long as commercial activities are perfectly in tune with the values, mission, and goals of higher education."[3] Among the activities that are presumably "in tune" with the mission of higher education are seven-figure compensation packages for celebrity coaches, the sale of broadcast rights to television networks, sponsorship deals with major corporations, and the construction of state-of-the-art stadiums and arenas that derive revenue from luxury seating, skyboxes, and other sources.

Brand's argument that revenue from high-profile athletic programs often provides young men and women in nonrevenue sports with an opportunity to participate is a valid one. He refuses to acknowledge, however, that athletic programs that produce the lion's share of the revenue are also the ones where commercialism is most likely to exact a heavy educational toll, especially on minorities. For instance, graduation rates were almost always higher for students in the general student populations at the schools attending bowls and the NCAA Basketball Tournament in 2006 than for the players.[4] In some cases the differences were striking. Connecticut, a school that won the NCAA national basketball championship in 2004, graduated 72 percent of its student body in 2006 but only 33 percent of its players. Duke, another basketball powerhouse, had a general student graduation rate of 93 percent. The graduation rate for the men's basketball team was 40 percent. The graduation rate for black basketball players at Duke was 17 percent. Graduation rates for football players at Texas, California, and Michigan were 34 percent, 48 percent, and 57 percent, respectively, about 30 percent below those of regular students at those schools.[5]

Derek Bok, the former president of Harvard University, has written eloquently in his book *Universities in the Marketplace* about the educational compromises that are made when universities put their athletic programs on the market. According to Bok, "the saga of big-time athletics reveals that American universities, despite their lofty ideals, are not above sacrificing academic values—even values as basic as admissions standards and the integrity of their courses—in order to make money."[6] Examples of lowering admissions standards for revenue-producing athletes are not hard to find. According to a survey of admissions data by the *San Diego Union-Tribune,* 70 percent of scholarship athletes at UCLA from 2004 to 2006 were "special admits"—students accepted even though their grades and test scores do not meet regular admission standards. By contrast, the percentage of special admits for the general student body was 3 percent. UCLA's policy on special admits reflects nationwide trends.[7]

University administrators readily admit that academic compromises are made to recruit exceptional athletes. UCLA's assistant chancellor, Tom Lifka, is quoted as saying, "In order to be competitive in Division I-A athletics, you're going to have to have some flexibility. We need those students if we're going to be competitive in certain sports." Dick Bestwick, a retired University of Georgia senior associate athletic director, says, "If you want to win, you're going to have to have some people who are at risk."[8] Dan Saracino, Notre Dame's admissions director, makes no attempt to hide the nearly 300-point SAT gap between football players and regular students. Few people would deny that academic compromises are made. The debate arises over whether the pressures of commercial sports allow players to receive a bona fide education.

Jim Harbaugh, Stanford's football coach, stated in a recent interview in the *San Francisco Examiner* that the University of Michigan, the school where he starred as a quarterback in the 1980s, makes substantial academic compromises when admitting players and assigning them to classes. In a statement unlikely to endear him to his fellow alums, Harbaugh charged that "the athletic department has ways to get borderline guys in and, when they're in, steer them to courses in sports communications."[9] Athletic director Bill Martin denied in an interview with the *Ann Arbor News* that Michigan players are funneled into particular majors. But according to data obtained by that newspaper, 3 percent of all undergraduate degrees conferred between 1 July 2004 and 30 June 2005 were in general studies, while 82 percent of players who declared a major in the 2007 spring football guide were in general studies.[10]

Although Martin denies that players are "steered" into this major by the Athletic Department, the clustering of so many players in one program, when there are more than two hundred from which to choose, raises serious questions about academic integrity. Admissions director Ted Spencer defended the quality of the classes in the general studies program and suggested that their popularity among football players probably stems from the wide range of course choices and the flexibility in scheduling this allows. Spencer also admitted in the *Ann Arbor News* article that "it's much harder to be a business major and go to practice and play 13 or 14 games a year, travel and yet be able to go to calculus and those kinds of classes." The attitude at Michigan and in other big-time college sports programs seems to be that a taste of "education lite" represents a fair return on athletic services rendered, and that athletes should be happy they're getting that much.

The NCAA cannot totally ignore cynics who ask, "How does playing major college football or men's basketball in a highly commercialized, profit-seeking entertainment environment further the educational purpose of its member institutions?" Such questions are especially likely to grab the NCAA's attention when posed by institutions such as the Internal Revenue Service and the courts. In 2006 the U.S. House of Representatives Committee on Ways and Means wrote to the NCAA asking precisely this question. Similarly, athletes and others are beginning to ask in court whether what athletes do on the playing field is education or entertainment provided by underpaid professionals. The NCAA has responded to these threats by intensifying its public relations efforts to brand big-time college sports as an educational activity.

The NCAA excels in brand management. To enhance the educational image of the business of college sports, the NCAA—since its first battle over workers' compensation in the 1960s—requires that the term "student-athlete" be used in all of its publications. Sportswriters now use the term widely, even though the requirement that all college athletes be matriculating students makes the term redundant. The term "student-athlete" creates positive spin by implying that all college athletes are good students. The NCAA also enhances its brand by insisting that big-time college football and basketball fit under the same amateur umbrella as sports in small liberal arts colleges that grant no athletic scholarships. All of these strategies—marketing gurus refer to them as "positioning a product"—are meant to reinforce the impression that a clear line of demarcation separates big-time college athletes from the pros.

Under Myles Brand's leadership, the NCAA claims once again to have imposed "tough new academic standards" on big-time college sports. Proposition 48 has been replaced by the academic progress rate (APR) as the industry's new public relations buzzword. Under this new system, teams must have a graduation rate of about 50 percent and show other signs of academic progress if they want to avoid the loss of scholarships. The APR is a move in the right direction, but it does not reduce the stress placed on coaches and athletes when college sports becomes professional entertainment. Nor does it reduce the number of classes athletes miss because of games, prevent midweek football contests, limit coaches' control over athletes' lives, or make it easier for freshmen to adjust academically. It does not reduce the pressure on athletes to take academic shortcuts. In fact, it increases that pressure. The APR is good brand management. It falls short of meaningful reform.

In another stroke of public relations genius, the NCAA has introduced its own method of calculating graduation rates called the graduation success rate (GSR), which raises graduation rates overnight. Unlike the federal graduation rate (FGR), which measures the percentage of all freshman athletes who actually graduate in a six-year period from their initial college or university, the GSR excludes from its calculation all athletes who leave college in good academic standing and could conceivably graduate elsewhere. Not surprisingly, the NCAA's methodology has boosted graduation rates without athletes having to so much as attend an extra study hall. Boston College's FGR for men's basketball in 2006 was a dismal 31 percent, but excluding players who left in good academic standing yielded a GSR of 60 percent.

The NCAA argues that the GSR is fairer and more accurate because it takes into account the possibility that transfer students may graduate elsewhere. If the NCAA can someday provide information on graduation rates of athletes who leave in good academic standing, the GSR would help to determine how many athletes graduate in spite of having been sidetracked for a while by sports. The strength of the FGR is that it helps admissions directors assess whether they have successfully recruited athletes who fit a school's academic profile. An athlete who jumps from one school to another in search of more playing time is unlikely to become an integral part of a university community and give back to that school after graduation. The FGR has proven its usefulness. The GSR, in its present form, provides little more than window dressing.

Intellectual Elitism, Disclosure, and the IRS

For those who accept what I have labeled the intellectual elitist model of college sports reform, the corporate takeover of college sports represents an assault on academic integrity, academic standards, and student-oriented sports. For some in the intellectual elitist camp, the solution is to kick big-time college sports off campus altogether and let them operate as independent professional sports franchises. Others are willing to acknowledge that commercial college sports has become a permanent fixture on many college campuses. Given this reality, the primary objective of reform, as they see it, should be to defend the academic integrity of college classrooms from intrusions by the burgeoning college sports industry. The Drake Group, founded in 2000, has adopted the latter approach.

The four proposals for change that the Drake Group presented in San Antonio during the 2004 Men's Final Four are remarkable in their simplicity, their potential educational impact, and their grounding in the collective wisdom of faculty, coaches, and educational leaders who have grappled with these problems for decades. I am personally committed to these proposals because they reflect policies that were supported by the NCAA when I played big-time college football in the 1960s. Although the NCAA does not currently support them, these proposals provide concrete strategies universities could use to meet the graduation requirements of the NCAA's APR legislation. Not only would adopting these proposals increase graduation rates, but their adoption would also ensure that athletes leave college as educated citizens.

One Drake Group proposal that could be adopted even without NCAA support would require that athletes have a cumulative grade point average of 2.0 every semester to be eligible for varsity sports. Because a 2.0 grade point average, which translates into a C, is the minimum grade that most colleges and universities require for graduation, requiring athletes who fall below that average to sit out a semester and get back on track seems like a no-brainer for increasing graduation rates. Failure to bring the cumulative GPA up to 2.0 during the semester out of competition would cost the athlete his or her scholarship. When I was being recruited by the University of Pittsburgh in 1963, a 2.0 requirement exactly like this one was included in the scholarship letter I received.

College faculty are well aware of the difficulties freshman athletes, especially those from educationally disadvantaged backgrounds, might have in maintaining a C average while at the same time dealing with the stress of big-time college sports. For this reason the Drake Group's second proposal would require freshmen and transfer students to sit out a year before playing college sports, thus giving them a chance to adjust to college and demonstrate their commitment to being there. As I mentioned at the beginning of this book, freshman ineligibility was a lifesaver for me. Had I not gotten off to such a good start academically at Notre Dame, I am not sure I would have ended up in graduate school. Highly respected former coaches, including Dean Smith, John Wooden, and Terry Holland support this proposal, as do scores of other coaches, college presidents, and faculty members.

The beauty of the freshman ineligibility proposal is that it institutionalizes a practice already quite common, called red shirting. Coaches often hold players out of action for one year and then give them four more years of athletic eligibility. In order to provide a fifth year of financial aid, the Drake Group's third proposal would replace one-year renewable scholarships with five-year grants whose only condition for renewal is maintaining adequate academic progress. This proposal amounts to "going back to the future." When I was at Notre Dame, I had a four-year no-cut scholarship. Our proposal simply adds a fifth year. The Drake Group believes that restoring multiyear grants reaffirms a university's commitment to athletes as students, regardless of how they perform athletically, and puts to rest any claim that athletes are employees under contract.

The Drake Group's first three proposals return college athletes to the academic mainstream while maintaining athletic excellence. Although perfectly crafted to meet academic needs, these proposals raise questions about costs and competitive advantage that would not make them popular with many coaches and athletic administrators. Thus substantial external pressure would have to be brought to bear to force the NCAA to consider, let alone pass, these proposals. The Drake Group's fourth proposal, which is to disclose information on how college athletes are educated, could provide the leverage needed to get the NCAA's attention. Consistent with higher education's current emphasis on outcome assessments, the Drake Group's disclosure proposal supports publicly disclosing such things as whether athletes are more likely than other students to "cluster" around easy majors or to take classes with faculty who ignore academic standards.

According to Jon Ericson, the founder of the Drake Group, information would be gathered only on aggregates of students to protect their rights under the Family Educational Rights and Privacy Act, often referred to as the Buckley Amendment. For example, information about whether athletes are overrepresented in certain academic majors, and on whether students in those majors generally have higher grade point averages than others, can be made public without mention of an individual student. Information on the number of grade changes on athletes' transcripts and the number of incomplete grades given to athletes compared with other students could also be revealed, as could the names of faculty members who engage in these practices. Published accounts of educational improprieties in the media, based on systematic nationwide information, would be explosive.

The *New York Times* reported in 2006 that eighteen Auburn football players had received high grades from a sociology professor who required no classroom attendance and little work. As a result of this fraudulent grade inflation, several Auburn players who were academically at risk were able to compete on a team that went undefeated and finished number two in the nation in 2004. A subsequent internal audit at Auburn revealed that the same professor had made about fifty-five grade changes for students between 2003 and 2006. The average for professors in that department during that period was twenty-two. The professor in question also gave twenty-four incompletes—a grade given to students who fail to complete a course on time but intend to do so later—during that period, 67 percent to athletes.[11] Because of this disclosure, Auburn has been forced to fix the problem.

The impact of disclosure as a catalyst for reform increases substantially if linked to questions regarding the tax-exempt status of big-time college sports. The NCAA's not-for-profit status allows it to avoid federal taxes on the $6 billion it receives from CBS for rights to the men's basketball tournament. Millions more flow into major conferences and universities from football, also tax free. According to the *Indianapolis Star* and reporter Mark Alesia, "tax exempt bonds give schools favorable financing when building stadiums and arenas. Donations for stadiums are 100 percent tax deductible."[12] In 2005 Drake Group member and former faculty fellow at Northwestern University Frank Splitt launched a congressional initiative to make the continuation of the not-for-profit status of the NCAA and its member institutions contingent on the disclosure of data on the academic performance of big-time college athletes.

In October 2006 William Thomas, chair of the House Committee on Ways and Means, responded to some of the Drake Group's concerns by asking Myles Brand to justify the NCAA's and its member institutions' not-for-profit status. According to a *New York Times* editorial, "The House Ways and Means Committee sent shock waves through college sports when it asked the National Collegiate Athletic Association to justify its federal tax exemption by explaining how cash-consuming, win-at-all-cost athletics departments serve educational purposes."[13] If the House Ways and Means Committee concludes that the distinction between big-time college sports and professional entertainment has become blurred, the NCAA would be far more likely to consider reforms not unlike those proposed by the Drake Group.

In January 2007 George Stephanopoulos asked Charles Rangel, the new Democratic chair of the House Ways and Means Committee, if he intended to follow up on the investigation of the NCAA's tax exemption that had begun under Bill Thomas, the previous chair. Rangel, one of the New York congressmen who befriended CARE when it was under attack by the Reagan administration in 1982, replied that he would take a hard look at the issue. The Drake Group's emphasis on the disclosure of academic fraud could lend support to the argument that big-time college sports has drifted significantly from its tax-exempt function. Just as Congress has threatened to revoke Major League Baseball's antitrust exemption to get it to take the players' concerns more seriously, threats to the NCAA's tax-exempt status could provide the leverage needed to implement modest proposals to help educate college athletes.

Many Drake Group initiatives have been embraced by other faculty. For instance, the Coalition on Intercollegiate Athletics (COIA), a faculty senate–based organization, supports the renewal of athletic scholarships on the basis of academic rather than athletic performance, tying athletic eligibility to a minimum grade point average and disclosing academic fraud by faculty and staff. A number of COIA's other proposals could have been taken right off of the Drake Group Web site. Perhaps the major issue separating the Drake Group and COIA concerns tactics. COIA believes the NCAA will embrace its proposals merely because they sound reasonable. Drake Group members believe that serious reform will require substantial outside pressure from the federal government or the courts. Regardless of these differences, faculty groups can work together.

Athletes' Rights in the Twenty-First Century

Academic capitalists focus on branding. Intellectual elitists live and die by traditional academic values. The athletes' rights model of college sports recognizes athletic scholarships as employment contracts. Athletes' rights advocates strive to provide fair compensation for the athletes who labor in the multibillion-dollar college sports industry. Their tactics have included legislative initiatives in state government, organizing college athletes, forming alliances with organized labor, challenging the NCAA on antitrust grounds, and filing lawsuits against the NCAA. Such actions will undoubtedly increase as college sports becomes more unabashedly commercialized in the decades ahead, and as athletes themselves absorb the entrepreneurial spirit that drives academic capitalism.

As mentioned in Chapter 7, Nebraska state senator Ernie Chambers stands out as a pioneer in the area of athletes' rights for college athletes. In 1980, the same year that I became director of the Center for Athletes' Rights and Education, Chambers introduced a bill that would mandate the payment of stipends to college athletes beyond room, board, tuition, and fees. He contacted me back then to congratulate CARE for receiving a federal grant, and we have followed each other's progress ever since. In 2003, after repeated efforts over the course of thirty-three years, Chambers finally succeeded in getting his bill signed into law. The bill in its original form stated that football players at Nebraska "shall be employees of the university who shall be covered by Nebraska Worker's Compensation Act and be paid compensation, the amount of which shall be no less than the federal minimum wage." Although the governor, Mike Johanns, supported the bill in this form, the bill passed by the legislature contained softer language and conditions that had to be met before the bill could become law.[14]

For instance, the final version says that football players at Nebraska "may be granted a stipend, the amount of which shall be determined by the university." In addition, before the bill can go into effect in Nebraska, a similar bill must be passed in four other states that field football programs in the Big Twelve Conference. According to Chambers, "no other states have shown interest as yet."[15] He admits that the final version was a substantial compromise but points to the message Nebraska's governor and legislature have sent to the NCAA. Written into the bill was the statement that "rules of the [NCAA] prohibiting compensation are unduly restrictive and unreasonable, promote unfairness, encourage dishonesty in recruiting and retaining players, and would not be tolerated if applied to all students."

Chambers has demonstrated that state legislatures can grant protections and rights to college athletes even when the NCAA refuses to do so. For instance, he got a bill passed that says that if an athlete is injured, his or her scholarship cannot be taken away, even though NCAA rules allow it. The legislature also approved his bill to require that injured athletes receive assistance equivalent to what they would receive under workers' compensation. "To get the insurance coverage through," says Chambers, "I said that if you are not going to pay them as employees, protect them as students, and that carried the day." Chambers takes pride in his small victories but thinks the hypocrisy will stop only when "these players become savvy enough to get a national network together to boycott some of these big games. But that is a big burden to place on these young men who have nothing to protect them from retaliation."

Although only a handful of graying sports activists from the sixties generation still raise their voices for athletes' rights, the current generation of big-time college athletes, many of them devoted viewers of shows such as ESPN's *Outside the Lines*, are far more sophisticated about these issues than athletes were decades earlier. For several years a quiet effort to organize college athletes to defend their rights has been under way in California. Under the leadership of former UCLA linebacker Ramogi Huma, an organization called the Collegiate Athletes Coalition—the name has since changed to the National College Players Association (NCPA)—has been pursuing goals similar to those proposed by CARE two decades ago. The NCPA wants better medical benefits for athletes, as well as financial compensation to cover the full cost of a college education.

Although more moderate than CARE was, the NCPA's alliance with the United Steelworkers of America, avoidance of fiery rhetoric, and disciplined focus on issues that have a strong appeal to college athletes have made the NCPA a major force that the NCAA cannot easily ignore. Huma says that at one point about a thousand athletes from fifty Division I universities were CAC members.[16] Although that mass support was good at the outset, Huma says that maintaining those numbers has been difficult because many players graduate, and others move on and off campus and change their addresses. Now the goal is to restructure the organization so that each school has an NCPA representative who is involved in strategic planning and stays in touch with team members and the NCPA council.

Huma refuses to get bogged down in a philosophical debate about the meaning of amateurism. "We call it what it is," he told me in response to my question about the NCAA's use of the term. "The players are already paid. They are just not paid a lot. It's like you see in any other job. If you stop going to work, you don't get paid. You can call it amateurism if you want, but it is what it is. Our concern is getting more—getting more health coverage, safety, and making sure the money is enough to get by with basic necessities." Huma is perplexed as to why the NCAA does not provide these things without having to be pressured. "If the NCAA would simply give in on stipends and healthcare," he says, "I do not see a huge need among college athletes to change a whole lot else." The NCAA will not budge on the stipend issue, even though Myles Brand has made supportive statements about raising the cap.

Huma, refusing to wait for the NCAA to make up its mind, has thrown NCPA support behind an antitrust lawsuit filed in Los Angeles in 2006 that seeks to prevent the NCAA from prohibiting its members from offering athletic scholarships up to the full cost of college attendance. Huma, who graduated in 1998, is not a plaintiff, but he helped line up athletes whose names are on the lawsuit. The class action was brought on behalf of current Division I football and major college basketball players, as well as any player in the past four years. The NCAA will pay a heavy price if the court finds that it capped scholarship costs illegally. "The lawsuit," says Tom Farrey of ESPN, "applies to 144 colleges, so 20,000 or so affected athletes would have been shorted a potential $117 million." Because damages are tripled under antitrust law, the penalty could be a staggering $351 million.[17]

In the years I have known him, Huma has insisted that his group is not interested in larger issues such as forming labor unions or free agency for college athletes. "We don't want to raise the floodgates to let in open professionalism," he has said in public. I tend to believe him, although part of me thinks he may be adopting this moderate line because he knows that the more openly radical approach taken by CARE in the 1980s got us little more than a lot of press coverage. "The current system is not fair," he told me, "and athletes should be able to sell their services in a free market, but progress is slow and the NCPA is doing what is possible." He is also very concerned that paying revenue-producing athletes openly might have negative effects on non-revenue-producing athletes.

I share Huma's concern that most colleges and universities, even the football and basketball powerhouses, do not make enough profit to pay players salaries and still support an entire athletic program. But I personally see no reason why scholarship athletes should not be able to engage in other forms of entrepreneurial activity, such as endorsing products, giving speeches for a fee, and sharing part of the revenue when a school uses his or her likeness in advertising. Athletes are currently asked by their schools to sign a waiver allowing their image and name to be used in marketing efforts, as long as the institution controls its use. Players are not allowed to be compensated. Not long ago the University of Memphis organized a merchandise campaign featuring running back DeAngelo Williams. The school sold merchandise with Williams's name, jersey number, and picture.[18] The NCAA insists that it is defending Williams from commercial exploitation by cutting him out of the profits.

Few cases better illustrate the extremes to which the NCAA will go to defend its amateur myth than the case of Jeremy Bloom, an Olympic skier who was declared ineligible to play football for the University of Colorado when he refused to give up the endorsement deals that supported his skiing career. In order to compete at the World Cup and Olympic levels, Bloom depended on corporate endorsements to pay the costs of training, which can run as high as $100,000 a year. Bloom, whose good looks and star power earned him commercial opportunities even before he entered college, had also dreamed of someday playing football for the University of Colorado, a school not far from his hometown of Loveland. He was aggressively recruited by the University of Colorado to play football but deferred his enrollment to pursue his dream of skiing for the U.S. Olympic team.[19]

NCAA rules allow a professional in one sport to play for a college or university in another sport. For instance, teenagers sometimes sign with Major League Baseball teams and come back to college to play in some other sport. The athlete remains an "amateur" in the sport played in college as long as benefits do not exceed the NCAA's salary cap. Following this logic, Jeremy Bloom should have been able to continue as a professional skier and play college football as well. NCAA rules, however, which often defy logic, prohibit athletes from doing commercial endorsements, even if the endorsements are related to the athlete's professional sport. In other words, salaries are fine but endorsements are evil, even though in a sport like skiing, participation is virtually impossible without corporate sponsorships.

In 2002 the University of Colorado, in support of Bloom, asked the NCAA for a waiver of the no-endorsement rule and was turned down. Bloom dropped his endorsements, modeling, and other media activities in order to play football for Colorado. In the off season he resumed his skiing career at his own expense. But he filed a lawsuit against the NCAA after his sophomore season, seeking a preliminary injunction that would allow him to play for the University of Colorado while accepting sponsorship money needed to ski and to begin preparation for the 2006 Winter Olympics in Turin, Italy. Judge Daniel Hale of the Colorado district court in Boulder denied the injunction on the grounds that the NCAA rule supported amateurism. Bloom resumed his endorsement deals, rendering him ineligible to play college football. He left college and set his sights on winning an Olympic medal.

Ramogi Huma and Jeremy Bloom do not fit the mold of bomb-throwing anarchists trying to bring down the NCAA. Bloom's case was so circumscribed that the NCAA could easily have granted him a waiver without compromising its rules. Bloom argued that an athlete in a professional sport whose only compensation comes in the form of prize money or endorsements from that sport should be able to compete in a different sport in college. That the NCAA sent a team of seven attorneys to Boulder to intimidate a judge into ignoring the merits of Bloom's argument suggests that the organization viewed any compromise as the start of a slide down the slippery slope toward open professionalism. The NCAA did not want to encourage college athletes to demand the same rights to cash in on college sports that their celebrity coaches have.

The case of Maurice Clarett, a running back who led Ohio State to a national championship in 2002, also raises serious legal and ethical questions about big-time college sports. Clarett's college football career peaked in January 2003 when he led the Buckeyes to an overtime victory against Miami to give Ohio State its first national title in thirty-four years. Several months later the *New York Times* reported that Clarett and other players had received preferential treatment in the classroom, an allegation consistent with Clarett's own description of his academic life at OSU. Clarett also reported in his interview with ESPN's Tom Friend that boosters regularly funneled money to him and other players under the table and allowed him to borrow automobiles whenever he requested them.[20]

What led to an NCAA investigation of Clarett were NCAA findings that Clarett and his mother had accepted improper benefits while Clarett was in high school and that he had lied to police about the cost of items stolen from a car he had borrowed, which led to his suspension for his sophomore year.

After the suspension Clarett became persona non grata in the Ohio State community for tarnishing the school's image. But he was given an opportunity for reinstatement after a year if he could maintain a high GPA, repay the money he had accepted in high school and donate it to charity, and engage in an intensive conditioning program. When Clarett began to find these conditions too onerous, he quit school and applied for the NFL draft, thus touching off a court battle that had substantial implications for the NCAA, the NFL, and the future of college sports. The only thing preventing Clarett from playing pro ball was the NFL's rule limiting eligibility to players three seasons removed from their high school graduation. The question before the court was whether this rule violated antitrust laws.

Although Clarett had problems off the field, his physical ability to compete safely in the NFL seemed beyond dispute. At the time of the 2004 draft, Clarett was six feet tall and weighed 230 pounds, bigger and stronger than Walter Payton, Emmitt Smith, and Barry Sanders were in their NFL playing days. Clarett would have been twenty-one years old at the start of the 2004 NFL season, whereas Emmitt Smith was only twenty years old when he was drafted. In the end, arguments about strength, speed, and maturity had far less to do with the outcome of the case than whether the three-year rule was the result of a collective bargaining agreement between the NFL and the players' union, and therefore immune to antitrust scrutiny. A district court found for Clarett, making him eligible for the NFL draft. Subsequent court rulings reversed that finding, however, leaving Clarett barred from the NFL and unable to return to college sports.[21]

Clarett's saga continued in 2005 when the Denver Broncos made Clarett a third-round draft pick and then released him on waivers during the preseason. Things turned very ugly for Clarett on 1 January 2006. On the day before the Ohio State Buckeyes took the field against Notre Dame in the Fiesta Bowl, Clarett, who would have been playing in that game if he had stayed in school, robbed two people at gunpoint outside a dance club in Columbus. Later that year, Columbus police stopped him for a driving violation and found a cache of weapons, including a loaded AK47, in the SUV he was driving. In September 2006, Clarett, potentially one of the finest running backs in Ohio State history, was sentenced to seven and a half years in prison on robbery and concealed weapons charges. He is currently serving time in a close-security prison in Toledo, Ohio.

Maurice Clarett must accept responsibility for his tragic free fall from highly regarded athlete to prisoner in the Toledo Correction Facility. But his case says a great deal about structural flaws in big-time college sports. Recruiting athletes with marginal academic skills and little interest in education invites academic fraud, especially when such athletes are thrown into the world of big-time college sports as freshmen. In Clarett's case, the battle for a starting position as a "true freshman" began in the spring of what should have been his senior year in high school. By the time classes started in the fall, Clarett had already been introduced to the eligibility game, replete with "no-show" classes, friendly faculty, and tutors and academic counselors who often cross the line into doing athletes' work for them.

The three-year rule that denied Clarett an opportunity to sell his remarkable athletic skills in an open market is a poignant example of the hypocrisy that sustains the current system of corporate college sports. Regardless of the various justifications the NFL and NCAA give for this rule, it exists primarily to provide the NFL with free minor league training and to ensure that universities have a lock on marquee athletes they need to fill their giant stadiums, keep television ratings high, and make alumni and donors happy. Absent this collusive arrangement between the NFL and the NCAA, the rare athlete with Maurice Clarett's abilities could sign a lucrative contract with the NFL right out of high school, and, like soldiers on the GI Bill, go to college later. Young men and women currently enter the military at age eighteen and fight, and sometimes die, for our country. The argument that athletes with exceptional ability must be out of high school for three years before they are mature enough to play pro football is absurd.

Putting the Amateur Myth to Rest

Toward the end of my interview with Myles Brand, he suggested that the term "amateur" may have outlived its usefulness. The term, he said, was the creation of the nineteenth-century British leisure class and was not a very good fit for college sports in the new millennium. "If the term is not a good fit," I asked, "why not just delete it from the NCAA manual? What would happen if you just dropped the term?" Brand responded, partially in jest, "We can define a new term. We are always good at defining new terms here at the NCAA." "Would dropping the term have legal consequences?" I asked. "It might," he said. "I don't know." Although there was

no need to say it, Brand and I were both well aware that the legal consequences of dropping the term would be dramatic.

The myth of amateurism, as I have argued throughout this book, serves
as the lynchpin of professionalized college sports. It has held off tax col-
lectors seeking unrelated business income taxes, defended universities
from athletes filing workers' compensation claims, and allowed universities to set a cap on financial benefits to athletes. Under common law, "an
employee is a person who performs services for another under a contract
for hire, subject to the other's control or right to control, in return for payment."[22] The myth of amateurism has allowed universities to exercise control over athletes' lives comparable to that of employers, without having to
provide rights and protections that other workers take for granted.

Although some faculty deplore the NCAA's exploitive use of the term
"amateur," the main assault on the amateur myth in the coming decades
will be launched by athletes themselves. The wave of academic capitalism that has buoyed Myles Brand's confidence in building the business
of college sports will invariably wash over the athletes who work in the
industry. The athletes' rights model of reform is actually a mirror image
of academic capitalism, except that athletes want a cut of the action. Faculty members hustle for research grants from major corporations and
hire agents to handle lucrative book contracts. Celebrity coaches endorse
products and are models of entrepreneurship in action. Regular students
work in paid internships for college credit. Soon, athletes too will discover
the joys of academic capitalism.

Myles Brand's clever rhetoric about amateurism defining the athletes,
not the sports enterprise, may have drawn applause at the NCAA convention, but among many big-time athletes it sounds like a formula for exploitation. Ramogi Huma and the National College Players Association, in my
opinion, represent the kind of organization that will define the relationship between athletes and professional college sports in the decades to
come. If the NCPA-inspired antitrust suit against the NCAA to increase
athletic scholarships to cover full educational expenses is successful, the
NCAA cartel will take a hit. Regardless of the outcome, similar cases can
be expected in the future, as athletes imbibe the same business values
that drive the NCAA.

In 2006, just before the start of football season, I joined a group of
former athletes, players, journalists, and college administrators on ESPN
Classic to debate the issue of pay for college athletes.[23] I have done scores
of these debates over the years. What surprised me about this one was
that most of those interviewed agreed that college athletes are already
being paid. The central argument was over whether they should be paid

more. Among those who supported a raise in the salary cap were former athletes and coaches such as Tom Osborne, Nolan Richardson, Patrick Ewing, Sheryl Swoopes, Reggie Bush, Jim McMahon, and Ramogi Huma. The arguments in favor of increasing compensation for athletes focused on the fact that athletes generate millions of dollars for the college sports industry but receive scholarships that do not even cover the full cost of a college education.

Tom Osborne pointed out that the value of a scholarship today is probably less than when he was coaching football at Nebraska. CBS sports commentator Tom Brando said that "today's athletes, like USC's Reggie Bush, see jerseys with their numbers, and sometimes their names, being sold to fans and they're saying, 'why can't I even get a stipend for my laundry?'" According to Huma, athletes see coaches with multimillion-dollar salaries, and money from television contracts soaring into the billions, and ask, "What about us?" Among the former athletes on the program who supported higher compensation, the sentiment was that universities do not need to pay lavish salaries, but they do have an obligation to do more than they are doing now. Leo Gerard, who represented the United Steelworkers Union on the show, characterized big-time college athletes as "sweatshop workers."

The second half of the show presented arguments against blaming the NCAA for not paying college athletes more. The argument ESPN gave the most prominence was that athletes are already paid quite well by the subsidized education they receive. "Education," said John Thompson, Georgetown's former coach, "has value. They [athletes] are already being paid. If you get a scholarship, it is extremely important that you understand that it has a money value to it." The average yearly cost of an education, as ESPN's Brian Kenny pointed out, ranges from about $12,000 at a public school to $30,000 at a private school. Another argument against paying college athletes more than room, board, tuition, and fees was the damage it would do to women's and other nonrevenue sports.

It seems beyond dispute that limiting revenue-producing athletes' compensation to room, board, tuition, and fees keeps program costs down and subsidizes the athletic experiences of thousands of other students. If revenue-producing athletes were merely amateurs engaged in sports to round out their education, this distribution of revenue would be no different from taking money from a very popular academic program and using it to subsidize another. In reality, big-time college sports, as a form of mass commercial entertainment, has very little to do with education except that it offers athletes a way to work their way through school. As students—as I have argued repeatedly in this book—they deserve the same quality of education that other students get. As professional athletes they should have the same rights and protections as other workers.

Although ESPN edited out some of the comments I made about labor unions and employment, others on the show blasted away. According to Doug Gottlieb, a former Oklahoma State University basketball player, "It's going to take some well-versed student-athlete in world affairs and in the world of negotiating, or maybe a Don Fehr, to come in and say, what are you guys doing? You guys are an incredibly profitable business and you guys are the product. The only way to get your way is to withhold services." Ramogi Huma echoed these sentiments and added that athletes have to band together to get this done. "No one is going to do this for us," he said. Huma and the NCPA have been organizing athletes with the financial backing and moral support of the United Steelworkers Union.

Forty years ago, black college athletes led the charge for an end to racial discrimination in sports and demanded that black athletes be treated with dignity. The revolt of the black athletes, and the civil rights movement that nurtured it, created opportunities that did not exist when I entered Notre Dame in 1963. The athletic revolt led by Huma, though less strident than the movements of the sixties, has the potential to take the struggle for fairness and equity another step further. Since the slave era, blacks have been expected to be grateful for things they have justly earned through hard work and sacrifice. The NCPA asks only that college athletes (both black and white) receive what they deserve.

Although I support the right of big-time college athletes to organize to protect their financial, medical, and educational rights, I have not given up on amateur college sports altogether. The term "amateur" accurately describes hundreds of athletic programs at colleges and universities that offer no athletic scholarships, where the educational needs of athletes take priority over the entertainment needs of paying spectators. The amateur ideal has survived in the NCAA's Division III and in the Ivy League, though even there it is under attack. The major purpose of this book has been to put the amateur myth to rest, not to launch an attack on amateurism in its truest sense.

As college sports moves further into the new millennium, challenges to the NCAA's counterfeit version of amateurism will undoubtedly increase. Players' associations representing college athletes will challenge the amateur myth in court, and an injured athlete will eventually win a workers' compensation case, giving legal confirmation to the obvious fact that scholarship athletes are employees. The IRS will most certainly continue to ask how million-dollar skyboxes and celebrity coaches contribute to college sports' tax-exempt educational function. A hundred Myles Brands, and all the high-priced lawyers at their disposal, will not be able to sustain the amateur myth forever.

The NCAA will have two alternatives when the amateur myth is laid to rest. One alternative, the one I prefer, is to replace counterfeit amateurism with the real thing. Adopting proposals like those presented by the Drake Group and other faculty organizations would be an excellent starting point for integrating athletes into the student body and reconnecting with amateur values. The other alternative is to adopt some form of open professionalism, and to ensure that athletes receive fair treatment as both students and workers. Although this approach is theoretically possible, very few colleges and universities could afford to run their athletic programs as unrelated businesses. Regardless of the outcome, the first step toward meaningful and ethical college sports reform will require the elimination of the amateur lie upon which big-time college sports is founded.

Notes

CHAPTER 1

1. Probably the best treatment of the politics and culture of the 1960s is Todd Gitlin's *The Sixties: Years of Hope, Days of Rage* (New York: Bantam Books, 1987). I have relied heavily on this book to refresh my memory of the broader social and political climate that shaped my thinking during the 1960s and for decades to follow.

2. Raymond Fleming and Chris Siegler offered their observations on the Wallace visit in e-mail communications to the author, 2 March 2004.

3. Theodore M. Hesburgh, with Jerry Reedy, *God, Country, and Notre Dame: The Autobiography of Theodore M. Hesburgh* (New York: Doubleday, 1990).

4. See James L. Shulman and William G. Bowen, *The Game of Life: College Sports and Educational Values* (Princeton: Princeton University Press, 2001), for a discussion of the widening gap between sports and academics over the past four decades. Notre Dame is among the schools included in this study.

5. Ara Parseghian, interview by author, 14 June 2005.

CHAPTER 2

1. For a summary of this case and the full opinion of the U.S. Supreme Court, see "U.S. Supreme Court Rules for TSSAA in Brentwood Case," *Chattanoogan*, 21 June 2007, www.chattanoogan.com/.

2. Knight Foundation Commission on Intercollegiate Athletics, *Keeping Faith with the Student-Athlete: A New Model for Intercollegiate Athletics* (Charlotte, N.C.: John S. and James L. Knight Foundation, 1991), 32.

3. Russell Adams, "Friday Night Luxe," *Wall Street Journal*, 9 December 2006, 1.

4. Julian Garcia, "New Transfer Rules," *New York Daily News*, 30 March 2005.

5. "Law Makers Asked to Reverse High School Transfer Rule," Associated Press, 8 February 2006, www.abcactionnews.com/.

6. Pete Thamel and Duff Wilson, "Poor Grades Aside, Athletes Get into College on a $399 Diploma," *New York Times*, 27 November 2005.

7. When Tose was questioned by editors from the New York Times about these payments, he said that "they were perfectly legal according to the NCAA." See Allen Sack, "Getting Up Close and Personal with Under-the-Table Payments," *New York Times*, 19 March 2000, 13.

8. Ed Gebhart, interview by author, 30 January 2004.

9. This discussion of recruiting services is based on a report by the American Coaches Federation, "Companies to Be Compared," 3 March 2004, www.americancoachesassociation.org/.

10. Bruce B. Svare, *Reforming College Sports Before the Clock Runs Out: One Man's Journey Through Our Runaway Sports Culture* (Delmar, N.Y.: Sport Reform Press, 2004), 69–70.

11. Lee Jenkins, "Schiano's Plan: Let the Sunshine State In," *New York Times*, 14 November 2006, D1, D7.

12. Jay Weiner, "Goin' Steady: Desperate Demographics Meets the Star Making Machine, or Why High School Sports and the News Media Were Meant for Each Other," paper presented at the "Sports Reform Summit: Assessing the Past, Planning for the Future," Lake George, New York, 7–10 November 2003.

13. John Gerdy argues that although some think it is a stretch to associate falling academic standards in the United States with the growth of highly commercialized sports in the school systems, sports has played a role. See John Gerdy, "If Reform Is Based on Need, Change Aid," *NCAA News*, 17 July 2006, www.ncaa.org/.

CHAPTER 3

1. Michael Oriard played football at Notre Dame a few years after I did. His reflections on his experiences appear in his book *The End of Autumn: My Life in Football* (Garden City, N.Y.: Doubleday, 1982).

2. Mike Celizic, *The Biggest Game of Them All: Notre Dame, Michigan State, and the Fall of '66* (New York: Simon & Schuster, 1992), 314.

3. Jay Coakley, *Sports in Society: Issues and Controversies* (Boston: McGraw-Hill, 2007), 521.

4. Richard Hofstadter, *Anti-Intellectualism in American Life* (New York: Vintage Books, 1963).

5. Richard Sandomir, "Not Everyone Wants a Channel That's All Big Ten, All the Time," *New York Times*, 18 June 2007.

6. Shulman and Bowen, *Game of Life*.

7. Pete Thamel, "For Some Auburn Athletes, Courses with No Classes," *New York Times*, 13 July 2006.

CHAPTER 4

1. Hesburgh, *God, Country, and Notre Dame*, 107.

2. Bernard B. Fall, *The Two Vietnams: A Political History* (New York: Richard A. Praeger, 1963).

3. D. Stanley Eitzen and George H. Sage, *Sociology of North American Sport* (Dubuque, Iowa: William C. Brown Publishers, 1978), 313–14.

4. Bob Minnix, quoted in Steve Delsohn, *Talking Irish: The Oral History of Notre Dame Football* (New York: Perennial, 2001), 159.

5. Ara Parseghian, quoted in John Underwood, "The Desperate Coach: Cut That Thing Off," *Sports Illustrated*, 1 September 1969, 22.

6. Bob Minnix, interview by author, 20 July 2005.

7. Tom Pagna, quoted in Celizic, *Biggest Game of Them All*, 14.

8. Quoted in Delsohn, *Talking Irish*, 159.

9. Michael Oriard, e-mail message to author, 20 July 2005.

10. Matt Eagan, "Belated Award in Fight for Fair Play," *Hartford Courant*, 21 October 2006.

CHAPTER 5

1. Intercollegiate Athletic Association of the United States, *Proceedings of the First Annual Convention*, 29 December 1906, 33, in author's files.

2. "Story of a Graduate Manager," 1925 transcript, Harvard University Archives, President Lowell Papers, 1922–25, folder 6B.

3. National Collegiate Athletic Association, *Proceedings of the Seventeenth Annual Convention*, 29 December 1941, 144, in author's files.

4. Walter Byers, with Charles Hammer, *Unsportsmanlike Conduct: Exploiting College Athletes* (Ann Arbor: University of Michigan Press, 1995), 73.

5. Everett D. Barnes to Walter Byers, 6 July 1964, NCAA Headquarters, Walter Byers Papers, Workmen's Compensation folder, Overland Park, Kansas.

6. Byers, *Unsportsmanlike Conduct*, 69.

7. Clyde B. Smith to Walter Byers, 6 December 1966, NCAA Headquarters, Walter Byers Papers, Long Range Planning folder, Overland Park, Kansas.

8. National Collegiate Athletic Association, *Proceedings of the Sixty-first Annual Convention*, 9–11 January 1967, 122, in author's files.

9. For a discussion of the 1.6 rule and how its being rescinded lowered academic standards in the early 1970s, see John Sayle Watterson, *College Football: History, Spectacle, Controversy* (Baltimore: Johns Hopkins University Press, 2000), 305. Watterson also discusses other changes that the NCAA made in 1973, including the creation of the three-tier divisional structure that exists today.

10. John William Ward to Walter Byers, 26 July 1972, NCAA Headquarters, Walter Byers Papers, Financial Aid, Special Committee folder, 1971, Overland Park, Kansas.

11. For a discussion of the AIAW's philosophy of sports and education, as well as the NCAA's takeover of the AIAW, see Allen L. Sack and Ellen J. Staurowsky, *College Athletes for Hire: The Evolution and Legacy of the NCAA's Amateur Myth* (Westport, Conn.: Praeger Publishers, 1998), chapter 7.

12. Joyce quoted in National Collegiate Athletic Association, *Proceedings of the Seventy-fifth Annual Convention*, 12–14 January 1981, 116, in author's files.

13. Ibid.

14. See Wells Twombly, "JV Coach's Version of Notre Dame Incident," *San Francisco Examiner and Chronicle*, 22 December 1974, 2.

CHAPTER 6

1. Much of the background information on the early years of Sports for the People was derived from Mark Naison, interview by author, 4 May 2004.

2. Alan Page, interview by author, 25 February 2004.

3. Don Cronin, UPI wire story, 28 September 1981, in author's files.

4. Dave Anderson, "James Madison Writes Again," *New York Times*, 2 October 1981.

5. Bart Barnes, "Group Plans Union of College Players," *Washington Post*, 29 September 1981, D1, D3.

6. "Garvey: Not a Try at Unionizing College Athletes," *Washington Post*, 30 September 1981.

7. When I walked into Garvey's office the day after the press conference, he jokingly said something like, "Look who it is, the Walter Reuther of collegiate sports." He then explained that the misstatement in the *Washington Post* had raised concerns among players that the NFLPA was launching a new labor-organizing initiative without informing the membership.

8. Byers, *Unsportsmanlike Conduct*, 342.

9. "Lawyers Examine Union Question," *NCAA News*, 30 November 1981, www.ncaa.org/.

10. Quoted in Byers, *Unsportsmanlike Conduct*, 342.

11. Leslie Hornig to Cary Goodman, 6 October 1981, in author's files.

12. Leslie Hornig, memorandum to Bob Atwell, Roscoe Brown, Cary Goodman, and Allen Sack, 30 December 1981, in author's files.

13. Sven Groennings to Robert Garcia, 7 July 1982, in author's files.

14. The final days of Sports for the People are well documented in Mark Naison, *White Boy: A Memoir* (Philadelphia: Temple University Press, 2002), 209–12.

15. Bob Herbert, "Feed the Billionaire, Starve the Students," *New York Times*, 15 November 2004, A1.

CHAPTER 7

1. *Rensing v. Indiana State University Board of Trustees*, 437 N.E. 2d 78 (Ind. App. 1982), filed 16 June 1982.

2. Allen L. Sack, "The Myth of Amateurism," *Notre Dame Magazine*, February 1983, 21.

3. *Rensing v. Indiana State University Board of Trustees*, 444 N.E. 2d 1170, 1173 (Ind. App. 1983), filed 9 February 1983.

4. Quoted in Scott Vance, "4-Year Sports Scholarships Proposed to Avoid Workers'-Benefit Disputes," *Chronicle of Higher Education*, 23 February 1983, 17.

5. Kevin Horrigan, "Simple Justice Goes Unserved in Rensing Case," *St. Louis Post-Dispatch*, 18 April 1983, C8.

6. Ernie Chambers to Allen Sack, 18 March 1983, in author's files.

7. Quoted in Allen L. Sack, "The Commercialization and Rationalization of Intercollegiate Football: A Comparative Analysis of the Development of Football at Yale and Harvard in the Latter Nineteenth Century" (Ph.D. diss., Pennsylvania State University, 1974).

8. This account was taken from Andrew Zimbalist, *Unpaid Professionals: Commercialism and Conflict in Big-Time College Sports* (Princeton: Princeton University Press, 1999), 94.

9. Allen L. Sack, "Players Ignored in Big-Money Deals," *New York Times*, 27 September 1981, sec. 5, 2.

10. *NCAA v. Board of Regents of the University of Oklahoma*, 468 U.S. 85 (1984).

11. See Zimbalist, *Unpaid Professionals*, 102.

12. *NCAA v. Board of Regents of the University of Oklahoma*.

13. For an overview of the findings of this study, see Peter Monaghan, "Some Athletes Found Troubled by Campus 'Role Conflict,'" *Chronicle of Higher Education*, 11 September 1985, 43. The findings were also reported by UPI and appeared in newspapers across the country.

14. Diane Ravitch, "Defining Literacy Downward," *New York Times*, 28 August 1996.

15. Brad Wolverton, "Graduation Rates Remain at Record High," *Chronicle of Higher Education*, 27 January 2006.

16. Myles Brand, quoted in Joe Drape, "N.C.A.A./ Men's Round of 16; Graduation Is Secondary for Many in Final 16," *New York Times*, 24 March 2004.

17. Dean Golembeski, Sports News column, Associated Press, 16 November 1989.

18. Quoted in Carolyn White, "Pay the Players; Study Notes Player Payments; Athletes, Colleges Doubt Results," *USA Today*, 21 November 1989, 9C.

19. Quoted in Robert Thomas Jr., "Illicit Pay in Wide Use, Study Contends," *New York Times*, 17 November 1989, A34.

20. Mike Fish, "Auburn Probe: Accusations Fly in Auburn Scandal," *Atlanta Journal and Constitution*, 13 October 1991, 16.

21. Roman Gabriel, interview by author, March 1991.

22. Caitlin Nish, "Basketball: Webber Avoids Jail, Pleading Guilty on a Contempt Charge," *New York Times*, 15 July 2003.

CHAPTER 8

1. Knight Foundation Commission on Intercollegiate Athletics, *A Call to Action: Reconnecting Sports and Higher Education* (Miami: John S. and James L. Knight Foundation, 2001), 21.

2. Theodore M. Hesburgh, C.S.C., interview by author, 20 May 2005.

3. Richard Conklin, "Edmund Joyce, C.S.C., 1917–2004," *Notre Dame Magazine*, summer 2004.

4. Much of my account of Notre Dame's role in the 1990 television negotiations is based on a discussion by Walter Byers, the former executive director of the NCAA, in his book *Unsportsmanlike Conduct*, 287–95. Byers was at the center of the NCAA's antitrust battle against the CFA.

5. Vince Dooley, quoted in ibid., 291.

6. Roger Valdiserri, interview by author, 17 August 2005.

7. Michael DeCicco, interview by author, 17 August 2005.

8. A discussion of the aftermath of Notre Dame's decision to go it alone in 1990 can be found in Zimabalist, *Unpaid Professionals*, 101–3.

9. Johnny Ray, interview by author, 18 August 2005.

10. James Baugus, interview by author, 17 January 2006.

11. Chris Kvochak, interview by author, 19 January 2006.

12. Dan Saracino, interview by author, 15 August 2005.

13. Mike Wadsworth, quoted in Delsohn, *Talking Irish*, 344.

14. Matt Dingens, quoted in Don Yaeger and Douglas S. Looney, *Under the Tarnished Dome: How Notre Dame Betrayed Its Ideals for Football Glory* (New York: Simon & Schuster, 1993), 217.

15. These graduation rates were compiled from *The Notre Dame 2002 Football Media Guide*, and from a study by the Institute for Diversity and Ethics in Sport at the University of Central Florida, "Report on APR Rates and Graduation Rates for 2005–6 Bowl-Bound Teams," 5 December 2005, http://bus.ucf.edu/sport.

16. Paul Hornung, quoted in "Hornung Calls on Notre Dame to Lower Academic Standards," *USA Today*, 31 March 2004.

17. Teddy Greenstein, "Davie Finds New Home in Booth," *Chicago Tribune*, 11 August 2005.

18. University of Central Florida, Institute for Diversity and Ethics in Sport, "Report on APR Rates and Graduation Rates for 2005–6."

19. Maturi, quoted in Rachel Blount, "Irish Still Want It Both Ways," *Minneapolis Star Tribune*, 31 October 2004.

20. Andrew Soukup, "N BC Extends Football Contract Through 2010," *Notre Dame Observer*, 14 January 2004, www.ndsmcobserver.com/.

CHAPTER 9

1. Some background information on Waldrep was derived from his book *Fourth and Long: The Kent Waldrep Story* (New York: Crossroad Publishing, 1996), written with co-author Susan Mary Malone. I also did an extensive interview with Waldrep on 25 March 2006 that focused primarily on his court case.

2. Byers, *Unsportsmanlike Conduct*, 376.

3. *Waldrep v. Texas Employers Insurance Association*, 21 S.W.3d 692 (Tex. App. 2000), filed 15 June 2000.

4. Ibid.

5. William Dowling, "College Sports: Faut-il Legaliser la Prostitution," *Academic Questions*, 2001, www.rci.rutgers.edu/.

6. Jay Weiner, "College Athletic Reformers Find It's a Daunting Task," *Minneapolis Star Tribune*, 23 October 1999.

7. Robert Lipsyte, "Forget X FL; Real Revolution Is on Campus," *New York Times*, 11 February 2001.

8. Liz Clarke, "Points Other than Baskets," *Washington Post*, 5 April 2004.

9. Myles Brand, "Back Talk: In Athletics, Level Field Must Begin in Classroom," *New York Times*, 9 May 2004.

10. Terry Holland, memo to Drake Group Executive Committee, May 2006, in author's files.

CHAPTER 10

1. See, for instance, Sheila Slaughter and Gary Rhoades, *Academic Capitalism and the New Economy: Markets, the State, and Higher Education* (Baltimore: Johns Hopkins University Press, 2004), and David L. Kirp, *Shakespeare, Einstein, and the Bottom Line: The Marketing of Higher Education* (Cambridge: Harvard University Press, 2003).

2. Myles Brand, "Commercialism Controlled When Activity Aligns with Mission," *NCAA News*, 24 April 2006, www.ncaa.org/.

3. Myles Brand, interview by author, 23 May 2006.

4. These data were derived from reports on graduation rates published by the Institute for Diversity and Ethics in Sport at the University of Central Florida. The graduation rates were based on federal graduation rates (F GRs) for schools that participated in bowl games and in the NCAA basketball championships in 2006.

5. Overall graduation rates for general student populations were derived from the *U.S. News & World Report* special issue, "America's Best Colleges in 2007."

6. Derek Bok, *Universities in the Marketplace: The Commercialization of Higher Education* (Princeton: Princeton University Press, 2003), 54.

7. Brent Schrotenboer, "Athletes Going to College Get Special Treatment," *San Diego Union-Tribune*, 10 December 2006.

8. Quoted in Rebecca Quigley, "University Eyes Admit Grade Woes," *Athens (Ga.) Banner-Herald*, 10 December 2006.

9. Quoted in Glenn Dickey, "Harbaugh Can Resurrect the Cardinal," *San Francisco Examiner*, 5 May 2007.

10. Jim Carty, "Harbaugh: U-M Should Hold Itself to a Higher Ideal," *Ann Arbor News*, 13 May 2007.

11. Pete Thamel, "An Audit Reveals More Academic Questions at Auburn," *New York Times*, 10 December 2006.

12. Mark Alesia, "Public Pumps $1 Billion into College Sports," *Indianapolis Star*, 30 March 2006.

13. "Top Grades, Without the Classes," editorial, *New York Times*, 20 December 2006.

14. Dustin Dopirak, "Nebraska Law Sends Message to NCAA," *Digital Collegian*, 1 May 2003, www.collegian.psu.edu/.

15. Ernie Chambers, interview by author, 6 June 2006.

16. Ramogi Huma, interview by author, 8 June 2006.

17. Tom Farrey, "NCAA Might Face Damages in Hundreds of Millions," *ESPN Magazine*, 21 February 2006, www.sports.espn.go.com/.

18. Brent Schrotenboer, "NCAA Lets No One Market Athlete for Profit, Except Schools," *San Diego Union-Tribune*, 24 November 2005.

19. This account of the Jeremy Bloom case relies on Gordon C. Gouveia, "Making a Mountain out of a Mogul: *Jeremy Bloom v. NCAA* and Unjustified Denial of Compensation Under NCAA Amateur Rules," *Vanderbilt Journal of Entertainment and Law Practice* 6, no. 1 (2003); Larry Bloom (Jeremy Bloom's father), interview by author, 8 June 2006.

20. Tom Friend, "My Side," *ESPN Magazine*, 10 November 2004, www.sports.espn.go.com/.

21. *Clarett v. National Football League*, 306 F.Supp.2d 379 (S.D.N.Y. 2004).

22. See Robert McCormick and Amy Christian McCormick, "The Myth of the Student Athlete: The College Athlete as Employee," Michigan State University College of Law, Legal Studies Research Paper Series, Research Paper no. 03-18, 2006, 91.

23. "The Top Five Reasons You Can't Blame the NCAA for Not Paying College Athletes," ESPN Classic. This show was aired repeatedly for several weeks in the late summer and early fall of 2006.

Suggested Reading

Acosta, R. Vivian, and Linda-Jean Carpenter. "Women in Intercollegiate Sport: A Longitudinal Study—Twenty-Seven Year Update: 1977–2004." www.womenssportsfoundation.org/.

Benford, Robert D. "The College Sports Reform Movement: Reframing the 'Edutainment' Industry." *Sociological Quarterly* 48 (2007): 1–28.

Bok, Derek. *Universities in the Marketplace: The Commercialization of Higher Education.* Princeton: Princeton University Press, 2003.

Bowen, William C., and Sarah A. Levin. *Reclaiming the Game: College Sports and Educational Values.* Princeton: Princeton University Press, 2003.

Brand, Myles. "Money Not Corruptive If Actions Uphold Collegiate Mission." *NCAA News,* 25 April 2005, 4, 22.

———. "NCAA State of the Association Address." January 9, 2006. www.i-aa.org/article_print.asp?articleid=75346.

Byers, Walter, with Charles Hammer. *Unsportsmanlike Conduct: Exploiting College Athletes.* Ann Arbor: University of Michigan Press, 1995.

Carpenter, Linda-Jean, and R. Vivian Acosta. "Back to the Future: Reform with a Woman's Voice." In *Sport in Contemporary Society: An Anthology,* 5th ed., ed. D. Stanley Eitzen. New York: St. Martin's Press, 1996.

———. *Title IX.* Champaign, Ill.: Human Kinetics Press, 2005.

Celizic, Michael. *The Biggest Game of Them All: Notre Dame, Michigan State, and the Fall of '66.* New York: Simon & Schuster, 1992.

Delsohn, Steve. *Talking Irish: The Oral History of Notre Dame Football.* New York: Perennial, 2001.

Dowling, William C. *Confessions of a Spoilsport: My Life and Hard Times Fighting Sports Corruption at an Old Eastern University.* University Park: Pennsylvania State University Press, 2007.

Duderstadt, James J. *Intercollegiate Athletics and the American University: A University President's Perspective.* Ann Arbor: University of Michigan Press, 2000.

Feinstein, John. *The Last Amateurs: Playing for Glory and Honor in Division I College Basketball*. Boston: Little, Brown, 2000.

Fried, Barbara H. "Punting Our Future: College Athletics and Admissions." *Change Magazine*, May–June 2007. www.carnegiefoundation.org/change/sub.asp?key=98&subkey=2352.

Gerdy, John. *Air Ball: American Education's Failed Experiment with Elite Athletics*. Jackson: University of Mississippi Press, 2006.

Gitlin, Todd. *The Sixties: Years of Hope, Days of Rage*. New York: Bantam Books, 1987.

Hawkins, Billy. *The New Plantation: The Internal Colonization of Black Student Athletes*. Winterville, Ga.: Sadiki Publishing, 2000.

Hesburgh, Theodore, with Jerry Reedy. *God, Country, and Notre Dame: The Autobiography of Theodore M. Hesburgh*. New York: Doubleday, 1990.

Hofstadter, Richard. *Anti-Intellectualism in American Life*. New York: Vintage Books, 1963.

Kaplan, Richard L. "Intercollegiate Athletics and the Unrelated Business Income Tax." *Columbia Law Review* 80, no. 7 (1980): 1430–73.

Kirp, David L. *Shakespeare, Einstein, and the Bottom Line: The Marketing of Higher Education*. Cambridge: Harvard University Press, 2003.

Knight Foundation Commission on Intercollegiate Athletics. *A Call to Action: Reconnecting College Sports and Higher Education*. Miami: John S. and James L. Knight Foundation, 2001.

———. *Keeping Faith with the Student-Athlete: A New Model of Intercollegiate Athletics*. Charlotte, N.C.: John S. and James L. Knight Foundation, 1991.

McCormick, Robert, and Amy Christian McCormick. "The Myth of the Student-Athlete: The College Athlete as Employee." Michigan State University College of Law, Legal Studies Research Paper Series, Research Paper no. 03-18, 2006.

Meggyesy, David. *Out of Their League*. Lincoln: University of Nebraska Press, 2005.

Naison, Mark. *White Boy: A Memoir*. Philadelphia: Temple University Press, 2002.

Porto, Brian L. *A New Season: Using Title IX to Reform College Sport*. Westport, Conn.: Greenwood Press, 2003.

Presidential Task Force on the Future of Division I Intercollegiate Athletics. *The Second-Century Imperatives: Presidential Leadership—Institutional Accountability*. www.ncaa.org/.

Rhoden, William C. *Forty Million Dollar Slaves: The Rise, Fall, and Redemption of the Black Athlete*. New York: Crown Publishers, 2006.

Sack, Allen L., and Ellen J. Staurowsky. *College Athletes for Hire: The Evolution and Legacy of the NCAA's Amateur Myth*. Westport, Conn.: Praeger Publishers, 1998.

Salzwedel, Matthew R., and Jon Ericson. "Cleaning Up Buckley: How the Family Educational Rights and Privacy Act Shields Academic Corruption in College Athletics." *Wisconsin Law Review* 6 (2003): 1053–1113.

Shulman, James L., and William G. Bowen. *The Game of Life: College Sports and Educational Values.* Princeton: Princeton University Press, 2001.

Slaughter, Sheila, and Gary Rhoades. *Academic Capitalism and the New Economy: Markets, the State, and Higher Education.* Baltimore: Johns Hopkins University Press, 2004.

Smith, Ron. *Sports and Freedom: The Rise of Big-Time College Athletics.* New York: Oxford University Press, 1988.

Sperber, Murray. *Beer and Circus: How Big-Time College Sports Is Crippling Undergraduate Education.* New York: Henry Holt, 2000.

Splitt, Frank. "The U.S. Congress: New Hope for Constructive Engagement with the NCAA and Intercollegiate Athletics." *Montana Professor* 17, no. 2 (spring 2007): 18–25.

Suggs, Welsh. *A Place on the Team: The Triumph and Tragedy of Title IX.* Princeton: Princeton University Press, 2005.

Svare, Bruce B. *Reforming College Sports Before the Clock Runs Out: One Man's Journey Through Our Runaway Sports Culture.* Delmar, N.Y.: Sport Reform Press, 2004.

Telander, Rick. *The Hundred Yard Lie: The Corruption of College Football and What We Can Do to Stop It.* New York: Simon & Schuster, 1989.

Ukeiley, Stephen L. "No Salary, No Union, No Collective Bargaining: Scholarship Athletes Are an Employer's Dream Come True," *Seton Hall Journal of Sport and Law* 6 (1996): 167–222.

Waldrep, Kent, with Susan Mary Malone. *Fourth and Long: The Kent Waldrep Story.* New York: Crossroad Publishing, 1996.

Watterson, John Sayle. *College Football: History, Spectacle, Controversy.* Baltimore: Johns Hopkins University Press, 2000.

Yaeger, Don, and Douglas S. Looney. *Under the Tarnished Dome: How Notre Dame Betrayed Its Ideals for Football Glory.* New York: Simon & Schuster, 1993.

Zimbalist, Andrew. *Unpaid Professionals: Commercialism and Conflict in Big-Time College Sports.* Princeton: Princeton University Press, 1999.

Index